BONNIE & CLYDE & MARIE

A Sister's Perspective on the Notorious Barrow Gang

JONATHAN DAVIS

STEPHEN F. AUSTIN STATE UNIVERSITY PRESS
NACOGDOCHES ★ TEXAS
2014

Manufactured in China by Everbest Printing Co.,
through FCI Print Group

First Edition

This paper meets the requirements of
ANSI/NISO Z39-48-1992 (Permanence of Paper).
Binding materials have been chosen for durability.

Library of Congress Cataloging-in-Publication Data
Davis, Jonathan
Bonnie & Clyde & Marie: a sister's perspective on the notorious
Barrow gang / Jonathan Davis. — 1st ed.
p. cm.
Includes bibliographical references and index.

1. Parker, Bonnie, 1910-1934. 2. Barrow, Clyde, 1909-1934. 3. Barrow, Marvin (Buck) 1903-1933. 4. Barrow, Marie 1918-1999 5. Criminals—United States—Biography. I Title.

ISBN-13: 978-1-936205-12-7
ISBN-10: 1-936205-12-2

Stephen F. Austin State University Press
P.O. Box 13007, SFA Station
Nacogdoches, TX 75962
sfapress@sfasu.edu

Designed by Ciara Umbrell
Copy Editors: Laura Davis and Brittany O'Sullivan

Dedicated to the memories of
Marie Barrow Scoma, Joseph Pinkston, and
Charles W. (The Crime Doctor) Stanley. Without their contributions, this book would not be possible.

PREFACE

WHETHER WE LIKE TO ADMIT it or not, most recorded history is a matter of best guess. Books about people and events decades or more in the past are generally written by someone who wasn't there; the participants are long gone, and what's left to sort through is a jumble of third-hand recollections and exaggerated or even entirely made-up articles from period newspapers and magazines. It's frustrating for writers, and even more so for readers. That makes the rare exception – fresh material coming directly from participants to the printed page – both welcome and precious. And that is why *Bonnie & Clyde & Marie: A Sister's Perspective on the Notorious Barrow Gang* should be greeted with all possible fanfare. You hold historic treasure in your hands.

Many years after her beloved brother Clyde's bloody demise on a back road in northwestern Louisiana, Marie Barrow set out with close friend Jonathan Davis to tell the real story of the Barrow gang. Previous books, magazine articles and films – even Warren Beatty's much lauded *Bonnie and Clyde* – didn't, to Marie's way of thinking, even remotely capture the sweetness of the love between Clyde and Bonnie, nor the desperation with their lots in life that drove them into crime. So over a period of time, Marie told Jonathan the Barrow Gang story from her perspective. She had plenty to tell about. Even as they tried to stay one step ahead of the "laws," Clyde and Bonnie made frequent visits to their families in the fetid slums known as West Dallas, and Marie even joined them on the road a few times to provide Bonnie with female companionship and an opportunity to engage in the "girl talk" she enjoyed so much. Jonathan, a gifted historian and relentless researcher, wrote down everything Marie had to say and doubled-checked it wherever possible. The result was a riveting, insightful manuscript that throbbed with energy. No dry-as-dust, best-guess history here!

And Marie hated it. She was less interested in facts than in presenting Clyde as a sort of Depression-era saint, near-faultless and forced into criminality by a corrupt legal system that hounded decent young men into mistakes that often cost them their lives. (Marie was less concerned with polishing Bonnie's reputation; like the other Barrows, she considered the pert Miss Parker to be a bit too flighty for her own – and Clyde's – good.)

Over Jonathan's protests, Marie shelved the whole project and eventually published a watered-down book with another writer. She died just as that collaboration began, so the results were far removed from insightful first-hand remembrances.

Meanwhile, Jonathan Davis retained the original Marie Barrow manuscript, generously making it available to other historians bent on telling the real story of the Barrow Gang. I'm proud to number among them. In the process of studying the Marie manuscript and getting to know Jonathan, I discovered that he was one of the very few Bonnie and Clyde scholars who refused to buy into their mythology. Based on his friendship with Marie, and with Clyde's nephew Buddy and Bonnie's niece Rhea Leen, Jonathan understood the outlaw couple as real human beings rather than one-dimensional legends; acknowledging their quirks and flaws made them more rather than less interesting. His participation made my book much, much better.

Now, finally, it's Jonathan's turn to tell the Bonnie and Clyde story, and he does so with the original Marie Barrow manuscript bolstered by his own diligent research. The voice you'll encounter is authentically Marie's, and it's unfiltered in the matter of her expressing opinions. For instance, the Barrow family's dislike of Bonnie's snooty mother Emma comes through loud and clear, as does Marie's unrelenting enmity toward Henry Methvin, the chunky Louisiana con who, with his family, betrayed Clyde and Bonnie to hulking ex-Ranger Frank Hamer. History simply doesn't get any more immediate or more powerful than this.

Bonnie & Clyde & Marie makes no claim toward telling the definitive Barrow Gang story. Rather, it allows readers to see through the eyes of a first-hand observer who regularly spent time with the couple that is still celebrated as the ultimate Romeo and Juliet of American crime. Marie's is certainly a subjective perspective, but it's an informed one, and, most importantly, it's as close as the rest of us can ever come to actually interacting with Bonnie and Clyde, joining them on their bloodstained road trips or chatting with them during family picnics in isolated spots far from the prying eyes of pursuing lawmen. Marie was there, and now, thanks to Jonathan Davis and Stephen F. Austin State University Press, so are we.

Jeff Guinn
Author of *Go Down Together: The True, Untold Story of Bonnie and Clyde*

INTRODUCTION

IN 1996, THE DOWNTOWN DALLAS Public Library had a public exhibition of artifacts pertaining to Clyde Barrow and Bonnie Parker. These items included the blue, western-style shirt Clyde was wearing when he and Bonnie were slain by a posse of peace officers eight miles south of Gibsland, Louisiana, on Wednesday, May 23, 1934. The shirt and the other things on display had been kept in matriarch Cumie Barrow's cedar chest for the previous 60-plus years. The cedar chest was now in possession of Marie Barrow Scoma, Cumie's youngest child and the last remaining member of Clyde's immediate family.

Part of the activities involved with the public exhibition involved a book signing which was held by the widow of Barrow gang member Ralph Fults and John Neal Phillips, a noted author/historian who had written a book about Fults' experience with Bonnie and Clyde. Marie attended this book signing and became interested in publishing her own account of the lives of her brothers Clyde and Buck. She contacted me and asked me to work with her on this project.

I had known Marie since autumn, 1993, after both of us had worked on a documentary titled Remembering Bonnie and Clyde. She brought in the "death shirt" and other items to be photographed for this program. I watched her being interviewed and was impressed by the story she had to tell. A few days afterward, I sent her a small thank-you card with a note telling her how much I enjoyed meeting her and that if I could ever be of assistance, she should call and I would help her in any way I could. I didn't expect a response.

Marie called me and asked to meet with me and thus began one of the richest and most interesting times of my life. I began to go over to Luke's and Marie's home in east Dallas regularly to call on them. Over the last five-and-a-half years of her life (she and her husband Luke Scoma passed away within days of each other in February, 1999), I was at their house every other weekend, primarily on Saturday evenings. When I did go over there, I knew I had to arrive by 6:30 because Luke and Marie were serious watchers of "Wheel of

Fortune" and I didn't dare walk in on them when that show was being broadcast. If I couldn't get there before "Wheel" started, I would goof around in the neighborhood for 30 minutes to arrive sharply at 7 o'clock.

The first time I went to their house, I told Marie that if she did not want to talk about her brothers Clyde and Buck, that was okay with me because I knew the memories were undoubtedly painful. Marie did want to talk about them. The memories concerning their lives were indeed painful, but her pain continued beyond the normal grieving process after their deaths. Her pain continued because of the effect that their criminal careers had on her parents and her siblings. Her pain continued because of what the press and the authors and the TV shows and the movies said about her brothers in the decades afterwards. It is true that Clyde, Buck, Bonnie, and Blanche were involved in many activities which deserved public condemnation. But a lot of what was being written, published, and broadcast went beyond what really happened and turned her family members and friends into monsters and unrecognizable ogres. Marie wanted to leave the world with a more reasonable perspective of her brothers and get her side of the story out.

I began to introduce Marie to people I knew who could assist her in doing this. One of the best people I knew who could help her was Joe Pinkston, owner and operator of the John Dillinger Historical Wax Museum in Nashville, Indiana. Joe was a nationally recognized authority on Dillinger and he had known members of the Indiana outlaw's family for many years. He was a one-man clearing-house and crossroads for those people across the country who were interested in the outlaws of the 1930's. He certainly understood the continuing grief that the family of a notorious outlaw had to deal with throughout the years. Also, Joe had co-authored the first (and still one of the best) nonfiction book about the life and career of John Dillinger. In addition, Joe had worked with major TV documentaries about Dillinger and could therefore assist Marie in any visual media projects with which she became involved. Joe and Marie began to communicate regularly by phone and letter; in fact, Marie was planning on coming to Nashville, Indiana, in the autumn of 1996 to see Joe at his museum. Tragically, Joe's death in June, 1996, eliminated that opportunity.

There was a major contribution that Joe made towards the manuscript which Marie and I wrote in 1996-7. Joe was also well-acquainted with Charles Wiley Stanley, the "Crime Doctor" of the 1930's and 1940's who owned the Barrow-Parker "death car" from 1934 to the early 1950's. Marie also knew Charles Stanley from the 1930's when the Barrow family toured with his exhibition. Stanley settled in Cincinnati, Ohio, which was close to central Indiana where Joe lived. During that time period, I would visit Joe three times a year when I flew back to Indiana to visit with family. I would spend a day at his museum where we would talk about Bonnie & Clyde. Joe related quite a bit about the Crime Doctor's recollections of people like Frank Hamer and some of that information became a part of this manuscript. I would take notes on what Joe told me and would go over that information with Marie when I returned to Texas. Both Marie and Joe had a high opinion of Charles Stanley.

Marie and I talked quite a bit about the books that had been written about Bonnie and Clyde. Some of them she had read; I got her copies of those she hadn't seen yet. She expressed disappointment with all of them, but it was not until the 1996 Bonnie and Clyde exhibit at the Dallas Public Library that she specifically took action towards getting her story told. I began to ask her about her early years and to take notes. I offered to tape record her memories, but she did not want to do so and so I took hand written notes, much as I had with Joe Pinkston.

Some people have total recall of details; unfortunately, Marie was not one them. She recalled memories about her own family (a lot of which I couldn't use due to her concern for the privacy of her non-outlaw siblings), but seemed to lack recollection about the specifics of many of the gun battles, prison breaks, and bank robberies of the Barrow gang. Knowing that those items would be the reason most people would purchase her memoirs, I tried to jostle her memories of 1933-4 by referring to the books about Bonnie and Clyde which had been published by 1996. I would re-read these books and outline what each of them said concerning things like the Joplin and Platte City shootouts, the Eastham prison break, and the killings with which Clyde's and Buck's names were connected. I would show these outlines to Marie and tell her: "Now, this is what the writers and historians said about these things, but what do you recall Clyde telling you about what happened?" What is contained in this volume is what Marie said she recalled Clyde telling her.

Marie also gave me a copy of Cumie Barrow's manuscript to use. Shortly after Clyde and Bonnie were killed, Cumie attempted to tell the true story of her sons' lives, and began to write. What Cumie had completed was what Marie gave me to use. There was some original family information in there; other parts of it seemed to be taken from "true crime" magazines of the period. I had to do the best I could with it due to the fact it was a rough – very rough – draft.

There were other sources outside of Marie's recollections, Cumie's manuscript, and the historical books which Marie distrusted so much. I did quite a bit of research with the microfilmed Dallas newspapers from the years when Bonnie and Clyde were on the road. There were a couple of audio resources which were available: in the late 1960's both Billie Parker (Bonnie's only sister) and Charles "Crime Doctor" Stanley made recordings during the public uproar over Warren Beatty-Arthur Penn movie. Whatever I gleaned from the microfilms and the records were brought to Marie for her opinion.

After 16 months of work, a 230 page rough draft was completed and was presented to Marie for her review. Unfortunately, she was unhappy with the result due to the fact that there was too much information concerning outlawry, both involving her own brothers and other fugitives with whom they were compared and paralleled. I had a very specific reason for doing it that way because of my discussion with another family member of a noted fugitive of the 1930's. For ten years, from 1993 through 2003, I corresponded regularly with a gentleman named Bruce Barnes. Bruce wrote a very interesting book about his father, who is known in popular history by name of George Ramsey "Machine Gun" Kelly. Machine Gun's real name was George F. Barnes, Jr. Bruce visited his father while he was serving a life sentence on Alcatraz and got a lot of information. He decided to use this information to write a book and tell the story of his dad as a person and not a gangster. Unfortunately, publishers were not interested in the family story of George F. Barnes Jr.; they wanted the story of the "crimson career" of Machine Gun Kelly. Bruce had the book privately published. If a person wants to know the story of the real man behind the "Machine Gun," I would wholeheartedly advise getting Bruce's book.

Another reason why I included information about other gangsters of the 1930's was because Clyde and Buck were frequently disparaged by writers when compared to these other fugitives. For that matter, the Barrow brothers were disparaged by many of the contemporary "big time" bank robbers and crooks like John Dillinger, Alvin Karpis, Herbert "Deafy" Farmer, and Urschel kidnapper Albert Bates. Clyde and Bonnie were never trying to be among the nation's top Public Enemies and never aspired to be known as "big timers." Comparing them to Dillinger and Karpis was like comparing apples and oranges.

Anyhow, my arguments did not impress Marie and she made the acquaintance of another writer and began collaborating with him on her memoirs. Unfortunately, just a few weeks after work began on this second project, Marie died suddenly. But her son Shawn Scoma continued on and the outcome was a book titled The Family Story of Bonnie and Clyde. But the original manuscript did not remain in mothballs forever. It was used as a significant source in two well-received books: James R. Knight's *Bonnie and Clyde: A 21st Century Interpretation* (2003) and Jeff Guinn's *Go Down Together* (2009). In fact, it was Jeff who recommended that this original manuscript be published because he regarded it as a significant contribution to the history of Bonnie and Clyde.

The book which you now hold in your hands is the result of Jeff's recommendation.

Chapter 1

In early autumn of 1934, a particular volume appeared in bookstores across America. This book was titled *Fugitives: The Story of Clyde Barrow and Bonnie Parker*. Supposedly "written" by my older sister Nell Barrow and Bonnie's mother Mrs. Emma Parker, in actuality it was "compiled" by Jan Fortune. Jan Fortune was a screenwriter for the motion pictures back in the 1930s. This book was published by the Ranger Press of Dallas.

Most of what has been written in books and magazines about my older brother Clyde's early life was taken from *Fugitives*. I eagerly awaited the publication of this volume, hoping it would tell the truth about Clyde's life. But, when I read it, I was shocked at all of the fiction it contained. I was furious about the untruths that appeared in this book as hard fact. I confronted my sister Nell about it. It turned out that Nell was just as surprised at what was in it as I was. She told me she never told Jan Fortune any of the stuff that appeared in *Fugitives* as Barrow family memories. Mrs. Parker's story was the same. She told me she had never given the information Fortune claimed she did.

I believe *Fugitives* was the first thing to appear in book form about Clyde Barrow and Bonnie Parker. As bad as it was, things seemed to go downhill from there concerning the telling of the truth about my brothers, Clyde and Buck. Most of the stuff that has appeared in books, magazine articles, and newspaper accounts has been the wildest form of fiction. Of course, those who created these works apparently had no reason to try to deal with the truth of Clyde's life; after all, they never knew him or any of the Barrow family. In addition, they're typically only doing it for the dollars to be made from the exploitation of Clyde's and Bonnie's names. It seems to be the case that the more bizarre their accounts are, the more the public is ready to "shell out the bucks" in response. There is an adage which has been credited to both P. T. Barnum and H. L. Mencken, "Nobody ever went broke underestimating the taste of the American people." This statement perfectly captures the mentality displayed by most of those who have written about Clyde and Buck for the edification of the public; if anything, it's an understatement.

It's probably too late to change the overall perception that the American public has of Clyde and Buck, as well as Clyde's sweetheart Bonnie Parker and Buck's wife Blanche Caldwell Barrow. The public's perspective on my family members and friends has been reinforced by over 60 years of caricature and exaggeration through the output of the publishing houses and the Hollywood studios. It began during the days of the old newsreels in the movie houses and has continued unchanged up through today's modern cable television networks and satellite communications. No matter which medium carries the message, the message itself is typically 100% pure baloney.

As I said earlier, *Fugitives* was the first of these "true accounts" to hit the public. It was the original item which got the misinformation concerning the so-called "Barrow Gang" snowballing into the avalanche it has turned into. The books, articles, and stories which have appeared throughout the last 60 years have compounded the errors which initially appeared in the Jan Fortune book. I consider *Fugitives* to be Jan Fortune's book because it sure can't be considered as a production of the Barrow and Parker families. Most of the "family information" in there was not gotten from any members of the Barrow family.

Accounts of Clyde's life were wrong from the get go, starting with his date of birth. Now, I know the marker in the Barrow family plot at the Western Heights Cemetery says Clyde was born in March, 1909. But the entry in the Barrow family Bible plainly states that Clyde Chestnut Barrow was born in March, 1910, and the Barrow family Bible should really be taken as the definitive source for this matter. When Clyde was ambushed and killed, my mother was so distraught and upset she gave the stonecutter the wrong date of birth. The same thing happened with Buck. Although Buck's marker states that he was born in 1905. His actual year of birth was 1903. It was my sister Nellie Mae Barrow who was born in 1905. The gravestone was not put in the family plot until after Clyde was killed in May, 1934. By that time, Buck had already been buried for almost ten months. My mother knew Clyde's fate was similar to Buck's, therefore she requested the marker he wanted. My mother waited until Clyde was brought back home for burial and then used Clyde's preference for both he and Buck. Her emotional state was such at the time that she gave the wrong years of birth for both of my brothers. The family Bible really has the correct dates.

Now, I can understand how the mistake concerning the year of birth could be made. But even that "understandable" error could have been avoided if these writers would have bothered to contact any member of the Barrow family. There's a lot more I could say about the so-called "authoritative" Jan Fortune book, but I think the best way to handle this matter is not to continue to point out other people's mistakes concerning my brothers and my friends. The best thing to do is to tell the story myself from the beginning, depending on the best sources with which to tell it: family records and my own personal memory.

The proper place to begin to tell the story of my brothers, Clyde and Buck, is with our parents, since my father and my mother played such a big part in all of our lives. Henry B. Barrow, my father, was born in Pensacola, Florida, on January 10, 1873. He spent the early years of his life in Pensacola. Sadly, Henry's mother died while he was still a boy. After this tragedy, Jim Barrow, my grandfather, decided to relocate from Florida to Texas. In addition to this change of locale, my grandfather also desired a change in vocation. While living in Pensacola, Jim was a shoemaker, but he wanted to take up farming when he moved to Texas. The Florida Barrows relocated to Texas when my father was just beginning his teenage years.

Back in those days, mandatory school attendance was taken pretty lightly. In fact, my father only went to school one-half-day in his life. The day he attempted to go, he was brought back home in a buggy after getting sick at school. Early in his life, he was afflicted with chills and this condition stayed with him throughout his childhood years. I've always felt that my father was a victim of a malaria attack back in his Florida days, to which he developed a severe reaction. He was extremely sickly as a child in Florida, and this condition carried over to his early adolescent years in Texas. However, he was able to assist on his father's farm in his later teen years. Apparently getting away from the mosquito-infested Pensacola region of the 1880s eventually improved my father's health.

It is a real tragedy that my father could not take advantage of what educational opportunities were available at that time. Due to his lack of schooling, he could neither read nor write. This is a tragedy for any individual, but especially for my father, as he displayed a real aptitude for mathematics. His mind was like a calculator; nobody was ever able to out-figure him when it came to numbers. If circumstances had been different in that schooling hadn't been denied to him, the history of his offspring might have been drastically different. His natural ability with numbers might have really advanced him in life.

As my father recovered his health and became involved in his father's farm, his interests began to parallel those of any other teenage boy in Texas: he wanted a fast horse more than anything else in the world. My father liked horses and cattle, but his desire for a fast horse was more connected with racing and not with breeding stock on the farm. At this time, the Jim Barrow family was living in Grimes County, Texas.

It is important to note at this point that neither my father nor any of his brothers ever had any serious trouble with the authorities. I know my father had one full-blooded brother named Frank and two half-brothers named Ed and Jim. One of Henry's brothers was arrested in Grimes County for fighting, but nothing ever came of the charges. Henry himself was involved in occasional scraps with other young men in the neighborhood, but, again, these were never any kind of serious crimes. Whenever these occurrences did come to Jim Barrow Sr.'s attention, all my grandfather would do was to talk to Henry and try to get him to see the error of his ways. My father was seldom whipped for anything he ever did.

Some of these disagreements and scuffles among the young men of the community were the natural by-products of the horse races. In fact, the only time my father was ever in any legal trouble was when he was hauled into court once in connection with a horse race. But nothing ever came of this charge.

Nevertheless, the occasional fights caused my grandfather quite a bit of uneasiness and concern. Horse racing was considered as the first major step downward towards a life of debauchery, debasement, and dereliction. Most Texas citizens were still familiar with the story of the noted train robber Sam Bass from Denton County. Bass was mortally wounded in a gunfight with Texas Rangers and county officers in Round Rock, Texas, in July, 1878. On his deathbed, Bass admitted that his descent to a life of crime began with his participation at Denton County horse races and his ownership of the famous "Denton Mare." The tale of Sam Bass was still being used by fathers to their sons to illustrate what evils could be born from eager participation in the business of horse racing with its attendant gambling and fast money.

Grandfather Jim gave my father quite a series of lectures concerning Henry's behavior and tried to influence him to attend both Sunday School and church. My father did attend the church at Whitehall in Grimes County at my grandfather's insistence. He also reduced his activities involved with horse racing in deference to my grandfather's wishes.

It was at this point in Henry's life that he decided to get out on his own and seek his fortune. In the late 1880s, he gravitated towards Nacogdoches County from Grimes County, and found employment at a sawmill in the county seat. But Henry found much more than just a sawmill job at Nacogdoches. As Henry's involvement in the horse racing business declined, other interests took its place. The most important and special piece of business was a young Nacogdoches County lady named Cumie T. Walker.

Unlike Henry, my mother Cumie was born and raised in Texas in Nacogdoches County. She was born on November 21, 1874 and grew up on a farm with several siblings. The members of her family that I was familiar with were her sisters Belle and Sallie, and her brother, Walter.

In terms of her farm background and her schooling, my mother's early life paralleled that of my father. My mother liked cats and other animals. She had a bit more schooling than my father did, of course, but farm life took precedence over her schooling, as it did with so many other farm children at that period of history, and Cumie attended only sporadically.

The one big difference between my mother's upbringing and my father's was strictness. My father's early interest in and involvement with horse racing would not have been tolerated, in the slightest, in the Walker family. While my grandfather Jim influenced and encouraged my father towards the Baptist church, the inducements towards Sunday School and church attendance in the Walker family would've been much more direct and emphatic. My mother was baptized early in her life and the Baptist church in Nacogdoches played a very big part in her early years.

Cumie's life in terms of social activities was also quite strict. Make-up on women was not permitted, being considered an outward manifestation of inward worldliness. Her dating life was also taken quite seriously by her family. Henry Barrow was one of the earliest beaus in Cumie's dating career. As a result of their meeting, Henry began to court Cumie in late 1890.

Chapter 2

On December 5, 1891, Mr. Henry B. Barrow and Miss Cumie T. Walker were united in the bonds of holy matrimony. The wedding took place at the home of Cumie's parents in the small town of Swift, Texas, in Nacogdoches County. Their wedding was something that my mother always remembered "like it was just yesterday."

My father decided to quit his job at the sawmill at this point and go into farming full-time. Their ultimate dream was to own a successful farm of their own. Henry and Cumie began to fulfill this dream by renting a farm in the Nacogdoches area. By doing this, they figured they could begin to build up enough funds to one day acquire their own establishment.

Then, the children began to come along. And I want to stop right here and comment on another one of the popular myths concerning our family that was initiated by Jan Fortune in the book *Fugitives*. In it, Fortune states that there were eight children in our family. There were only seven of us Barrow kids. Most of the writers that have followed since Fortune included her initial mistake in their works. Many people come up and ask me who the eighth child was in our family. Quite frankly, that eighth child is over with the four children that Blanche supposedly had, in the land of the writer's imagination.

Moving away from the fictitious "eighth" Barrow child, the first child born to Henry and Cumie was Elvin W. "Jack" Barrow. He was born while my parents were living and farming in Nacogdoches County in 1894. Just a very few years later, my sister Artie was born.

Henry and Cumie found that operating a farm, whether renting someone else's or owning your own, was an "up-and-down" proposition. The "down" aspects of the farm in Nacogdoches County were rapidly becoming apparent to both of my parents. So Henry began to look elsewhere for another opportunity with which to build his fortune.

My father decided that Milam County, Texas, definitely had greener pastures and more productive agricultural possibilities than Nacogdoches county, so Henry, Cumie, Jack, and Artie packed up and left. They settled themselves near Jones Prairie and rented another farm. It was here, Jones Prairie, that my brother Marvin Ivan Barrow was born in 1903, and then, two years later, my sister Nell was born. I mention these two together to re-emphasize the fact that Buck's birth date on his tombstone is in error. That gravesite is one of the most visited locations in the city of Dallas, and one of the most photographed. I just want people to know the dates on the grave marker are incorrect.

Just as Elvin was nicknamed "Jack," my brother Marvin was also given a nickname in early childhood. One of my aunts called him "Buck" because he was so playful. Buck was indeed a playful little boy; he always liked a good romp. He liked to make-believe he was a horse in some of his games. Buck was also especially fond of playing with wagons.

After a few years in Milam County, Henry began to get restless again in terms of his farming activities. It was becoming apparent to both of my parents that their dream of someday owning their own large farm was diminishing due to the realities of raising a family. But Henry still had it in his blood to make a "go" at farming. So my parents and their four children moved north to Ellis County, Texas. Henry rented a farm near the little hamlet of Telico and began to give agriculture one more try. It was here in the Ellis county area that the final three Barrow children were born: Clyde in 1910, L.C. in 1913, and, finally, me in 1918. With Jack, Artie, Buck, and Nell, the sequence of births in the Barrow family was finally complete.

Now that the cast of main characters is assembled, it is time to examine the early years of my brothers Buck and Clyde. So much has already been written about their growing-up years that to cover the subject again might seem repetitive. But just about everything that has been written has been untrue or exaggerated. I, as the remaining member of the Barrow family, feel it necessary to try to correct the misinformation concerning both my parents and my siblings.

For example, one published account stated that my father was short and fat, which was totally untrue. My father was a rather tall individual, and he certainly wasn't anything remotely resembling corpulent. Henry B. Barrow was a dignified, hard-working individual who held the respect and regard of everyone who knew him.

I mentioned that my father was rather tall. My mother was of medium height, and all of the Barrow children identified with one or the other. Jack, L.C., and Nell were rather tall, while Artie, Buck, Clyde, and myself were of more medium stature.

Some writings have said that my mother had children on an annual basis. If that were true, I would've had two dozen siblings, instead of only six, since Jack was born in 1894, and I was born 24 years later. In fact, I'd like to point out that ours wasn't really that big of a farming family by turn-of-the-century standards. Many farm families of the period had ten, twelve, or even fourteen children. If anything, the family of Henry and Cumie Barrow had less than the average number of farm children. In those days, farming families were larger due to the work that needed to be done, as well as increased infant mortality rates in the rural areas where quality healthcare was often not obtainable. Since farms were worked by the same family from generation to generation, there had to be some way to ensure that there would be heirs to inherit the establishment.

I've pointed out earlier that there was no notable criminal activity in the families of both my father and mother, outside of my father's one appearance in a court of law concerning a horse race. For that matter, at that time period if everyone who had any connection with neighborhood horse races was arrested, it would have resulted in the incarceration of the majority of the male population of the county. As we Barrow kids were growing up in the Ellis County-Navarro County area, there was no criminal activity occurring in which we were involved.

My brother Buck attended school at Midlothian and Ennis. He was considered a good student and fast learner in public school, whenever he went. He attended regularly through the third grade, but only sporadically after that. Buck was attracted to outdoorsy type activities, like hunting and fishing, not the indoor and desk-bound atmosphere of the schoolhouse. His personal temperament, coupled with the rather lenient outlook of the farming community towards mandatory school attendance, pretty much guaranteed that Buck would not make the full twelve years of formal education.

Unfortunately, Buck's interests were also pretty lax towards other institutions, like church. He was a regular church attendee as a youngster, much to the delight of my mother. But as he grew older, Buck wandered away from it.

Clyde, on the other hand, was a fairly enthusiastic attendant of the Baptist church. He regularly patronized both Sunday School and church. In fact, Clyde was baptized at the little Baptist church in Eureka, Texas, in 1924 at the age of 14. The fact that Clyde was interested in the Baptist church may surprise many people, but there are many things about Clyde's early years which would surprise a lot of people. What would be surprising is not what did happen during those growing-up years of his, but what didn't happen.

After Clyde and Bonnie were killed, reporters covered all aspects of Clyde's life, including things that didn't really happen. For example, a reporter for the Associated Press interviewed several people in Houston Heights who supposedly were neighbors of ours back around World War I. They stated that they could recall that when Clyde was a little boy, he was consistently in trouble for abusing and maiming small animals. It was stated that Clyde would break birds' wings and then watch and laugh at their suffering. He also supposedly abused household pets in much the same fashion.

It is stories like this that make me the angriest. First of all, we never lived in Houston or in Houston Heights. Clyde was born and raised around Ennis, Waxahachie, and Corsicana. My father and mother had the farm at Telico from before Clyde's birth until they moved into west Dallas in the early 1920s, and they never lived anywhere else during that period.

Second of all, the idea that Clyde Chestnut Barrow, son of Henry and Cumie Barrow, would ever intentionally inflict pain and suffering upon an animal is outrageous. Every member of the Barrow family was an animal lover. My father liked horses. My mother was fond of cats. My sister Artie inherited my mother's love of cats and raised Persian cats. I've raised Yorkie dogs. The only trouble that Clyde ever had with animals was that he was frequently bringing them home with him. He'd find a stray out there in the woods somewhere and would invariably fetch it back to the house.

There is a second myth concerning Clyde's non-existent Houston years. This is the story that his first "stretch in the pen" occurred at age nine at someplace called the Harris County School for Boys. This account includes the fact that Clyde was already classified as an inveterate thief and an all-around rascal. Again, this tale is untrue because of the simple fact that we never lived in or around Houston.

But I guess it shouldn't surprise me that stories like these circulate about the early lives of bandits. In an 1883 account of the lives of Frank and Jesse James, it was stated that the childhood amusements of the James boys included burying animals alive and cutting off the ears and tails of dogs and cats. The Jameses were also supposed to be the terrors of their childhood neighbors. But since Zerelda James (Frank and Jesse's mother) was as religious and strict as Cumie Barrow, I don't believe there were too many animals or people that were abused in either case.

The hard fact of the matter is that there was nothing extraordinary in the early lives of either Buck or Clyde Barrow. They were exactly what would be expected from the time and place in which they were raised. And this attitude is reflected by all who knew either of them in their early years.

Now, it would be expected that Clyde's immediate family would come to his defense and state he never had any criminal or violent tendencies during his childhood years. But we're not the only people who knew Clyde who maintain this belief, which extends members of the extended family. I recall reading a newspaper interview with one of Clyde's cousins with whom Clyde spent time when he worked on our uncle Frank's farm. My cousin described him as a good boy from a good family who worked hard in the fields. He said Clyde was an intelligent youth.

On top of the testimonies of various family members, the opinion of the communities where Clyde was raised was that he was no different than any other young man. When Clyde and Bonnie were ambushed in Louisiana, a reporter went down to Waxahachie, Texas, to talk to people who knew of Clyde and Buck when they were young men. The "Barrow Boys" were known in all three towns. Yet all people could recall was that there was no difference between the Barrow brothers and any other young men in Waxahachie. There were no memories of animal torturing or any childhood terrorism. All that was meant by the term "Barrow Boys" was a reference to the sons of Henry and Cumie Barrow.

One would get the impression from reading Jan Fortune's book that Clyde and Nell had uncles and aunts in just about every county in southeastern Texas. They seem to be moving around from relative to relative all of the time. Actually, the only uncle that we kids ever really stayed with was Uncle Frank near Corsicana, Texas, in Navarro County. Clyde always enjoyed staying there, as did we all. He worked hard on Uncle Frank's farm. But it wasn't all work on the farm; there were fun things to do, also. We liked to fish with Uncle Frank's kids. I never knew my Aunt Rosie, Frank's wife because she died when I was too young to know her.

There is one more thing worth mentioning concerning our happy days at Uncle Frank's. He had many guns, as he and his kids liked to hunt. But, although Clyde liked guns, he was hesitant to go hunting with his cousins. At this time in his life, he was unable to aim a gun at a living creature. But he did enjoy target shooting and "plinking," which was something I immensely enjoyed also.

Clyde's education wasn't neglected during his early years. Although farm work occupied part of the year, Clyde still attended school fairly regularly at two different locations. When living at my parents' farm near Telico, he went to school at Ennis. When living at Uncle Frank's, Clyde went to school at Corsicana.

All in all, Clyde's early years were primarily based in the country. All aspects of his life, whether working on the farm or attending school and church, were typical of most other young men of his time and locale. If Clyde would've stayed in this early environment, the rest of his life would've probably been totally different.

However, things changed for the Barrow family in the early 1920s, and these changes would re-route the direction of Clyde's life. And these changes were not for the better.

Chapter 3

Most history books say that the Great Depression began in October of 1929 with the stock market crash. That may have been when the world of stocks and bonds was affected, but for the American farmer, the Great Depression began ten years earlier. After World War I ended, farm prices plummeted and the agricultural industry was hit hard.

Farmers at all levels were economically devastated. The people who were rental farming were hit the hardest initially, and many just gave up. It happened all around us in Ellis County.

My parents still tried to make a go at farming after the bottom had dropped out of the agricultural market. Henry supplemented what he made on the farm at Telico with earnings from working at the brickyard in Ennis. But it still didn't seem to be enough.

There were other factors that caused my parents to consider giving up on farming. In the early 1920s, when I was becoming aware of my family surroundings, the four older Barrow kids had already left home. None of them were staying in the Ellis County area to make their livings.

The depressed agricultural market had soured my older brothers and sisters on getting their own farms to work. They wanted things that didn't seem to be available to those who made their living from the soil. My older siblings wanted secure employment and comforts and conveniences not found in the country. The nearest big city was just one county to the northwest, Dallas, Texas. When kids were tired of the farm life, they gravitated towards Dallas.

By 1922, my four older siblings had already gravitated into Dallas. My oldest brother Jack and his wife Drusilla were living there. Jack ran a garage on Forest Avenue, to support his family of four daughters. My sisters, Artie and Nell, went into the beauty parlor business in downtown Dallas. The shop was located in the Sanger Hotel. Artie had lived in Denison for a while, but later returned to Dallas. Buck's life remained a series of ups and downs. At the age of 19, Buck married his first wife. Together they had twins. Sadly, tragedy struck, claiming the life of one of the children.

It was in 1922 that my parents finally gave up on their dreams of owning their own productive farm. By this time, both my father and mother were closing in on 50 years old. They were at a point where it would have been too hard for them to try to take up another rental farm elsewhere. They decided to follow their older children into Dallas. Henry and Cumie wanted to open a small business of their own to provide an income capable of supporting them as they grew older.

So they finally left the farm at Telico and moved into west Dallas. Of course, the Barrow family was not the only farming family to pull up stakes and head into the city. There was a steady stream of urban immigrants from all over north-central Texas.

These urban immigrants had no place to stay when they first arrived in Dallas, so they had to make what temporary arrangements they could until more permanent living arrangements were available. Therefore, there were many tent-cities and shanty-towns all over.

At this time, the Barrow family consisted of Henry, Cumie, Clyde (age 12), L.C. (age 9), and me (age 4). During the transition to Dallas, Clyde was alternating between living with us and with Uncle Frank near Corsicana.

Anyhow, we didn't directly move into the service station from Telico. We first moved into the campgrounds in west Dallas, where a lot of other farming families were temporarily residing. It is at this point that I'd like to debunk another myth about the Barrow family which I've seen in many books and articles: that we lived under some bridge somewhere when we first moved into Dallas. That is untrue; our family went directly to the west Dallas campgrounds, where so many other families in the same predicament lived.

Our family could not expect to depend on welfare programs, and this was for two reasons primarily: there were no such government programs in those early days of the twentieth century, and most people wouldn't have availed themselves of them anyway if they were able-bodied and were capable of active work. My father was one of these people.

When we first hit the west Dallas campground, my father immediately began to earn funds to support the family by peddling, i.e., buying and selling commodities like brass. At this time, his mode of transportation was his horse and wagon. It was an old white horse that had been with the family for some years.

Times were still pretty hard there at the campground, despite what my father could bring in from his peddling activities. All of us who lived there had to do the best we could. We lived in tents under very primitive conditions. The only form of public assistance that we ever knew of was free bread brought into the campground by an unknown benefactor. It was brought in by the wagon load and was gratefully received.

My father knew his peddling activities were only being done on a temporary basis, to keep body and soul together while we were residing at the campgrounds. It was while we were living there that my father began to build a small wooden house, which he intended to move to the location where he and my mother had chosen to settle for good. The house was built as the accumulation of money and materials permitted.

Finally, my parents found a location on Eagle Ford Road where my father believed a gas station would provide a liveable income. And then came the big day when we moved the house from the campground to the Eagle Ford Road site.

The moving of the house is one of the most notable memories I have of life in the Barrow family. I got to ride inside of the house as it was moved, and I thought it was quite a grand adventure! The actual moving of the small house covered only a trip of a few blocks, but to a little girl, every foot of the trip was exciting.

The house itself contained the essentials for living: bedrooms and a kitchen area, and that was about it. Many of those who are reading this account will undoubtedly have seen the photo of the old Barrow service station which has been published many times. The service station portion of it was added onto the living quarters after it was located on the site. What we called my father's "oil room" was added on to my parent's bedroom to the west. The "oil room" was the area where the business for the service station was carried on.

My bedroom was across from my parents' bedroom, and L.C.'s bedroom was behind mine. Clyde, when he was home with the family, would share L.C.'s room. My father built this small house with his own two hands. He didn't include any amenities like a living room or a family room or anything like that because of the urgency of the situation at the campgrounds. He couldn't take his time and plan out a big dwelling because he knew we couldn't live in tents very long. The house had to provide for our basic needs, which would have been shelter and a place to sleep.

At the campgrounds, my mother cooked and washed outside. At the Eagle Ford Road site, my father added on a small kitchen with an old iron cooking stove in it. But my mother still had to do her washing outside. Even though we did have a form of permanent housing, living on Eagle

Ford Road still had many aspects which would be considered as primitive by today's standards. One thing that I can still recall very well was how cold it got at night in the wintertime. Insulation for houses was unknown in those times, and many people who lived back in those days remember the winters as being much colder than the winters now. It's probably because we felt the cold so much more back then. Many houses in the early 1930s were little more than multi-room sheds.

We dealt with the night time winter cold by home-made methods. My mother would take the old irons that were used to press clothes (and I do mean irons, which is what they were: just molded lumps of cast iron) and heat them on the old stove, just the same way she would do if she was going to press some clothes. She would then take these heated pieces of heavy metal and wrap them in some clothes. Then the whole bundle would be tucked under the covers at the sleeper's feet.

There was no indoor running water. When it came to taking baths, there were no bathtub fixtures. We used a big old wash tub on the kitchen floor. The water was heated on the stove and poured into the wash tub.

Of course, since there were no bathtub fixtures, other such bathroom necessities were also lacking, like commodes. When nature called, we used the outhouse in the backyard- way far back in the backyard. It was equipped to meet the physical needs of two people simultaneously, i.e., a "two-holer." The big Sears-Roebuck catalogs were also kept out there; the pages were handy for reading and other purposes.

There was one area in which our family had an advantage over many people in west Dallas: we had our own well at the side of the house. In running a service station, it was necessary that my father have the facilities with which to service the radiators of his customer's cars. So he set up a pump at the side of the house by which to draw up the water from the well. That's also where we got our drinking water and our water for our baths.

My father made a little extra money from the well and the water pump. He sold barrels of water for 25¢ each to the other families out there. It was through the selling of these barrels of water that we met many of the other residents of west Dallas.

Despite the urban location, life was still as hard as it was out on the Telico farm in many ways. Even with most of the Barrow kids out on their own, the income generated by the service station and the water barrels only provided the barest of necessities for our family. Luxuries were an unknown commodity. Toys at Christmas time were only dreamed of by L.C. and myself. What we did get at Christmas was obtained by my mother from the Salvation Army. She would get apples and oranges, and sometimes Cumie would get clothing for our family. Quite frankly, I don't know how we would have made it through those tough times if it hadn't been for the Army's aid. Because of their help, I've always tried to support the Salvation Army in whatever ways I could in the years since.

As I was growing up during the mid and late 1920s, my brothers and sisters were having their share of ups and downs. Jack and Drusilla were doing all right during that time, and Nell and Artie continued in the beauty parlor business. But Buck's life was still troubled. His marriage failed after the death of one of his twins. Buck continued in some of the practices he had learned down in Ellis County. While down there, he had become very involved in dog fights, involving pit bulls, and cockfights. He continued this activity when he moved up to Dallas. In fact, he had one pit bull which was unusually ferocious. This dog was kept tied up on the side of my parents' house. It was so ill-tempered that no one except Buck could go near it. One day, while I was outside playing ball by the side of the house, I got too close to the dog, and it went after me. Mercifully, I wasn't close enough for it to knock me down and maul me, but I was close enough that it ripped a large part of my dress with its jaws. That was it for my mother; she made Buck get rid of the dog immediately. My parents took a dim view of the "sports" of dog fighting and cockfighting. After the ripped-dress episode, that was it: no more animals of that type on the premises. Before that incident, they would occasionally let Buck keep his fighting animals at their house.

Our family hoped that Buck's life would change for the better when he remarried. It looked that way for awhile, and then a daughter was born to Buck and his wife. Unfortunately, after the birth of this daughter, the restlessness that seemed to be a part of Buck's personality reappeared. Sadly, his second marriage also came to an early end.

There seemed to be marked differences between the personalities of my four brothers. Both Buck and L.C. were more hot-tempered and pugnacious than Jack and Clyde. None of my brothers ever really sought out trouble or tried to create strife. It just seemed that Buck and L.C. were there when it happened, and neither of them believed in backing down when faced with a potential confrontation.

Buck moved from job to job. Before he first got married, he was in the poultry business, buying and selling chickens. Then he went into the commodities business with some other young men in west Dallas. Buck also moved his home around quite a bit. He lived with my mother's sister Belle for a time. Buck and his first wife also lived at the Eagle Ford Road service station with my parents on occasion, and in rented rooms when financially able.

While Buck was rambling around, Clyde steadily gravitated between the family home in west Dallas and Uncle Frank's farm. When my parents moved into Dallas, Clyde had made it through the sixth grade. It was these years in which I began to really know him. Everything I can recall about him in this point of his life was good. Everything about his earlier years was perfectly normal.

Clyde's ambition during this period was to be a musician. He liked music and showed a real talent for it. He could play just about any instrument he picked up. Clyde also could sing and dance. He and my sister Nell could do a really good "Charleston," which was the rage back in the 1920s. As for myself, the "jitterbug" was my dance. Clyde and L.C. were also big on marbles. They just loved to play, as did most boys growing up in those years. Clyde and L.C. kept their marbles in those old "Bull Durham" bags. In short, they were like any other kids, with no hint of the troubles to come.

One of the areas in which they were like so many other boys in the mid-1920s was in playing "hookey" from school. This was a holdover from their earlier years in the country. Down around Ellis and Navarro counties, farm kids attended school less rigidly than did children in the city, due to planting and harvesting and all of the work in between. The work a youngster would have to do on the farm was known and understood by all parties, so absences were not particularly noted. If a child decided to take a day or two to spend the time at the "old fishin' hole," it wasn't considered anything to get excited about.

But Clyde and L.C. found the attitudes of people in the urban areas were much different than those of the more relaxed countryside. They became acquainted with the hard realities of compulsory education. They learned to keep an eye out for the creature known as the truant officer when they decided that a day was just too nice to spend within the stuffy confines of a classroom.

Although just a little girl at the time, I was also learning the ways of the urban jungle. When the three of us headed off to school in the morning,

Clyde and L.C. would bribe me with a quarter not to tell my mother that her two sons were going to take a day off from the educational grind. To prove to my brothers the truth of the Biblical injunction that "the way of the transgressor is hard," I not only took their quarter, but also forced L.C. to give me "bicycle rights." Which is to say, he had to let me ride his bike whenever I wanted. I drove a hard bargain with those boys.

When the boys would take off, they wouldn't hang around their home neighborhood, of course. Clyde and L. C. would sometimes head for the hilly area outside of west Dallas and sometimes they would go over to Kiest Park in Oak Cliff. While they were out on these excursions, they went to the places where most other boys did their hanging around. At this time, Clyde was in his mid-teens and L.C. was in his early teenage years, those years in which kids begin to think somewhat independently. It was while he was out on these truancies that Clyde would sometimes find a small dog or cat in the countryside. Instead of butchering or mutilating it as the people down in Houston said he did, Clyde would pick it up and bring it home with him. There was one such animal that I especially remember. Once Clyde found a kitten out there in the woods and brought it home with him. It seemed to "meow" all of the time, so Clyde and I thought we'd name it "Kitty Meow." "Kitty Meow" wound up living several years at the service station with our family.

Before I leave the relatively placid and peaceful early years of Clyde and Buck in this chapter, I want to mention one more notion that many people have about Clyde. I want to eliminate the misconception as to just who Clyde grew up knowing out there in west Dallas.

Clyde did not run around with either Raymond or Floyd Hamilton when he was growing up. I recall hearing Floyd Hamilton telling about how he knew Clyde out there at the Cedar Valley School. First of all, the only public school Clyde attended in Dallas was Sidney Lanier. I've read accounts of how Clyde went to just about every public school there was in Dallas. I've even read about how he went to school at the Carroll School up in Grapevine. All of these stories are totally untrue. He only attended school at one place: Sidney Lanier.

Second of all, I know Clyde didn't associate with either Raymond or Floyd because I was the primary contact between the Barrows and the Hamiltons, and it happened because my father sold those 25¢ barrels of water to Floyd's and Raymond's mother and sisters. There were four Hamilton sisters, with Lillie being the oldest. Then came Lucy and

Maggie. Audrey Hamilton, the youngest of the family, was the same age I was; we became fast friends But none of my brothers ran around with either of her brothers during these earlier years. The only contacts there were between our families were between Audrey and myself. At this time, Audrey's mother Alice was married to Steve Davis; she had divorced her husband John Hamilton a few years previously. The Hamilton girls lived one street over, except for Lillie who lived a couple of blocks away on County Road.

Clyde also never had any association with Ted Hinton as a youngster. Ted Hinton, in his book, says that he knew Clyde somewhat, but that he knew Buck and my parents much better. I can't recall seeing Ted Hinton anytime or anyplace during those early days. I don't recall Buck ever mentioning him, and I know he never came out to visit my parents socially before Clyde and Buck took to the road after they left prison. There's just no early close connection between Hinton and the Barrow family, despite what his book indicates.

Finally, Clyde never knew Bonnie Parker while he was growing up. I've heard stories of them as teenage lovers "pledging their troth" on the banks of the Trinity River. Clyde knew nothing of her before 1930. The only connection the two of them had was indirect. Clyde did run with a boy named Clarence Clay in west Dallas during the 1920s. Clarence's sister married a boy named Buster Parker, who was Bonnie's older brother. But there was no contact between our family and any of the Parkers before Clyde met Bonnie.

Chapter 4

Bonnie Parker included the following verse in her poem "The Story of Bonnie and Clyde:"

From Irving to west Dallas viaduct
Is known as the Great Divide,
Where the women are kin,
And the men are men,
And they won't "stool" on Bonnie and Clyde.

This was a bit of social commentary on the neighborhood where many of the kids who later became noted as fugitives came from. West Dallas viaduct was indeed the "Great Divide" between the two areas. In terms of geographical distance, west Dallas was only a short distance from the office buildings and businesses of downtown Dallas, but in socioeconomic terms, west Dallas was a million miles away. This circumstance was recognized by the residents in both areas.

West Dallas, although it bore the name of the city, was not formally incorporated into the surrounding metropolis until the early 1950s, thirty years after the Barrow family moved out there. Dallas really didn't want any part of the area west of the "Great Divide," and west Dallas was just county territory. It was under the jurisdiction of the Dallas county sheriff's office.

But the jurisdictional situation never stopped the Dallas city police from coming out and rounding up "the usual suspects" when a crime against property was committed in the city of Dallas. It was automatically assumed that some predator from west Dallas committed the robbery or burglary.

But, in reality, I've always considered west Dallas as a generally decent, law abiding place, a lot more civilized than it was typically given credit for being. Back in the days when our family lived on Eagle Ford Road, people could leave their doors unlocked at night. You can't do that anywhere in the city of Dallas now during either day light or dark. We could walk down the streets at night and consider ourselves a lot safer than many high-income neighborhoods in Dallas are today. I wish today's Dallas was as "rough and tough" as west Dallas truly was back in the 1920s and 1930s. We'd be a lot better off.

Now, I'm not saying that there was never any crime whatsoever out there, but just that it was a lot less plentiful than it was portrayed back in the days of Clyde and Buck. The people out there knew that they were regarded as being from "the wrong side of the tracks," but they still did the best they could. That was all anyone could do back in those days. People across the "Great Divide" looked out for each other as people everywhere do. They took care of other people's needs when illness struck, supplying food and other support. When someone passed on, friends and neighbors out in west Dallas gave all of the assistance they could to the bereaved family.

But, in socioeconomic terms, west Dallas was still regarded as consisting of the "have nots" as opposed to the "haves" in the city of Dallas. This is where the west Dallas viaduct did its great dividing. West Dallas was the area where the newly arrived rural-poor and dispossessed usually settled. No other part of the city wanted the burden of dealing with the droves of relatively unskilled and under-educated farm people who relocated to the urban areas to better their circumstances. I use the terms "unskilled" and "under-educated" guardedly; quite frankly, I think many of the farm people had more common sense and more innate ability than a lot of the city dwellers who looked down on them.

Of course, coupled with such prejudicial attitudes was the belief that poverty and criminal tendencies walked hand-in-hand. This belief, of course, was untrue; the vast majority of people in west Dallas were honest and law-abiding. A number of those who did have criminal careers later in life had no initial intent to do so. They had already been pegged the criminal type by both the Dallas police and the county authorities.

The bad reputation of west Dallas reached such a level that it was eventually burdened with the nickname of "Little Cicero." The nickname means nothing now, but back in the 1920s and 1930s, Cicero, Illinois, was considered the crime capital of the country because Al Capone had his headquarters there. The name "Cicero" became synonymous with gangsterism and lawlessness and boot-legging.

Speaking of boot-legging, let me make an emphatic point on the subject. During the Prohibition years, moon-shining and bootlegging were activities that were done just about everywhere else in the country. But there was one establishment out there in west Dallas where no moonshine or boot-leg liquor was sold and that was the Star Service Station owned by Mr. and Mrs. Henry Barrow. I've seen it in print that my father sold moonshine "under the counter" at his station. Nothing could be further from the truth; my father had no involvement with any aspect of the bootleg business. My mother wouldn't have tolerated it one bit. The only businesses that my parents ever had out there in west Dallas were totally legitimate and honest.

During the mid-1920s, I was attending the Cedar Valley School, which was a grade school with classes from the first through the fourth grades. The next step for the west Dallas scholar was the Cement City School, which went from the fifth grade through the seventh grade. After graduating from the seventh grade, high school was the next level. For those who went, going to high school required taking the bus to downtown Dallas to attend Tech High School. Both L.C. and I went to Cedar Valley and Cement City schools. A lot of west Dallas people chose not to make that trip to downtown Dallas and figured that it was now time to begin making their way in the world. Many people married at sixteen and seventeen and began to set up homes, jobs, and families.

It was around 1925 and 1926 that Clyde stopped spending a lot of time at Uncle Frank's farm. He was becoming more and more involved with the people in west Dallas. By this time, Clyde was almost fifteen and was thinking of what most young men did at that age: girls and jobs.

Clyde's first Dallas-area wage-earning job was with the Brown Cracker Candy Company for one dollar a day. He began to scale the ladder of success, moving to his second job at Proctor and Gamble where he made more money. From Proctor and Gamble, he went to the United Glass Company, where he was a glazier.

It is at this point in the story that I want to stop to clarify something. Our family, for over 60 years, has kept in its possession a hand-held mirror that Clyde made while he was at United Glass Company. On this mirror are the initials of a young woman, the first girl that Clyde ever had any serious involvement with - and it wasn't Bonnie. Her first name was Eleanor; initials were E.B.W. Clyde made the mirror for her as a gift. Clyde's involvement with this young woman occasioned the first time he got into a serious situation with the law.

This initial conflict occurred when Clyde and this girl's mother went to a town in east Texas to pick her up. Clyde didn't have a car to drive over there. He used what money he had to arrange for a rental auto. He and this girl's mother drove over there, and they decided to stay longer than anticipated. The car's owner reported it stolen. Eventually the matter was all sorted out, and Clyde received no sentence, once the authorities figured out that no intentional theft was involved. But the Dallas police began to take an interest in Clyde.

Clyde and this young woman continued to go together after the rental car episode was settled. In fact, the young couple decided to elope, with another couple going along to share in the festivities. But something went wrong during the trip; there was no marriage. The girl figured that the whole purpose of the trip was defeated when no marriage occurred; and she returned to Dallas first. A day or two later, Clyde came back, and then the other couple returned to town. I never found out what happened to cancel the planned marriage. Clyde just never talked about it. But after this, the relationship cooled down, although they continued to go together for awhile. Then it finally died out completely. Clyde got his hand-held mirror back, and this hand-held initialed ("E.B.W.") mirror has stayed in our family.

It was around this time that Clyde's second brush with the law occurred. It happened the same year as the rental car episode, 1926, and it involved Buck this time. As I mentioned previously, one of Buck's earliest jobs was dealing in poultry, buying and selling chickens. Towards the holidays, Buck had the opportunity to buy a load of turkeys from a couple of boys in west Dallas. Of course, turkeys are in demand around Thanksgiving and Christmas, and Buck figured he would have no trouble selling them off at that time of year. Besides, he was able to get them for a surprisingly good price - which may have been a tip-off right there that something wasn't quite right about the matter. But the need for money was such that Buck decided that he wouldn't "look a gift horse in the mouth," and he went ahead and bought the flock of turkeys. Knowing that Clyde was also needing money, Buck cut him in on the deal.

So Clyde and Buck bought the turkeys in good faith from the other boys. But the "gift horse" should've been looked in the mouth. The turkeys were indeed stolen and Buck and Clyde were caught with the goods. The charges were dismissed in this case also, but the interest of the Dallas police in both Buck and Clyde greatly increased. The cops began to regularly pick up both of my brothers after the turkey episode.

Clyde eventually moved on from the United Glass Company. During this time period he worked at the Bama Pie Company with my sister Nell's husband. Finally, Clyde began work with the A&K Top and Paint Shop.

There are a couple of things that I'd like to point out concerning Clyde's job experience. There's one place that he never worked, despite claims to the contrary; he never was a messenger boy for Western Union. My brother L.C. did work for Western Union in this capacity, though. Of course, just about every place in Dallas in the late 1920s had Clyde for an employee, according to some people. But, in all honesty, the handful of places that I've mentioned are the only establishments where Clyde ever really worked. Another point that I'd like to make is that Clyde was always rated as an excellent employee, no matter where he worked. He never had any trouble on the job, never was charged with stealing anything from a place of work, and was never fired from any employment. I've found that this was true of many of those who later became bandits and outlaws.

In the mid and late 1930s, I came to know John Wilson Dillinger, the father of desperado John Herbert Dillinger. I found out that John Dillinger Jr. was always rated well at any place he ever worked. History bears this ironic fact out in other cases. Texas train robber Sam Bass worked in Denton County for Sheriff "Dad" Egan in the mid 1870s. The only trouble Sam Bass ever had with Sheriff Egan was that Bass was too scrupulous with Egan's money. Bass would deny himself and Egan's team of horses while he was working as a teamster. When Billy the Kid was a youngster, he worked for a woman along with several other hired boys. This woman always especially remembered Billy because he was the only boy that never stole from her. Then, one has to ask, just why did these obviously honest young boys like Clyde, Billy the Kid, Sam Bass, and John Dillinger Jr. wind up taking the wrong road in life? It seems that many of them began in life with so much promise. I can't answer for any of the Old West people or for the Dillinger family, but I believe that I can give some possible clues as to what caused Clyde to eventually take the outlaw trail in life.

My mother always believed that Clyde's first step towards a career as an outlaw came as a result of his association with some "wild women" in west Dallas. But to her, any woman who wore makeup would be classified as a "wild woman."

I do believe female associations did play a part in Clyde's descent towards banditry. But these associations were only a part of the whole picture. I think you have to look at the times in general, west Dallas in particular, and Clyde's own unique personality to arrive at an explanation for what later happened in the life of my brother.

First of all, Clyde was born and raised on a farm when the bottom dropped out of the agricultural market. He spent the early years of his life alternating between the Henry Barrow farm near Telico and Uncle Frank's establishment near Corsicana. The area that he grew up in was agriculturally based. The towns of Ennis, Waxahachie, and Corsicana all served the area farmers, and the financial well-being of all of the businessmen and merchants of these cities depended on crops like cotton. Clyde did as well as any other young man in this time and place for the first twelve or thirteen years of his life.

But then, when my parents moved into west Dallas, the picture began to change for Clyde. When he got more and more involved in west Dallas, he found out that the game of life was played by different rules. Out there in Ellis and Navarro counties, working on the farm was the rule and not the exception. But in west Dallas, factory workers and merchants were the norm. Out by Telico, no one paid that much attention when you took some days off from school. But in west Dallas, truancy was taken much more seriously by the police and the school officials. The skills that enabled one to successfully work on a farm meant nothing in west Dallas; a person had to think in terms of a professional career to scale the ladder of financial success. The ability to accumulate money was what counted. The rules of life were altogether different in an urban environment.

This change in rules was especially emphasized by many of the girls Clyde tried to favorably influence. My mother especially remembered one girl who Clyde liked that really demanded a lot in terms of material things. Her choice in men was primarily determined by who could give her the most in terms of "things," i.e., who had the biggest income. Many girls would have nothing to do with any boy who they thought would never have anything. And Clyde, with his rural, nonprofessional background, must have felt like he was beginning the race for accomplishment at the back of the pack.

Then, a person had to look at the time in which Clyde was living out there in west Dallas, i.e., the middle and late 1920s. It was the era of get-rich-quick schemes and of the accumulation of overnight fortunes in terms of the stock market. The newspapers were full of daily accounts of people who had hit it big by making the right investment on the margin. This all-pervasive mentality of getting rich by being at the right place at the right time with the right amount of money influenced many people.

Then there was the influence of the movies and the stars they created. Many people aspired towards the lifestyles they saw portrayed in the movies and the actual lifestyles of the movie stars themselves. People wanted to dress like their favorite movie stars and drive the same cars they did. Now, out in west Dallas, believe it or not, we had no movie houses. But many people out there still went to the picture shows in downtown Dallas, at theatres like the Queen Theatre and the Fox Theatre. All it took was to catch the bus that ran from the courthouse out through west Dallas. It went out to Cement City and then retraced its route back to downtown Dallas.

As a side note, although there were no movie theatres out there in west Dallas, we still had some neighborhood entertainments. I especially remember the annual Fischer's Carnival that came through west Dallas. It set up out there at Carpenter's Grocery. It was something that I always looked forward to each year. We also saw a lot of the old fashioned "medicine shows" that came through our neighborhood.

Anyhow, young people back then, both boys and girls, were influenced by the general "get rich quick" mentality of the times and the examples portrayed by those in the movie business. But that had been true of many eras. But there was another area that also influenced many young people back in the late 1920s, and that was Prohibition.

Although no bootleg whiskey or moonshine was sold through my parents' service station, we did sell soft drinks, and that was it. We never sold booze of any sort. For that matter, we never had any kind of a grocery store either, despite what has been printed in many articles. But there were other places that weren't so circumspect, and these places were regular conduits for bootleg liquor.

Although west Dallas was nicknamed "Little Cicero,"after Al Capone's Illinois headquarters, Prohibition didn't bring any outlandish lawlessness to our neighborhood, like up in Chicago. In fact, none of our family ever got involved with this business, and if Clyde and Buck had any serious intentions of a career in crime, Prohibition was the golden time in which to do it. Bootleggers and rumrunners rode around in big cars and wore fancy clothes, and lived in a style that many people would've liked to have lived. Even with the temptations of fast and easy money, Clyde and Buck still never were drawn into rum-running.

But these were just three of the circumstances that influenced many people back in the late 1920s, and still Clyde never turned to an active life of crime. But there were yet two more factors which were needed to complete the explosive mixture: police activity in west Dallas and Clyde's own personality.

The police activity has already been alluded to, but it needs to be focused on again. Mention has already been made to the misadventures involving the rental car and the flock of turkeys. By the way, when renting the car, Clyde gave his own name and his correct work and home addresses, evidence that he didn't plan to make off with the auto. But the fact that both episodes occurred in short order in late 1926 made Clyde an item of interest to the Dallas police. Starting in early 1927, it seemed that anytime the Dallas police or the county officers were investigating a particular crime or were just needing something to do, they began picking up both Clyde and Buck wherever the boys were in west Dallas. No matter if they were working at their jobs or not, both of my brothers were summarily hauled off by the authorities, as were many other young men out there in west Dallas who had previous brushes with the law.

Buck had initially aroused the interest of the area police shortly after my parents moved into Dallas in the early 1920s. As I previously mentioned, my father immediately initiated a peddling business, buying and selling salvage and the like. Buck also got into this line of work at about the same time. He was approached by someone who had a load of brass that they wanted to get rid of real cheap and in a hurry. Buck's financial circumstances at the time were extremely bad. Since he could always find people who needed brass, he agreed to buy the load. This deal seemed too good to be true, and it was, of course: the brass turned out to be stolen and Buck was left holding the bag.

I'd also like to point out that in the case of both Buck's brass and the turkeys, the Barrow boys were not accused of initially stealing the goods, but they were picked on possession of stolen goods. The turkey episode is not even listed on Clyde's FBI criminal record. At this time, neither of my brothers had any intentions of a life of predatory crime.

Beginning in early 1927, police interest greatly increased, and the boys' attitudes began to change. Previous mention has been made to the differences in their emotional makeup, that Buck was quicker to anger than Clyde. But now both personalities began to play a part in the situation.

My mother began to note a change in Clyde beginning around 1925 or 1926, about the time he began to work full-time. She observed that Clyde seemed to be continuously dissatisfied with his circumstances. He was never happy with the wages he made, and began changing jobs to increase his earnings. She saw that he began to get very concerned with his personal appearance in terms of grooming and the clothes he wore. He seemed to become greatly preoccupied with things that were needed to impress the girls out in west Dallas, which meant good clothes, cars, and nice gifts. The money he made at the jobs he worked at never seemed to be enough to reach a level of satisfaction.

So I guess it could be a combination of factors which led to the escalating circumstances which finally ended in a career of banditry for Clyde. His early years in the slower, more laid back, agrarian areas like Waxahachie had conditioned him in the same way, and he seemed to fit in fairly well. Then the complete turn around to the lifestyle of the city caused Clyde to realize how ill-equipped he was to deal with what it took to be considered a success there. He was faced with a choice: he could either go ahead and play the cards that life had dealt him as best as he could, or he could try to change the rules of the game. He chose to change the rules. Clyde initially tried to play his hand the best way possible, getting legitimate jobs and trying to get money on the side, as with the turkey deal. Then, when it seemed that over-interest on the part of the police was unfairly changing the rules against him, Clyde resolved to do a little rule changing of his own.

Chapter 5

So it was that the end of the year 1926 had drawn the battle lines in the conflict between Clyde and Buck and the constabulary of both Dallas city and Dallas County. Although the boys were frequently picked up throughout 1927, they were not charged with anything and were always released. As for me, I would turn nine years old in 1927 and didn't understand all of this which was going on with Buck and Clyde.

My older brother Jack and my sisters were doing well with their jobs and families. Jack was still operating his auto garage out of the back of his house on Forest Avenue, supporting his family. His four daughters would all graduate from Forest Avenue High School. Jack would never be classed with the Barrows of west Dallas during the early 1930s.

Nell and Artie were continuing with their careers with beauty parlors. Artie had an operation going in Denison, Texas, while her husband worked at the Denison newspaper. Nell's husband was a band leader.

Clyde and Buck were still trying to hold legitimate jobs, although the frequent rides to downtown Dallas courtesy of the police made such jobs harder and harder to maintain. One of the jobs Buck had at this time was helping to make willow furniture for an operation in downtown Dallas. The furniture itself was made at the old campground where the Barrows initially stayed when first coming to town. The manufacturers of this willow furniture would give kids a percentage to sell this furniture in some of the better neighborhoods around Dallas. The kids would make anywhere from 10¢ to 25¢ for each piece of furniture they sold.

My parents were worried sick about the turn that events were taking concerning Clyde and Buck, but there was little that they could do concerning the frequent police pickups. All they could do was pray that things wouldn't get any worse.

But 1927 turned into 1928, and things did become worse for both of my brothers. According to Clyde's FBI record, he was formally arrested in Ft. Worth on February 22. The charge was one of "investigation." The fact that the charges were dismissed still didn't give my parents any significant peace of mind.

Then, several months later, Buck got into trouble down in San Antonio. He was jailed, and a trial was set up. My parents resolved to go down there and supply whatever moral support they could give to their son. So, the four of us (Henry, Cumie, L.C., and myself) left west Dallas to go to San Antonio. Except we didn't drive down in a car, nor did we go down by train. We didn't have the financial means to travel by auto or railroad. My father made the 1928 trip down to San Antonio by horse and wagon.

Now this was the same horse that we had when we lived at the campground. Later this same horse was in an accident with a car on the viaduct. It was run through by a piece of metal from the automobile, but it still galloped all of the way back to the campground. At the campground it dropped down dead. When my father relocated to the service station on Eagle Ford Road, he got himself a Model T. That's the only auto my father ever drove, and that was the car that I first learned to drive with.

The Barrow family didn't go down to San Antonio alone, though. We were accompanied by three members of the Jones family: Mrs. Jones and two of her three sons, Leroy and William Daniel. We first got to know the Jones family when they lived on the campground at the same time we did. The three Jones boys paralleled the last three Barrow kids: Clyde Jones was about the same age as our Clyde, William Daniel (whom we called W.D.) was around L.C.'s age, and Leroy Jones was my age. I never knew Mr. Jones, though, as the Joneses had separated before we got to know Mrs. Jones and her sons.

That trip to San, Antonio is another one of the best-remembered experiences of my childhood. As I said, we could not afford auto or rail transportation. We really didn't even have the money beforehand to afford the expenses of the journey. We were able to make a living by working on farms along the road that we took down to San Antonio.

Although we did do some odd jobs on these farms, our primary work was chopping and picking cotton. My father was one of the best cotton-pickers that I ever saw. He really put effort into it, working down on his knees. But picking cotton was really hard on my father's hands: his fingernails would always come off after he'd been picking a long time. My career as a cotton picker only lasted one performance. There is apparently a science and a skill connected with the proper picking of cotton, but at the age of ten, I sure wasn't aware of that process. Everything I picked up in my hands got put into my cotton sack. We were paid by thc pound when they weighed our sacks. The people we worked for went ahead and paid for my poundage, cotton, leaves, twigs, and all, but that was it for my cotton picking career. After that, it was determined that there were other things that I could do to earn money on the trip than the picking of cotton. But the rest of the Barrows and Joneses chopped and picked a lot of cotton.

The money that was earned from the odd jobs and the cotton work was used to buy food for both families and feed for the horse. I can still clearly remember my mother and Mrs. Jones cooking our food out there in pots and pans over a campfire. Our meals primarily consisted of fried potatoes, fried cornbread, and a big pot of beans. The seven of us camped out at night around the wagon. It was quite an experience for a ten-year-old girl.

Buck's case involved an attempted car theft. It was dismissed in January, 1929. I don't know if my parents' and friends' presence there had anything to do with it, but I know that they were very relieved and happy when the charges were dropped, and everyone returned to Dallas.

But, just as Buck's fortunes seemed to be improving, Clyde's fortunes were starting to take a turn for the worse. It was about this time that Clyde made the acquaintance of the first truly bad influence of his life. Up until now, Clyde's friends and acquaintances had been those other boys he'd ran around with in west Dallas like Clarence Clay, who never had any trouble with the law at all, and Clyde Jones, of whom I don't recall any law-related trouble. Clyde also ran with the sons of many of the other west Dallas business owners. None of these boys ever got into any significant trouble either. But when Clyde fell in with Frank Clause, he fell in with his first truly bad companionship. Frank Clause made Clyde's acquaintance when they worked together at one of Clyde's later jobs. Frank was a very nice looking young man who didn't look in the slightest like the person he truly turned out to be. He wasn't even from west Dallas, but lived close to downtown Dallas. Frank was very familiar with the shady side of life, and he was the first person that Clyde ever got into trouble with concerning predatory criminality.

It was in his activities with Frank Clause that Clyde began to use a gun. While growing up, Clyde had always been around guns. He showed a great interest in them at Uncle Frank's farm, although he never cared for hunting with them. Clyde liked to fire rifles and revolvers at targets. Later, he always kept a rifle at our parents' home. I still have that rifle. It is an 1892 Winchester, and it has been in the possession of the Barrow family since the late 1920s, when Clyde first acquired it. I learned how to shoot with it myself. Clyde always could pick out a good gun for whatever use he needed. This old Winchester rifle still works as well as when Clyde used it, almost 70 years ago. We even still have the old leather cover, still initialed "C. B."

But this type of lever-action Winchester rifle could in no way be considered as a gangster-type gun; it was strictly a rifle that could be used for hunting or for self-defense or for recreational-type uses like target-shooting. Clyde showed no interest in the acquisition of any Tommy guns or Browning Automatic Rifles or sawed-off shotguns at this time.

Many accounts have Clyde moving in with Frank Clause almost immediately and going on a crime spree all over the state of Texas. These accounts have Clyde teaming up with Clause and Raymond Hamilton, with the trio traveling to Houston to join up with something called the "Root Square Gang." There are several things wrong with this scenario. First of all, Clyde still had no acquaintance with Raymond Hamilton at the time he began to associate with Clause. Second, Clyde was still trying to hold down a regular job in Dallas at this time. Third, I don't believe the story that Clyde was living with Frank Clause, because he was alternating his living arrangements between my parents and my sister Nell and her husband Leon Hale. I'll get back to Frank Clause later, but let me describe why I believe that Clyde was with Nell and Leon on Pear Street in Dallas instead of with the "Root Square Gang" in Houston.

Nell's husband and Clyde both had something very much in common: natural talent in the area of musical ability. Clyde was fascinated by anything that had to do with music. He had already become proficient with the guitar. It was at this time, while staying with Nell and Leon, that he learned to play the saxophone.

Contrary to some accounts, Clyde never played saxophone in any professional bands around Dallas back in the 1920s. He became a pretty good sax player during this time. Nell gave him ukulele lessons during this period and he came to play fairly well. Clyde must have inherited some of his musical ability from my mother. Cumie could play both the French harp and the jews-harp.

So Clyde couldn't have learned the saxophone and the ukulele while living at Nell's and Leon's and couldn't have struggled to hold down an honest job while, at the same time, terrorizing the southwest with the likes of Frank Clause and Raymond Hamilton. Yet he was associating with Clause around the Dallas area.

I believe Frank got Clyde involved with his first professional crime at this time. I don't, however, believe that Clyde was roaming the countryside, a full-fledged brigand with machine gun in hand. I do think Clause got him involved in activities like burglaries and second story jobs. These types of crimes seemed to have little risk both of gunplay and of innocent people getting hurt. Frank emphasized that the goods they stole were covered by insurance and that nobody would really be hurt, except for the insurance companies, and they deserved to be hit anyway. Frank also argued that since the police had already given Clyde the name, he might as well play the game. This second argument was the one that evidentially hit home with my brother, and he began to work with Clause "to even the odds," from Clyde's perspective, in the game of life.

Ironically, while Clyde was falling under the bad influence of a career criminal, Buck was about to come under the good influence of the one person who could have made a big difference for the better in his life, had he met her a few years earlier. After Buck's second marriage failed, he didn't immediately enter into any serious relationships. Buck was casually dating a west Dallas girl when he met another girl who was visiting his date. This visitor's name was Blanche Caldwell. When Buck and Blanche met, sparks flew, and Buck immediately forgot his west Dallas girlfriend. They became an immediate item.

Many accounts state that Blanche came from a farm in Missouri, but this was not the case when Buck made her acquaintance. At this time, she was living with her father up in Oklahoma, where he was a preacher. Blanche's parents were separated. Since she was really close to her father, she elected to stay with him after the separation.

Some accounts have tried to portray Blanche as a gunwoman and someone who was very familiar with the ways of the underworld. Out of all of the people who ever associated with Buck and Clyde, Blanche was the last person in the world anyone would have expected to run with my brothers in their days out on the highway. Blanche was a good, nice, sweet, gentle person and was as proper and respectable as a preacher's daughter could be expected to be. Yet, she and Buck were attracted to each other immediately. I often wished that he could've met Blanche much earlier in his life. If he had, his life story would've been much happier. But, as it happened, Buck met her after his trial in San Antonio, and several years after the Dallas police had taken an interest in him.

In fact, it was just a few months after Buck met Blanche that he and Clyde got in to the first serious trouble that I ever knew of them being involved with. In October, 1929, both of my brothers were involved with two other boys in an attempted burglary in the town of Denton, Texas. They were surprised by the police as they attempted to get away and a chase ensued. My brothers' car tried to make a turn at high speed around a street corner. They didn't make it: their auto smashed into a curb and broke an axle. Buck and one of the boys stood their ground by the car and were arrested. The police came in shooting, but Buck was not seriously wounded. Clyde and the other boy got away from the wreck on foot. This other boy was captured shortly after they fled, but Clyde managed to hide under a vacant house. After waiting under this house for a full day, Clyde made his way back to west Dallas the following evening.

Buck took full and sole responsibility for the affair at Denton. He was put on trial, convicted, and received a sentence of four years. The boy who was arrested with Buck received a sentence of 10 years. Buck never implicated Clyde and, in fact, took responsibility for some of the things Clyde and Frank Clause had been involved in.

Clyde laid low in west Dallas for several weeks after the Denton affair. He was thoroughly shaken and unnerved. This was the first time that any of his activity involved a police chase, an automobile crash, and hostile gunfire. He heard the officers shoot as he ran away from the wreck, and it terrified him. Clyde had heard Buck cry out in pain from the police bullet. He thought his older brother had been fatally wounded.

Up until the Denton incident, I believed that Clyde and Buck were still just young men trying to make their way in the world as best as they could. I still looked at them as working boys, despite their previous run-ins with the law. I think the shock of both Buck's sentence and his narrow escape caused Clyde to walk the straight and narrow for weeks afterward. He went back to his pre-Clause cronies and his teenage friends. One of Clyde's oldest and best friends was Clarence Clay.

One night in early January, 1930, Clyde and Clarence went over to Clarence's sister's house for a visit. There were several other people there, including some of Clarence's in-laws. This was strictly a social gathering, a bunch of friends and relatives getting together for an evening of fun and talk. One of the guests was the sister of Clarence Clay's brother-in-law. Since Clarence's brother-in-law was Buster Parker, so happened the first meeting of Clyde Barrow and Bonnie Parker.

Chapter 6

Throughout the years, I've read many different stories as to how Clyde first met Bonnie. The way it really happened was the way I just described it. Let me list the ways it didn't happen.

Just about everyone has seen the 1967 movie *Bonnie and Clyde* somewhere along the line. In that film, the couple first meets when Clyde tries to steal Bonnie's mother's car from in front of her house. I'm surprised at the number of people who think that's really what happened.

Then there's the story about Clyde and Bonnie meeting in a small town in Louisiana. According to this tale, both of them are there visiting mutual friends when their paths cross. Clyde had no interests in any Louisiana small towns, and I wish it would've stayed that way. Nothing good ever came from any contacts or connections they had in Louisiana.

Another story has Bonnie working in a café up in Kansas City. One day she sees a hungry-looking young man peering into the restaurant's big plate glass window from out on the sidewalk. It's cold, and the young man (Clyde, of course) is obviously down on his luck. Good-hearted Bonnie naturally invites him in for a bite to eat. Sparks are generated by their initial contact, and then, Bonnie takes off with Clyde into the wild blue yonder. This cafe scenario also takes place in Dallas in some accounts of Clyde's life.

Yet another story is that Bonnie was going with Raymond Hamilton when she meets Clyde, a pal of Raymond's. She immediately falls for Clyde and gives Raymond the heave-ho. Hamilton stays with the couple thereafter, trying to win back Bonnie's affections.

Still another story has Bonnie walking down the sidewalk in downtown Dallas when Clyde happens to pass her. He is thunderstruck by her "striking yellow hair" and is stopped dead in his tracks. He stands there open-mouthed and bug-eyed, gawking at this vision of beauty. Bonnie is naturally flattered by his attention and stops to talk to him. Introductions are made, and then, the couple walks off together to make history. I suppose there are more stories making the rounds as to how Clyde Barrow met Bonnie Parker. But other accounts, as well as the ones I've mentioned, undoubtedly have one thing in common: they're all hogwash and there's not a bit of truth in any of them.

When they met at Clarence Clay's sister's house, the attraction was immediate; much like it was with Buck and Blanche. There had been no previous contact between them as a couple or between the Barrow and Parker families. I'm sure that about all Clyde knew about the Parkers before this was that Clarence Clay's sister had married a boy named Parker.

Clyde never brought Bonnie over to the service station after they first met. I suppose it would've happened if things were allowed to proceed along their natural course. But now Clyde's association with Frank Clause had caught up with him. Several days after meeting Bonnie, he was arrested by police while over at the Parkers' house in connection with several burglaries around north-central Texas. It was getting known around the neighborhood that the couple was becoming quite an item. The police, finding this fact out, just watched the Parker house until they knew Clyde was there.

So, two of my older brothers were now in the clutches of the law. Buck had just begun his four-year sentence down at Huntsville when Clyde was arrested. Buck was apparently going through the same reformation Clyde did after his narrow escape in Denton. Just before he was shipped down to Huntsville, Buck wrote us a letter from the Denton jail. In the original letter, Buck's early disinterest in schooling is readily apparent. For the benefit of the reader, the following rendition of my brother's letter is edited for clarity. It was dated January 12, 1930, and goes as follows:

> Mr. and Mrs. H. B. Barrow,
> My dear Mother and Father and all home folks,
> It is with pleasure that I send this letter to you in answer to your sweet letter which I received today. However, it grieves me to be compelled to send it to you from prison. Mother, the days drag on here now and it seems like six years since your tear-stained face looked in the jail here at me, your son. I can fully realize that if I had heeded yours and Father's kind loving advice, I would not have been here on this dreary lonesome day. Oh, Mother, if God gives me one more chance I shall try to do the best that is in me to lead a worthwhile life in

> the future and to be a man that the people will respect and that my relatives will honor. I know the heartaches and sorrow that my crookedness has given to you and Father.
>
> Mother, tell B------ that I am going to whip her year down if she doesn't write me, and also tell Elvin to send me gloves when I get down on the farm, but don't send auto gloves for there is no cars to drive down there and send me two big
>
> red handkerchiefs also. This is all for this time. I send you all of my love.
>
> Your son, Buck Barrow.

Buck included as a postscript "All for my dear mother," with a whole line of "x's" afterwards. It was just after this letter that Buck made the trip from the Denton jail to the Texas prison system farms down around Huntsville. This really devastated my mother.

Not only were two of her sons in trouble again, but one was already sentenced to a term in the penitentiary and it looked like the other was headed in the same direction right behind him. The boys had been in trouble before, but they had never been found guilty and sentenced to any jail terms. But now, one of them was already in the state pen and it didn't look good for the other one.

My mother felt better when she got the first letter from Buck written from the Huntsville-area prison farm. This letter has also been edited for the benefit of the reader. This letter was dated January 16, 1930.

> Dear Mother and all,
>
> Will write you a few lines to let you know that I have made the trip. Mother, I am in the hospital now and my legs are hurting pretty bad. It sure looks hard but I am going to take it. Mother, try to get me a furlough, and don't fail to write often and don't forget to tell Blanche to write me and to tell me all of the news that happens in the outside world. Send me some stamps and envelopes that I can write every day and I wish you would do the same. Mother, tell sister to send my shoes and send me some more pajamas because they

> burned mine up, but they will let me have some more now if you send them to me and tell her to help me all she can to get out on a parole or a furlough while you are so sick. I hope that the outside world don't forget me because I am in the walls.
> Goodbye Mother and don't worry -
> (signed) Marvin Barrow

Buck also included a postscript on this second letter: "Don't send me any tobacco but send me some money. Because they won't let any tobacco come in."

The trouble in Denton was the first time that I knew both my brothers to be involved in professional criminality but it turned out that Clyde had been involved with Frank Clause in quite a few burglaries around north-central Texas. Shortly after his arrest, Clyde was sent down to the jail in Waco where he was to be put on trial. Bonnie began to come over to our service station after Clyde was arrested and jailed. These visits were the first time that I'd ever met her. Bonnie could have been characterized as cute, even pretty when she fixed herself up. She was several inches shorter than Clyde, and was just under five feet tall. She was slender in stature, probably weighing under 100 pounds. I don't recall hearing anything about her around west Dallas before she met Clyde, so she'd never been in any significant trouble herself. But she had a husband named Roy Thornton that couldn't make that same claim. He was in prison at the time Bonnie was socializing around west Dallas. Bonnie and Roy had married back around 1926, but they had separated for good a couple of years later. Bonnie wouldn't consider getting a formal divorce, though, as she felt that it wouldn't have been right since Roy was in prison. It would've been like kicking him while he was down.

We all liked Bonnie, but she never made the impact on us that Blanche did. My mother especially liked the fact that Blanche's father was a minister. Bonnie's father had died when she was a little girl, and her mother moved her little family from the small town of Rowena, Texas, into the Dallas area. Bonnie had a younger sister named Billie Jean, as well as her older brother Buster. Bonnie had a pleasant personality and liked to laugh. She had a good mind, having had a number of years of schooling around Cement City. She had been deeply impressed by Clyde, and found a degree of solace by being around his family while he was in jail.

When Clyde was transferred down to Waco, Bonnie followed him there, and she stayed with a friend. She had visited him when she was allowed to do so, and wrote him a lot of letters.

So it was that in January, 1930, Buck was sent to the Huntsville area prison farm and Clyde was arrested, jailed, and transferred to the Waco jail. The month of February came and went with no changes in the status of my brothers. Buck continued to serve his time and Clyde was being set up for trial on both car theft and burglary charges. Then, in early March, everything changed drastically: both of my brothers made successful jail breaks within a few days of each other.

Buck's prison break came first. It certainly couldn't be considered as a classic "bust-out" with machine-gun wielding guards and bloodhounds, searchlights, and wailing sirens. Buck merely walked away from his prison job. During the first week of March, Buck was working as a trustee in the kitchen area of the prison farm. He and another boy just walked out of the kitchen, got into one of the guards' cars and drove away, disappearing in the maze of country roads and wooded areas around Huntsville.

It took Buck and the other boy about five hours to make their way from the prison farm to west Dallas. The first thing he wanted to do was to come back home. Buck wore his white prison uniform all of the way home. I remember that day very well: we heard someone walk up on the porch and open the door to the house. When Buck stuck his head in the door way and gave a good-natured laugh, all of us just about fell over in a dead faint. Buck was the last person we ever expected to see (except maybe for Clyde) on a casual visit. Buck's last letter to us was dated on February 24, 1930, and was postmarked from Midway, Texas. In this letter, Buck seemed to be adjusting tolerably well to prison life:

> My dear mother -
> I am sorry I have not written you sooner. I am well and hope you are the same. The guards and the Captain down here treat me awfully good. So I see no reason why I should not get along. You must write me often and with all of the good news. Tell Marie I will send her something pretty when I get some money. My Captain's name is Mr. W. R. Crume and anything you want to write him for

> me will be alright. You ask me if I needed anything - I am doing fine and don't need a thing, only lots of sweet letters from you, Mother Dear. Will close with all of my love to you -
> Your son Buck
> c/o Ferguson Farm, Midway, Texas

So you can understand my family's shock when Buck broke out of prison just a few days after such a reassuring letter. My brother seemed to take the whole thing lightly as he told of how he just walked and drove away from the Ferguson farm. My father just smiled, shook his head, and said, "That's Buck." My mother, like myself, was both delighted to see him safe and sound at home again and frightened by the circumstances under which this unexpected reunion took place. Buck didn't forget these circumstances, either. He just came by long enough to reassure us and to get out of those prison clothes. The other boy was still with him, and they were still in the guards' car. Buck left his prison clothes and shoes with us and told us to burn them, but my mother never did. Then he and the other boy disappeared into the night.

Later, I found out that Buck picked up Blanche after his visit home, and they hid out for awhile in a rooming house somewhere. The other boy separated from Buck shortly afterward and was rearrested a short time later.

I'll get back to Buck's adventures later, but now it's time to return to Clyde's rather dire circumstances. Unlike Buck, Clyde didn't send any reassuring letters. He knew that he might very well face a long prison sentence for his activities with Frank Clause. Clyde began to make his own plans for an escape from the Waco jail.

Clyde's plans were more elaborate than Buck's relatively simple getaway. One of the boys in jail with Clyde was from Waco, and he knew of a house where a gun was hidden. Unfortunately, the boy's friends were well-known to the Waco police and would be carefully watched when visiting the prison. But Bonnie Parker was a nobody to the Waco police department, making her the best candidate to sneak a gun into the jail.

One day when Bonnie was visiting Clyde, he slipped her a note which contained a chart showing where the gun was located in the particular house. She followed the instructions explicitly and smuggled the gun into the jail under her clothing.

There's a little historical anecdote concerning this note. Bonnie always kept it with her as a keepsake for years afterward. In fact, this note came into our possession a few years later. In early 1934, Bonnie left one of her purses at the service station after she and Clyde paid a visit. My mother found the purse and opened it to determine to whom it belonged. She found this Waco jail note in the purse. It was written on a piece of rough tablet paper. There was a rough diagram of the house in which the gun was hidden. Under this diagram, Clyde wrote a little message to Bonnie: "You are the sweetest baby in the world to me - I love you."

Anyways, Clyde finally got his hands on this gun after Bonnie's cooperation. Clyde's next step was to ask the jailer for a bottle of milk. There were two other boys who were to be in on this escape attempt and all three were in Clyde's cell when the jailer returned with the requested milk. When the jailer opened the door, one of the boys threw himself in the doorway, with the other two following. They grabbed the jailer, shoved him in the cell, and locked the door.

Unlike Buck, Clyde didn't immediately return to our house, nor did he contact Bonnie, who was still in Waco. In fact, the three boys didn't spend any time contacting any friends or family, instead stole the first car they could get their hands on and headed north. Between Waco and the state of Ohio, Clyde and his associates stole three autos. It was in Ohio that the three boys checked the newspapers and found that the law was looking for them in the same area. That seemed too close for comfort, and the trio decided to head back towards Texas.

The boys had made it through the town of Middletown, Ohio, when the inevitable happened. The car they were riding was spotted by the police. Clyde's two associates were captured, but Clyde jumped from the car before the other two were arrested and made his escape. He hid for several hours under a house, just like he did in Denton. Clyde got concerned that one of the police or that a regular citizen might catch a glimpse of him, so he decided to make a break for it. Clyde was spotted as he made his way from his hiding place. With the police on his tail, he ran toward a river. Clyde was cornered - and he still had the gun Bonnie had smuggled to him. The last thing he did before the cops grabbed him was to pitch the gun into the river. Clyde and his two friends had been out of the Waco jail for a week before they were rearrested. All three were returned to Texas.

The newspapers in Waco had a field day with the jail break. The press characterized my brother as Clyde "Schoolboy" Barrow in some articles. The boys were called "Baby Bandits" and "Baby Thugs" in news stories. A few of the reports even called them "Dumbell Bandits." The reason Clyde and his two fellow prisoners were characterized as such was because they were recaptured in Middletown, Ohio, just four hours after robbing a railroad station in that same town. They were trying to get money with which to finance their return trip to Texas. They had made their getaway but had gotten lost in the Ohio countryside. They accidentally found themselves in Middletown again after four hours of driving. Of course, the papers made it sound like a well-planned heist instead of a spur-of-the-moment action. If the boys really wanted a well planned big score, there were places closer to Texas where they could've gotten money.

The Waco newspapers even came up to our house in west Dallas to interview my parents. My mother had quite a bit to say on the matter. She said Clyde was a good boy before he got involved with this Waco crowd. My brother had to have met these boys through Frank Clause, who was well-known throughout underworld circles in several north-central Texas towns. Clyde's transfer to Waco was the first inclination that any of us had concerning his involvement with Clause's crowd. My mother told the Waco newspapers that Clyde's involvement in this jailbreak was unnecessary in that he probably wouldn't have gotten a severe sentence from the Clause-related burglaries. But since his escapade had involved firearms, interstate flight, and armed robbery, Clyde had forfeited any leniency he might have gotten from the Waco courts. This statement proved to be prophetic; Clyde was hit with the maximum for his criminal activity. The judge sentenced him to seven two-year terms which were to be served cumulatively, which meant a total of fourteen years. Adding insult to injury, the judge delivered these sentences with scathing words.

My mother had spoken to the jury at Clyde's trial, and she asked them to make the sentence as light as they could seeing as it was his first conviction. They still gave him the maximum. The court's sentence was later overturned by the Texas Supreme Court in Austin. They said that these seven sentences should run concurrently, reducing Clyde's sentence to two years.

While all of this was going on, Bonnie Parker had returned to west Dallas. She left Waco shortly after the three boys broke out of jail, and frequently visited us at the service station. In fact, she was with my mother when she was interviewed by the Waco newspaper. She and Clyde wrote to each other for the first several months of his jail term. Then her initially frequent letters began to taper off somewhat because she became involved with other boyfriends in west Dallas. Her visits to our house on Eagle Ford Road became more and more infrequent as time passed, finally stopping altogether. I know Bonnie's mother was pressuring her to end her relationship with Clyde due to his troubles with the law.

My mother knew what she was doing when she asked the jury to consider leniency in sentencing Clyde. She knew that a harsh prison sentence in one of the hellish state prison farms would be counterproductive in that it would harden and embitter Clyde. My mother was aware of his last-ditch commitment to personal reformation after his scare with the Denton police chase, car wreck, and Buck's injury. It turned out that my mother was one hundred percent correct in her concerns.

The devastating nature of Clyde's prison term became apparent during the first week of his confinement. Clyde was a handsome young man of medium height and of slender build. He attracted the attention of an older, bigger, heavier, stronger inmate with depraved instincts. For the price of three packs of cigarettes, this deranged inmate arranged to "purchase the rights" to Clyde from the guards. These coffin nails bought the pervert the uninterrupted right to have his way with Clyde. During his first week, and for some time after, Clyde was sodomized by the inmate.

What the prisoner didn't realize was by sexually abusing Clyde, he had made a fatal mistake. He was later found dead. Some believed Clyde evened the score with a lead pipe. But no formal investigation was started on the death of the prison bully.

Clyde's prison difficulties went well beyond dealing with the twisted mentalities of other prisoners. There was the way the Texas prison system was run throughout the 1930's. The prisoners were disciplined for infractions by many extreme measures. One of these punishments sounds simple enough; it was called "riding the barrel" and all it involved was standing on top of a pickle barrel. A prisoner would stand on top of the barrel for hours and hours which could stretch into nights and days. Inevitably, the prisoner would sooner or later collapse. There was one time when Clyde was forced to "ride the barrel" for a long period of time. While he was on the pickle barrel, he had to endure the direct effects of a violent thunderstorm.

There were also the harsh disciplines of everyday prison life. Mention has already been made to Buck concerning the fact that he was serving his time on the Ferguson farm. These prison farms, like the Ferguson farm and the Eastham farm, were at one time cotton plantations that were owned by families that were named Ferguson and Eastham. These farms were given to the state of Texas. The state continued to run these plantations as cotton-producing facilities, using convict labor. The prisoners spent all day from sunup to sundown working in the cotton fields, hoeing and picking cotton. The guards always rode horses to oversee the prisoners, and they would run the prisoners from the buildings out to the fields every morning and back to the buildings every evening. And I do mean "run;" the prisoners were forced to run at a fast clip for quite a distance between the fields and the prison buildings. These prison buildings were not cell blocks like one would see on Alcatraz. These were dormitory-like arrangements with a big room full of bunk beds where the prisoners slept.

There were no individual, barred cells. Meals were cooked and served outside. Prisoners received their visitors outdoors also. Although communication between Clyde and Bonnie had decreased substantially as 1930 turned into 1931, Clyde always wrote to his mother, trying to put the best light possible on his circumstances. One of his letters, dated December 3, 1931, mailed from Weldon, Texas, illustrates his outlook:

> Dear Mother -
> Will drop you a few lines to let you know I haven't forgotten you. Say, what is wrong? I haven't had a letter from you in over a week. I have been worried about you all. This leaves me ok, except a little cold. Well, how is everything in big Dallas by now? It is raining down here and has been for three days. How is little Marie and L.C. and have you got your station fixed up yet? I sure wish I was there to help you. After you get everything going okay, Papa should build him a little place and handle used auto parts. You can buy them for a song. Well how is Elvin and Drucie? I sure would like to see you all. Have you heard anything

> from Blanche or not? Be sure and make her bring you down here and another thing, it isn't long until Xmas, so remind them all of that old cake and chicken. Well, Mother, I don't know any news. So will close for this time hoping to hear from you real soon. Your loving son,
> (signed) Clyde Barrow
> Weldon, Texas
> Route 16
> Camp No. 1

Clyde's reference concerning Blanche in his letter was really a veiled reference to how Buck was doing. Clyde could hardly mention his older brother directly, since Buck was still on the lam. Ironically, while Clyde's prison break was short and violent, Buck was free for almost twenty-two months. During this time period, Buck and Blanche went up to Oklahoma, where they were married.

Blanche's influence on Buck was extremely good. My brother was at last becoming the person he so wanted, to become in his letters from prison: "to lead a worthwhile life in the future and to be a man that the people will respect and that my relatives will honor."

Despite Buck settling in well to a respectable life with Blanche, the fact that he was still an escaped convict hung over everyone's head like a dark cloud. Reverend Caldwell, Blanche's father, began to try to influence Buck towards going back to prison to finish his debt to society. Blanche took up the same chorus. Whenever Buck and Blanche came back through Dallas to visit us, my mother would add her voice to those who were advising Buck to go back to prison, finish his term, and then live an upstanding life afterward. If Buck didn't feel that he could live around Dallas without being picked up by the police all of the time, then he and Blanche could start all over again up in Oklahoma with Blanche's people.

Finally, all of the family pressure paid off. Buck agreed to go back to prison to finish his term. However, he wanted one condition before he would go back: he wanted to spend Christmas on the outside with his family. Once the holiday was over, he would return to prison at the mercy of the penal system. Everyone agreed to this condition, and Buck spent Christmas Day, 1931, in the presence of his family.

Therefore, on December 27, 1931, Buck, Blanche, my mother,

and my sister Artie and her husband drove down to the main prison building in Huntsville, Texas, to re-introduce Buck to prison life. It was not the happiest of occasions, but everyone knew it had to be done before Buck and Blanche could begin their lives truly together. We went to Warden Waid and told him that Buck wanted to finish up his term, and asked the Warden to keep him at the "Walls," the main prison actually in the town of Huntsville. The health complications that caused Buck to go in the hospital during his initial few months in prison still plagued him.

Warden Waid agreed to all of these requests and seemed real impressed that Buck had come back on his own. My mother thought the Warden was a nice man. He seemed proud that Buck had chosen to return and finish his sentence and told all of us that it was a mighty fine thing to do. Buck was allowed to take up where he left off and was not penalized with additional prison time for his escape. Buck wasn't even put back in prison stripes.

Knowing Blanche would have assistance from his parents and sister, Artie, Buck, was able to return to prison quietly. It was arranged that Blanche would live part of the time with our family at the filling station. Part of the time she would live up in Denison with my sister Artie and would work some at my sister's beauty salon.

Ironically, just as Buck was re-acclimating himself into prison life, Clyde was finally released. Just thirty seven days after Buck went back in, Clyde was paroled.

Chapter 7

CLYDE WAS PAROLED from the penitentiary on February 2, 1932, after spending sixteen and a half months in the prison system. He was transferred from the Waco jail to the Huntsville pen in the early autumn of 1930. Outside of the week he was free in March, 1930, my brother had spent just over two years in jail.

Clyde's prison experience had scarred him both physically and psychologically. By January of 1932, he was so distraught by the prison farm that he tried to get a medical transfer back to the prison hospital. He intentionally mutilated his own left foot. Just a few days after this happened, Clyde was paroled. He came home on crutches.

The physical scars he bore from his experience were small compared to the psychological changes Clyde had undergone. Clyde had spent much of his time at the brutal Eastham prison farm and had seen many things which had made an indelible impression on his mind. Of course, what he personally underwent made the biggest impact of all, from the sodomy assault Clyde suffered the first week he was at Huntsville to the harsh discipline of the prison farm. My brother absolutely refused to talk about his experiences to anyone. All he ever said about it was that the Eastham prison farm was "a burning hell." He was more subdued and quiet after his return home.

Clyde's attitude towards life seemed to change. He was more fatalistic. He frequently told my mother that everyone had just one time to die, and we all go when our time comes. Before he went to prison, he never dwelt on the mortality of mankind. His interests were those of any other young man, involving keeping a job, finding a girlfriend, and other such things. He kept up with his hobbies, especially his musical development. But after his stint in prison, that all changed. This change in Clyde made all of his family uneasy.

But my brother did try to pick up his life where he left off. In fact, he did try to address where the future might lead. Clyde talked about putting up an automobile garage on the empty lot next to our service station. He even purchased that empty lot as a first step towards this dream. Clyde was a pretty good mechanic and could've made a "go" at his car repair shop if he could have followed through with it.

But the hard facts of life were that the worsening Great Depression made honest labor hard to come by, and Clyde's status as an ex-convict just made it that much harder.

I knew the father of one such young man, and we frequently compared family histories when he and I met a few years later. The father was named John Wilson Dillinger. Mr. Dillinger, Mrs. Emma Parker (Bonnie's mother), and my parents and I went on a tour with Mr. Charles Stanley, who was nationally known as the "Crime Doctor" in the 1930s. He owned the so-called "Death Car" in which my brother and Bonnie were slain. He had a traveling show with a theme of "Crime Does Not Pay," and my parents and the others would get up and speak about their famous offspring.

It was amazing how much John Dillinger's background paralleled Clyde's. I have mentioned previously about how both Clyde and Mr. Dillinger's boy were always highly rated as employees anywhere they ever worked. There were other similarities, also. Just as Clyde came under the bad influence of Frank Clause, young John Dillinger came under the bad influence of a man named Ed Singleton. Singleton persuaded Dillinger to help him in the sidewalk robbery of a grocer. The robbery was unsuccessful, and both Singleton and young John Dillinger were arrested.

The Dillinger family had no previous contact with any criminal activity and didn't have slightest idea of how the legal system worked. Mr. Dillinger's boy confessed to the botched holdup attempt, and his father told him to just plead guilty and throw himself on the mercy of the court. Young John never even got himself a lawyer. Mr. Dillinger figured that his son would get a light sentence since it was his first offence. Young John got hit with everything but the kitchen sink: one prison sentence of 10-20 years, another term of 2-14 years, long-term disenfranchisement, and a big fine. Young Dillinger served eight and a half years of this sentence.

By the way, Ed Singleton, the man who influenced Mr. Dillinger's son, was familiar with the ways of the legal system. He got a sharp criminal lawyer, got a change of venue, and received a light sentence of two years. Singleton was back out on the street in just over a year.

Like Clyde, after his prison term, John Dillinger was profoundly changed. And, like Clyde, he had a hard time trying to find work in those economically tough times.

Clyde managed to find jobs here and there, but police kept calling on his employers and informed them that their new employee was an ex-con and was likely to steal from them. The cops resumed their old habits and started picking Clyde up every time anything happened in the area. The same cycle started to perpetuate itself again: Clyde began to lose whatever jobs he was able to acquire.

My mother tried to encourage Clyde all she could. There was always an extremely strong bond between Clyde and our mother. For that matter, there was always an extremely strong bond between Cumie Barrow and all of her children. She and Clyde had many long talks about his good intentions to try to stick to the straight and narrow path in life. She told him that it truly was the best thing to do and she tried to get him to reflect on his earlier years, when he was under no strong temptations to do anything wrong. My mother asked Clyde to remember his days when he baptized and when he regularly attended the Eureka, Texas Baptist church.

But even my mother finally had to recognize that Clyde would not be able to maintain an honest job in the areas where he would always have his prison term hanging over his head. He was only about 22 years old in early 1932, way too young to have the rest of his life marked by his jail time. She recommended that he try to start over again in another state.

With the connections our family had, a job was arranged for Clyde in the construction business. About the only thing that went right for Clyde during this period was that Bonnie was willing and eager to take up with him again. Their communication through letters had eventually tapered off during his months in prison. Bonnie had moved in with her mother and was dating other men. The second day Clyde was back, he went over to Bonnie's mother's house to visit. Bonnie was overjoyed to see him and leapt into his arms, much to the chagrin of her current boyfriend who was also visiting there when Clyde came calling. This sudden ex-boyfriend immediately left.

Bonnie became a regular fixture around the service station again. She helped and supported Clyde until he was able to be free of his crutches. During this time, he was only able to do light work and so he helped our father around the service station, while Bonnie helped him wherever she could. He initially helped our father fill in with dirt around the station. As he got stronger, he began to try to find work outside the station, with the results described above. Bonnie also tried to encourage him, but verbal support only goes so far. So Clyde agreed to try the Massachusetts job option.

My brother left Texas in early March and traveled to New England to try to start his life over again. This was the first time that Clyde had been so far away from his family. It was also the farthest he'd ever been away from the state of Texas. As a result, his sojourn in Massachusetts only lasted about two weeks, due to loneliness and discouragement. But, while he was up there, he did send my mother one letter:

> Dear Mother -
> Just a few lines to let you know that I haven't forgotten you. I got here Monday night and I sure was tired out, but I like it up here and I guess I will go to work Monday. Well, how is everyone at home? I sure wish I could see you. I am lone-some already, but Jim is sure a good fellow and I am going to write to Nell over at Drucie's. I guess she will get it there. Have you seen Buck yet? Tell him hello for me. I am going to send him a box, soon as I work awhile. Well, Mother, I don't know anything much right now, but will write more when I hear from you, so answer real soon and let me know how everything is in Dallas. Tell everyone hello for me and send my mail to:
> FRAMINGHAM, MASS.
> General Delivery.
> Send it to Jack Stuwart- JACK STUWART, that is my name here

My mother received this letter in late March of 1932. Ironically, it was dated April 30, 1932, a date that would become ominous in Clyde's life.

Clyde's return from Massachusetts made us uneasy. We knew the trip was kind of a "last resort" type of action. Clyde was at a crossroads situation at this point in his life. He was unable to be away from his family in general and his mother in particular, due to his close family connections. Yet trying to get honest work around west Dallas seemed to be almost an impossible proposition, with the police keeping a perpetual interest in him. The Barrow family wondered what his next move would be. My mother hoped and prayed Clyde would again try to find a job and try to build a post-prison life.

When Clyde returned from the New England area, one of the

first things he did was try to get back with Bonnie. Also during this time, Clyde began to associate with Ralph Fults, a friend from his prison days. Ralph, after hearing Clyde had been paroled, travelled from McKinney to W. D. The boys had something of a bond after they had "pulled chain" down in the Huntsville.

Unfortunately, the combination of Clyde's despairing outlook on life and his re-association with old prison cronies had a predictable outcome: the robbery of the Simms Oil Company on March 25, 1932. Clyde's prison-generated anger would from henceforth be manifested in acts of predatory, armed criminality.

As with everything else that Clyde ever did, the Simms Oil company holdup has been exaggerated and misreport. Most of the popular accounts make this robbery a daylight holdup, with Clyde storming into that place of business brandishing a gun. He accosts the company manager and forces him to open the safe which Clyde empties. In some accounts, Raymond Hamilton is with him; in others, he is alone, but with Bonnie waiting in the getaway car just outside. Clyde gets away with several hundred dollars. Then, he and Bonnie and/or Raymond roar off down Eagle Ford Road in a cloud of dust.

The facts of the case, however, are as follows:"The Great Simms Oil Company Robbery" was a midnight burglary with Clyde and Ralph Fults. The boys didn't get anything, because the anticipated company payroll wasn't in the safe. They did tie up the few employees that were on duty at that time at night, hurting no one in the process. The boys left immediately upon finding that there was no money to be obtained. Now, I am sure that many readers will wonder why I didn't precede the Simms Oil affair with what happened down around Mabank, Kemp, and Kaufman. Most books put this occurrence as happening on March 22. However, it really occurred a month later, around April 19.

After the unsuccessful attempt in west Dallas at Simms, Clyde and Ralph decided they needed some more "business associates." Ralph knew a bunch of boys from up around Denton that would fit the bill nicely. So he introduced Clyde to them. One of the Denton area boys was almost a dead-ringer for Raymond Hamilton, who still remained an unknown associate of Clyde's at the time.

During this period of time, Clyde was still around home somewhat. His disappearances were attributed to his search for work. Bonnie was also still in the picture; she most certainly had nothing to do with the

Simms Oil holdup, as a getaway driver or anything else. Living with her mother at the time, Bonnie often worked as a waitress when work was available.

A few weeks after the Simms Oil affair, Bonnie was indeed with Clyde and Ralph when they pulled off their next Dallas-area activity. The three were casting about in the Mabank area, but their attempts down there proved about as financially successful as the Simms robbery. The trio didn't get anything except the interest of the authorities, and both Bonnie and Ralph were arrested near the small town of Kemp. Clyde got away unscathed, but Ralph was hit by police gunfire.

Bonnie and Ralph were first taken to the only jail building located in the town of Kemp: a small, one-room frontier calaboose. It was a small brick building with a heavy iron door and very small barred windows. Bonnie and the bloodied Ralph were kept there the first night they were arrested. Bonnie was very agitated by the lack of medical attention that Ralph was getting and was ready to let the local residents have it. Practically the whole town turned out to see the one-night residents of their little calaboose. Ironically, that little building has the status of being the only standing jail in which Bonnie was ever imprisoned.

After their miserable night, the two bedraggled bandits were transferred to larger accommodations in the county jail in Kaufman. Bonnie then finally contacted her mother about her current circumstances. Emma Parker always said that seeing Bonnie in jail was a terrific shock and she said that Bonnie felt the same shock about being in jail. She said that Bonnie was distraught by the fact that Clyde had "deserted" her and swore that she'd never have anything to do with him again. Yet, when members of our family went down to visit her in Kaufman, she was glad to see us and didn't seem to have the slightest bit of bitterness against Clyde or our family. We brought her some clothes and other items on these trips. We also brought Ralph some items he needed.

It was while she was in the Kaufman jail that Bonnie began to compose one of her two best-known works of poetry: "The Story of Suicide Sal." Her other oft-reprinted poem was, of course, "The Story of Bonnie and Clyde." Many writers who later tried to psychoanalyze Bonnie figured that the writing of this poem represented her feelings towards Clyde at this time.

The psychoanalysts figure that Bonnie saw herself as "Sal" and Clyde as "Jack." The poem deals with a young girl from rural Wyoming named Sal who runs off to the big wicked city. She gets involved with Jack, who is a professional killer from Chicago, and then gets involved with the underworld. Jack's gang hears of a fat payroll at a certain bank. Sal gets a job at the bank and feeds the gang all of the details of the bank's operation. Jack's gang stages a robbery and he is almost shot by a bank employee as he is the last to leave. Sal has to knock the gun out of the bank employee's hand, which gives her role in the affair away. She is put on trial and gets a prison sentence. Jack promises to spring her, but does nothing after Sal is sent up. In fact, Jack finds a new moll and writes Sal off. Sal is freed after serving five years. The first thing she does is to look Jack and his girlfriend up and kill them. Sal herself is gunned down days later by the mob. I simply cannot accept the notion that this cheery little ditty is Bonnie's attempt to get even with Clyde. Bonnie was an imaginative person, always dramatizing situations.

When she was younger, she aspired to be a stage actress or public performer. The account of "Suicide Sal" probably reflected a story she heard from another woman prisoner, with drama added by Bonnie's personal talents. We knew Bonnie probably wouldn't be sentenced to prison. But for Ralph Fults, it was another matter completely. Ralph hadn't been out of prison that long when he began to run with Clyde. His past record just about guaranteed that he'd get hard time. And that proved to be the case; Ralph was returned to the Huntsville prison. His time with Clyde lasted just about one month, and both their first and last forays turned out to be failures.

Clyde's first impulse was to try to free Ralph and Bonnie. He got back in touch with the rest of the Denton County boys after he left Kaufman County. To engineer a jail break for their two friends, Clyde needed money. The boys began to consider a place to rob. Somebody remembered a combination store-service station-garage on the outskirts of Hillsboro, Texas, that might have financial possibilities; since this store also dealt with jewelry, it was logical to assume that there would be both money and other valuables to obtain.

There wasn't enough time to thoroughly case the job, since they were unsure on how long Ralph and Bonnie would be held in Kaufman. This store was owned by John Bucher and was on the northern outskirts of Hillsboro, close by where the two highways would provide a fast getaway. The boys agreed to act immediately.

This Hillsboro store robbery was cased by one visit to get a general idea of where everything was situated. But Clyde was recognized by

Mrs. Bucher as a running buddy of her son from years past. Clyde now felt that the job was jinxed and wanted to pull out altogether. The other two boys said that Clyde wouldn't have to make another appearance inside the store; he could just wait outside in the car while they took care of business inside.

The hold-up was scheduled for the evening of April 30. The trio drove up to the Bucher store late that evening and honked the horn until they woke up Mr. Bucher. One of the Denton county boys yelled that they needed some guitar strings. Mr. Bucher agreed to sell them some and said he would come downstairs. The two Denton county boys got out to make the transaction while Clyde remained in the car, laying low as not to be seen. They intentionally planned to use a large bill to pay for the small purchase, which would force Mr. Bucher to open his safe to make change. Then, they would proceed to pull guns and take the safe's contents. Since they figured Mr. Bucher would be taken by surprise and would surrender his goods meekly, they anticipated no trouble, and certainly no gunplay of any kind.

So Clyde remained in the car at the wheel, expecting a quick robbery and swift getaway. The next thing he heard, though, was the sound of gunfire. Then, a few minutes later, the two Denton county boys came flying out of the store, and the trio took off in the automobile.

This Hillsboro robbery and shooting became a murder charge in the early hours of May 1, when John Bucher died of a bullet wound. This became the first killing officially charged against Clyde. Many accounts have him personally pulling the trigger on John Bucher. Some stories have Clyde, Bonnie, and Raymond invading the store; other accounts just have Clyde and Raymond inside; and yet other versions have Clyde and a blonde girl holding it up. Of course, at this time, Bonnie was in jail in Kaufman. Raymond Hamilton hadn't teamed up with Clyde at this time and, in fact, was definitely up in Michigan visiting his biological father.

The factor that involved Raymond Hamilton was the circumstance that one of the Denton county boys inside the Bucher store looked enough like Raymond to be his twin brother. Of course, this boy was identified as Raymond when Mrs. Bucher went through police photos of fugitives on the loose. Raymond had escaped from the McKinney, Texas, jail just a few days before Clyde was released from Huntsville. Hamilton was there in the McKinney jail on charges of grand theft auto.

Clyde's name was dragged into the matter due to the fact that Mrs.

Bucher had recognized him during his short visit to the store three days previously. Since Raymond was a later running mate of Clyde's and since he was "positively identified" by Mrs. Bucher, it was logical to assume the other man in the store with "Raymond" was Clyde. The trouble with this identification was that the other man with the Hamilton look-alike was almost six feet tall, much taller than Clyde's five-seven stature. This little fact was disregarded, however, and most popular accounts have Clyde pulling the trigger on John Bucher.

What really happened in the store was that, as expected, John Bucher had to open his safe to make change for the large denomination bill the Denton county boys had given him. The two boys hadn't taken into account two factors: that Mrs. Bucher would be with her husband and that the grocer would have a gun with him. Both unforeseen circumstances came into play. Mr. Bucher called his wife to come and open the safe. When the safe was opened, the Denton county boys pulled their guns on the couple. But John Bucher grabbed for a nearby pistol and the Raymond look-alike fired. Some stories say that the shot was a warning shot which ricocheted off of the safe door and struck Mr. Bucher. Then again, the bullet may have come from another source, which I'll mention later.

Whatever the source of the bullet, the effect was undisputed: John Bucher went down, mortally wounded. And for the first time, murder was connected with my brother's name.

Many people have believed that Clyde was lying when he said that Mrs. Bucher recognized him as a friend of her son. They point out that Mr. and Mrs. Bucher had married in 1902 and that they had run their establishment in Hillsboro for the thirty years before the shooting. It is automatically assumed that Clyde meant that he and the Bucher boy ran around together as children in west Dallas.

But I believe that it is indeed likely that Mrs. Bucher recognized Clyde as an associate of her son from years past. When Clyde hooked up with Frank Clause during the late 1920s, their associates ranged all of the way from Dallas to Waco and places in between. Hillsboro is between Dallas and Waco, and it is logical to assume that Frank would know people there. It is even more logical that Clyde would get to know them also, since he was running with Frank at that time. It is likely that Mrs. Bucher recognized Clyde from his days with Frank Clause and her own son.

It is the Bucher son which makes one question from where the fatal bullet was fired. Floyd Hamilton always said that the Hillsboro robbery was arranged by the Buchers' son and that he was the one secreted in the store who fired the shot that killed the grocer. There are still dark rumors circulating around Hillsboro that this may have been the case, due to stories that the son wanted the whole business or that John Bucher was an abusive father. Floyd stated that the ballistics showed that the fatal bullet came from elsewhere in the store than from the bandits in front of John Bucher.

Whoever shot and killed John Bucher, the end result was eventually the same: Clyde was blamed when he was identified as the six-footer in there with the Hamilton look-alike. As an ex-convict, Clyde knew that he would have a very poor chance of persuading a jury that he was innocent if he surrendered himself now. Although he wanted to abort the whole plan to rob the Bucher store after he was recognized, he still was in the car outside while a killing occurred inside. Clyde knew that Texas law holds that all parties connected with a robbery-murder would be held equally accountable. He figured that there was nothing to do but run after that conclusion was reached.

But Hamilton's identification (and by association, Clyde's) was still down the road awhile. The trio raced back to Dallas from Hillsboro and the two Dentonites returned to their home turf. Clyde came back to west Dallas, his concerns for Bonnie and Ralph now dwarfed by his connection with the Hillsboro robbery. He resolved that he was too far gone to go back.

Clyde decided to just lay low until Bonnie was released. Police were on the look-out for him, but they didn't really watch our service station too closely. In fact, they only came out of our house once to talk to my parents in the immediate aftermath of the Hillsboro shooting. One time Clyde brought a dress for Bonnie out to the house and asked my mother to buy her some more clothes, some shoes, and some underwear. My mother didn't know where this dress came from, so she switched and used one of my nicer dresses to send to Bonnie. I was just turning 14 years old at the time of the Hillsboro tragedy, but Bonnie and I were already interchanging clothes as we were both the same size. My mother did buy Bonnie some shoes as Clyde requested. Blanche took these items down to Bonnie at the Kaufman jail. Despite what has been written about her being angry at Clyde, she was always glad to see us and was pleased that my brother was still trying to look after her needs while she was imprisoned.

Chapter 8

THE HILLSBORO ROBBERY WAS initiated as a means to get money with which to free Ralph Fults and Bonnie Parker from the jail in Kaufman. In that regard, it was a miserable failure.

The Denton county boys only got $40 in cash and $2,500 in diamonds. But Clyde would have nothing to do with the ill-gotten gains and immediately severed his relationship with the Denton county crowd. He took no part in the division of the "loot" from the Hillsboro robbery.

Now that Ralph Fults was in jail, Clyde looked around for a new partner with which to operate. My brother really didn't plan on making a full-time career out of crime, but circumstances seemed to lead him that way. He had no deep contacts with the professional underworld himself. The only one of his past contacts that ever really was a hardcore criminal type was Frank Clause. So Clyde looked Frank up, and the two boys went out on the road.

Clyde and Frank were credited with robbing two service stations in Lufkin, Texas, on May 5, just five days after the Hillsboro tragedy. Then, one week later on May 12, the boys were charged with robbing a liquor store in Dallas. The bandits who committed the Lufkin robberies abducted the managers of both the Gulf and Magnolia stations in the course of the holdups. But they left the managers unharmed on the outskirts of town. The take from these robberies didn't even add up to $100. Clyde separated from Clause again, and this time it was for good. We wished Clyde had never met Frank Clause in the first place; it might have made a world of difference in the course that Clyde's life took.

After my brother separated from Frank, he laid low around west Dallas for awhile, waiting for Bonnie to be released from the Kaufman jail. Our family continued to visit her and to keep her supplied with clothing and other needs. Bonnie's mother also visited her, but Mrs. Parker went to Kaufman on her own. While being visited by her mother, Bonnie would swear off any further involvement with outlawry and ex-convicts and the like. When she was visited by members of our family, we carried messages back and forth between Clyde and Bonnie. Of course, Bonnie was only trying to keep her mother happy and to keep peace in her family by agreeing to her mother's urgings. There was no way that she would've ever stayed away from Clyde.

Our family visited a lot of jails during this period. At the same time we were keeping up with Bonnie's needs, we were also visiting with Buck down in Huntsville. We took him items he needed and gave him what support we could. We also kept him informed of what was happening in connection with Clyde.

Buck listened to the news about what Clyde had gotten involved in with a heavy heart. Since Buck had returned to prison, he had stayed out of conflicts and was successfully impressing the prison authorities with his personal reformation. His romance with and marriage to Blanche had totally turned his attitude towards life around. Buck was extremely worried about what was happening to his younger brother. He had learned quite a lot about the virtues of walking the straight and narrow path in life from Blanche and her minister father. His prison sentence was also a great influence on him and he determined that he never wanted to see Clyde back at Huntsville.

One time when my mother was talking to him, Buck asked her whether we could try to get Clyde to stop what he was doing and to try to change the course of his life. Buck said he couldn't stand the thought of Clyde being caught, brought back to Huntsville, and executed there at the main prison, especially if Buck was still there.

Buck had always felt bad about what was happening with his younger brother during those tempestuous months in early 1932. My older brother had always believed that one of the reasons that Clyde was in trouble was because of the police interest that Buck had initially attracted due to the stolen brass that he had purchased ten years earlier. But all we could tell him was that the Bucher killing had made it impossible for Clyde to come in and surrender.

It was about this time that Mrs. Bucher had made her identifications of Clyde and Raymond as the murderers of her husband. Ross Sterling, the governor of Texas at that time, put a reward of $250 out for the killers of John Bucher. After Mrs. Bucher fingered Clyde and Raymond, the newspapers began to refer to Clyde as the triggerman there in Hillsboro as if he'd already been tried and convicted.

Throughout the rest of May and the whole of June, Clyde stayed out of trouble. He tried to visit with his family when he could, but he had to keep on the move due to the heat generated by the uproar over the Bucher crime. He traveled around, staying with friends and relatives. The Texas Rangers got a report that he was over in the Nacogdoches area, living out in the countryside and visiting with relatives on my mother's side of the family. They got some information concerning a purported "hideout" of my brother's and made a heavily-armed raid on the area. The Rangers found no one there. All they did allegedly find were many spent shells from rifles, shotguns, and pistols and some paper targets. They also claimed to have found some cigars with lipstick on them, which is what makes me doubt that Clyde had any such hideout there. Of course, the lipstick/cigar clue was an indirect reference to the fact that Bonnie was supposedly with Clyde there. At this time, she was still in the Kaufman jail until her release around June 17. She spent the rest of the month of June at her mother's house in west Dallas during which time she had no contact with Clyde.

I think it's possible, and indeed likely, that Clyde was brushing up on his acquaintance with firearms. Central Texas was in an uproar over the Bucher killing and peace officers were talking about dealing with the murderers in a "shoot on sight" fashion. Since Clyde and Raymond were identified as these murderers by Mrs. Bucher, Clyde figured that re-acquainting himself with the same guns that the police would come after him with was a good idea.

In late June, Clyde returned to west Dallas, feeling that it was time to re-establish his relationship with Bonnie. He knew that Mrs. Parker would know of his connection with the Hillsboro affair due to the newspapers and that she would be against him rekindling his romance with her daughter.

While Clyde was in west Dallas in late June, his path crossed with that of Raymond Hamilton. Hamilton had just returned after visiting with his father in Michigan for over two months. He returned to find that he was wanted for murder and robbery in connection with the Bucher murder. Of course, Raymond couldn't have possibly have been in the Buchner establishment, but he was put there by Mrs. Bucher anyway. Raymond was now in the same boat as was Clyde. The two boys had known of each other in earlier years, but they were never closely associated until the circumstances concerning the Hillsboro crime threw them together. As I previously noted, I was the main connection between the Barrow and Hamilton kids, due to my friendship with Audrey Hamilton.

Even then, I really only got to know the other Hamilton girls. There were times that Audrey and I played together after school and we'd go over to visit another one of the Hamilton girls who lived a couple of streets over from our service station. Lillie Hamilton lived on County Avenue and we were over there frequently after school had let out. She and I always enjoyed going over there to visit with her older sister Lillie. I knew Audrey and Lillie had a couple of brothers named Raymond and Floyd, but that was about it. At this time, in mid-1932, Lillie had married and was now Lillie McBride.

So it was in late June of 1932, the paths of Clyde, Bonnie, and Raymond converged. Clyde and Raymond decided to rent a flat up in Wichita Falls and plan their next course of action. Bonnie told her mother that she was offered a job up in Wichita Falls, which was located on the Red River between Texas and Oklahoma. Bonnie said she had a ride arranged already and would not have to spend any money on a bus. A car stopped in front of her house and honked. Bonnie hurriedly kissed her mother, grabbed her luggage, and left.

Clyde and Raymond were already up there, awaiting her arrival. Both boys had no prior connections up around Wichita Falls, and figured that they would be safe from any police interest in that town. In July, 1932, a couple of crimes were committed that the authorities pinned on Clyde and Raymond. On July 16, 1932, the Palestine Ice Company in east Texas was robbed. The bandits abducted the bookkeeper after taking almost $1,000 from the office of that company. Unlike the gas station robberies in Lufkin two months earlier, the bookkeeper was taken out in the country and was savagely beaten.

The managers of the two Lufkin stations were released unharmed; their temporary kidnapping was strictly to prevent them from spreading a quick alarm and to give the bandits time to get away. The slugging of the Palestine Ice employee was a completely unnecessary bit of thuggery, and was totally inconsistent with Clyde's temperament. But he and Raymond still got blamed for it.

The second crime was the robbery, the bank in Willis, Texas, on July 27. In this affair, the bandits got all of the bank employees into the vault and locked it on them after gathering all of the money the could find. The robbers got around $3,000.

The reason why I doubt Clyde and Raymond robbed the Willis bank was that just a couple of days after this lucrative holdup, the two boys robbed the Interurban Station in Grand Prairie, Texas, which is just west of Dallas. They had returned to their home area from Wichita Falls, intending to rob a couple of select targets. This Interurban Station was supposed to be one of them, but it was a bust. Just a few minutes before they committed this robbery, the big money they were hoping to get (over $700) was removed from the office. All they got was $12. If Clyde and Raymond had gotten $4,000 from

Palestine and Willis days earlier, they wouldn't have had to return to their hometown and focus on trying to obtain a few hundred dollars from place like the Interurban Station.

After the bust in Grand Prairie, the boys concentrated on another target: the Neuhoff Packing Company. This second attempt was definitely more successful than the Interurban job. The bandits got $440 from the job and disappeared.

Clyde and Raymond were hiding out at an abandoned farmhouse outside of Grand Prairie. Both boys were familiar with this area from their boyhood years. Raymond was especially familiar with the area, having lived around southwestern Dallas County for a number of years. The boys had taken Bonnie with them out there, and were using the farmhouse as their quarters while they were in the Dallas area trying to garner funds through the Interurban and Neuhoff holdups.

On the day they robbed the packing company, Clyde and Raymond brought Bonnie into the service station and told her to listen to the radio and to see what happened. My mother was somewhat puzzled by Bonnie's intense interest in the police broadcasts. I knew something was up, but I didn't know what. Then we heard the news broadcast about the Neuhoff robbery and saw Bonnie's reaction. She began to get anxious and continuously looked out the front door and window. Bonnie was concerned that the boys would make a safe getaway. Then Clyde, Raymond, and the third boy who accompanied them on this job pulled up. Bonnie saw them pull up in front of the station, grabbed her hat and ran out front to join them. My mother got out there just as she was climbing into the car. My mother was only able to say just a few words before Clyde had to take off. He said "See you in a few days, Mom." All my mother could say was for him to be careful, and then he sped off.

The group headed back out to the Grand Prairie farmhouse to cool off for a few days. They knew the police would be watching the roads leading out of the Dallas area, hoping to catch sight of the getaway vehicle. Clyde knew that after a few days, the police vigil would be relaxed and that it would be safe to try to drive out of the area. The kids remained out there for four days after the packing company action. Clyde, Raymond, and the third boy brought Bonnie back into west Dallas so she could visit her mother for a while. Bonnie made her way back to her mother's house from where they dropped her off. The three boys then left the Dallas area and drove towards Oklahoma.

While driving north, they picked up another man, crossed the

Red River and drove into Oklahoma. They also picked up something else which would cause a crisis later that same evening: some jars of moonshine. They had to get this, however, over Clyde's protestations, as he did not drink at all and did not knowingly and willingly associate with those that did imbibe. Clyde neither smoked nor drank, a holdover from his "honest and upright" days when he faithfully attended the Eureka Baptist church while at Uncle Frank's.

Aside from moral considerations, there were other reasons why Clyde didn't partake in the use of alcohol. He knew from his days in prison the reason why many of the men were jailed was because they were caught while under the influence. Clyde had already been convicted in the newspapers of personally shooting John Bucher and he knew that there was a $250 reward for the Bucher killers. $250 was a lot of money back in 1932. My brother knew that this reward would be too tempting for many people to pass up. He could be fingered by anyone who wanted the money. Clyde knew he could be jumped by the police at any time, and he needed a clear mind to escape any police traps.

Clyde made two compromises that evening. Allowing the other boys the use of the moonshine was the first compromise. The second compromise was that he allowed himself to be taken in by Raymond's desire to attend a country dance they saw along side the highway just north of Atoka. The other two boys, feeling loose due to the influence of moonshine, seconded Raymond's suggestion. Their car pulled into the parking area close to the open-air dancing area.

As with the Hillsboro robbery-murder, there are many different accounts of what happened there at that country dance on the evening of August 5, 1932 and just who was there. Clyde and Raymond were definitely there. Unfortunately, so were Sheriff Charles Maxwell and Undersheriff Eugene Moore. Finally, there was the moonshine, which became the catalyst that involved my brother directly in his first murder.

Most of the popular accounts have the bandits' car pulling into the parking lot adjacent to the dancing area. There were either three or four boys in the car. There was an argument amongst them whether or not to get mixed up with the dance. The boys got out of their car and moved towards the dance floor. They halted and argued some more. Then, not to attract the attention of any officers who might be there, they got into the nearest unlocked car to argue some more. This action had the opposite effect of their intent; the sheriff saw this odd maneuver and walked over to investigate. Clyde and Raymond, knowing they can expect to get the chair in connection with the Bucher shooting, opened fire on the sheriff. The undersheriff ran up, and he too was shot. The boys returned to their own auto and took off.

Another slight variation of this story has the Dallas boys sitting in their own car, everybody swilling moonshine except Clyde. The sheriff saw them drinking the shine out of the Mason jar and walked up and said "We don't allow that kind of thing here." The boys opened fire on the sheriff and the undersheriff and then fled in their auto.

There are other accounts that offer a little more in terms of variety. One story has them stopping by this dance because the Dallas boy who helped in the Neuhoff robbery knew he could get some more moonshine from a bootlegger there. He got out and went into the dancing area to look up his source. The sheriff saw Clyde and Raymond sitting there in the car trying to look inconspicuous and went over to check them out. He got shot for his interest and so did the undersheriff.

Then there's the story where Clyde, Bonnie, and Raymond all willingly go into the dancing area and the boys both took turns dancing with her. Other men took an interest in Bonnie but were rebuffed. One of the sore losers went over and made a complaint concerning the trio, and the officers decide to keep an eye on them. When the officers saw the trio head back out to their car, they followed them and accosted them as they got back into their auto. Then the guns go off.

About the most bizarre story of them all is the one in which Clyde, Bonnie, and Raymond go in to dance. Tempers flared between Clyde and Raymond over Bonnie's affections, and they went away from the dancers to fight it out. The cops saw the scuffle and went over to break it up. Bonnie attacked one of the officers while the boys headed back towards their car and the guns. The two officers went after them and were shot. I suppose there are other variations, but these are the most popular stories.

All I can do is to tell the reader how our family learned of the Atoka tragedy. After dropping Bonnie off in west Dallas and before heading up to Oklahoma, Clyde made a quick visit by the service station and told my mother to meet him the following morning at the home of one my cousins there in the Dallas area. My mother agreed to do so, and we didn't think anything of it at the time.

My mother was driven over to my cousin's house early the next morning. Clyde and Raymond were already there, laying across the bed and peering out the window. When my mother walked in, Clyde jumped up to meet her. He didn't seem to be notably upset. My mother noticed the absence of the third boy who was with them the day before. Clyde and Raymond answered in unison with the same response: "We lost him." Clyde then asked my mother if she'd seen the morning newspapers yet. All of our family had seen the account of the shooting of the two officers, but none of us had connected Clyde with it; we never thought that he would have been there carousing at a public dance while he was being sought by every cop in the southwest in connection with the Hillsboro killing.

My mother mentioned that we had read about the Atoka affair in a personally disinterested fashion. Then a peculiar expression came over the faces of both Clyde and Raymond. My mother became apprehensive; she knew her son well enough to know when something was drastically wrong. My mother asked Clyde, "You didn't do that, did you?" All Clyde said in response was that he'd never killed anyone.

My mother later got the particulars of what had happened at the dance. As the group was driving up through Oklahoma, Raymond saw that there was a dance going on along side the road. Both he and the third boy wanted to stop and participate. Clyde didn't want to stop, but he gave in to them and pulled into the parking lot.

Raymond and the other boy got out and sauntered into the dance area. The fourth boy who was with them also got out. Clyde stayed inside the car; he knew better than to get out and mix and mingle with the public while his picture was in newspapers all over the southwest in connection with the Bucher slaying. He didn't even want to be at a public function such as a dance.

Clyde, sitting there in the car by himself, got the attention of one of the patrons of the dance. This person sidled closer to the car and saw some of Clyde's guns there on the back seat of the auto. Figuring that the firearms could be connected with a possible robbery of the box office there by the dance floor, this citizen told the sheriff and the under-sheriff of his suspicions. Both officers began to walk over to Clyde's auto to investigate with the sheriff in the forefront.

Clyde was standing next to the car stretching his legs when the sheriff approached. My brother saw the intentions of the sheriff and got back inside his car, which was parked in between two other automobiles. The sheriff, thinking Clyde was planning to get away, pulled out his gun and yelled at him to stop. Clyde grabbed his gun and fired at the sheriff.

At the sound of the shot, pandemonium broke out amongst the dancers. Many of them headed toward the parking area to investigate the gunfire. Raymond Hamilton was a member of this crowd. Other people were heading out into the darkness, fleeing in blind panic.

Raymond saw the undersheriff heading towards where Clyde and the sheriff were having their confrontation. Raymond pulled a gun that he had on him and opened fire on the undersheriff. Clyde saw this and began firing at the other lawman also. Both the sheriff and undersheriff were hit by the boys' gunfire. Undersheriff Eugene Moore died at the scene, while Sheriff Charley Maxwell was critically wounded. Many accounts have Sheriff Maxwell dying a couple of days afterward, but he actually survived his injuries and was later invited to witness Raymond Hamilton's execution in Huntsville.

Raymond jumped in the car with Clyde already behind the wheel. Sheriff Maxwell continued to fire at them as he lay injured on the ground. One of the men who was attending the dance grabbed Eugene Moore's gun and fired after Clyde and Raymond as they sped out of the parking lot back onto the highway. One of these bullets from the lawmen's guns may have hit a tire on the boys' car. Clyde lost control of the auto right in front of the dance site, and the auto crashed and turned over. My brother and Raymond got out and headed onto the MKT railroad embankment on the other side of the road and yelled for the other boy who had helped them in the Neuhoff robbery four days earlier. This boy had fled with the rest of the crowd, so Clyde and Raymond went across the railroad tracks and out into a field. The boys crossed the field and went through the woods that laid beyond the field. Then they came to a little town.

Clyde's first priority was to get an automobile as fast as possible and get out of that area. Because the law would be coming after them in full force. My brother knew that he didn't have time to be particular about the make of car, just as long as it had the horsepower to take them out of the area in short order.

While walking through the little town, Clyde and Raymond caught up with the night watchman. Clyde didn't beat around the bush: he wanted to know where he could get the best car in town. The night watchman didn't hesitate and immediately said the local doctor had the best and fastest car around. Clyde and Raymond got the directions to this doctor's house. Then they told the night watchman that it was in his best interest not to say anything about their business for awhile.

Clyde and Raymond went to the doctor's house and banged on his door, claiming a medical emergency. When the doctor opened the door, they drew down on him with their guns and told him they had immediate need of his auto. This doctor told them to go ahead and take it. The boys did so and tried to get out of the Atoka area through the back country roads.

Clyde' sense of direction was not as finely developed as it would be later. As was the case up around Middletown, Ohio, the boys drove around all night only to find themselves just 35 miles from the Atoka area early the next morning. Once they got their bearings, though, they drove back down towards Dallas, where they met my mother at my cousin's house.

The boy who had helped them rob the Neuhoff plant had fled with the rest of the crowd at the dance. He hopped a freight and made his way back towards Dallas. He was arrested as he was coming back through Texas. The boy was definitely identified as being there at the Atoka dance. He immediately identified Clyde and Raymond as the gunfighters there at the scene.

The news of what Clyde had gotten himself involved in there at Atoka made my mother sick at heart. She knew he had not shot and killed John Bucher there at Hillsboro, but now Clyde had been positively identified at the scene of the shooting of two peace officers with a gun in his hand. My family knew now that there were no more opportunities for Clyde to try to turn his life around for the better. We knew that the manhunt for the Hillsboro killers was focused on my brother and Raymond Hamilton, but we knew that Clyde was not directly involved in that murder. But we had no such solace regarding what happened up at Atoka. All my brother could do now was to try to stay ahead of the pursuing forces of the law until the chase reached its inevitable conclusion.

Clyde and Raymond had not returned to Dallas to hide out for any length of time. My brother wanted to pick up Bonnie to go out on the road with them. He finally talked Raymond into going over and picking her up at her mother's house. Clyde did not go over there himself. The two boys left to make the arrangements with Bonnie. My mother then left my cousin's house and returned to the service station and told the rest of the family about what Clyde said concerning the Atoka tragedy. All the rest of us could do at that point was to wonder and worry about what would happen next.

Chapter 9

After the killing of the undersheriff near Atoka, we knew it was too late for Clyde to ever hope to live on the right side of the law. This knowledge hit my brother L.C. and me especially hard. Clyde was the one older Barrow child with whom we had really grown up, the only one that we ever really knew as a big brother. Jack and Buck were already away from home by the time that I became aware of my family life, but Clyde and L.C. were still part of the home circle that I knew.

Clyde always had a positive impact on people in those early years before he got involved with Frank Clause. He always had a wide circle of friends out in west Dallas. My big brother also impressed many people he met due to circumstances. For example, there was a time in the mid- 1920s when typhoid wrecked havoc among the citizens of west Dallas. At that time, my father, Clyde, and myself were all admitted to Parkland Hospital in Dallas with this illness. The nurses at Parkland who dealt with Clyde while he was hospitalized were all impressed by him. They treated him well and he responded in kind. He was like that with most people; on a one-to-one basis, Clyde would be 110% square with anyone who treated him fairly. That Clyde Barrow was the one L.C. and I grew up knowing.

But now it seemed that the Clyde we knew was gone forever. He could never return home to live as he did in the past. Our contact with him would now be quick and quiet. This sad state of affairs was confirmed when Sheriff Maxwell positively identified my brother as the man who shot him. Raymond Hamilton was also identified as the other shooter by Sheriff Maxwell and other people at the dance.

Our family followed the turn of events closely. Of course, we felt pain due to the knowledge that Clyde would be forever beyond the law, but we felt extremely bad for those who were injured due to the things in which Clyde became involved. For example, we were hit hard when we found out that Eugene Moore wasn't even a regular deputy. He had a part-time job as an undersheriff: he would assist the sheriff only when help was needed. Moore was doing this work for extra money during the Great Depression. He just happened to be there that night at the dance trying to earn some extra cash to support his family. Moore left a young wife and a couple of small children, a fact that hit my mother extremely hard.

After the Atoka tragedy, Clyde, Raymond, and Bonnie knew that they could not stay around north-central Texas due to their connection with the Bucher murder. The trio could not head north up into Oklahoma due to the intense manhunt that had been generated by the Moore murder. They needed someplace to get off by themselves and to figure out what their next step would be.

Bonnie's mother's sister lived out near Carlsbad, New Mexico. Since this was well beyond the normal range of police interest, the boys figured maybe it was time for Bonnie to pay a visit to her aunt. They decided to spend a few days out there. Yet even this attempt at a quiet vacation erupted in screaming headlines. And, as always, there are several different accounts of what happened.

The most traditional account has the trio making their way to the farm of Bonnie's aunt. It has all of the makings of a pleasant visit; in fact, everyone decided it would be desirable to have a big dinner with homemade ice cream afterwards. Bonnie's aunt went out into her garden to pick vegetables for dinner while Raymond took their car into Carlsbad to purchase some ice for the ice cream.

While in Carlsbad, the local sheriff saw the car with the Texas license plates. He decided to follow Raymond, either out of idle curiosity or because he recognized it as a stolen automobile. Either way, he arrived out at the farm and began to poke around.

Clyde and Raymond saw him, and they realized they were in a fix because their guns are locked up in the truck of their auto. Bonnie saw the situation and grabbed a hunting shotgun out of a closet in the farmhouse and got the drop on the sheriff! Clyde and Raymond then removed the sheriff's pistol, herded the lawman into their car, and then the boys and Bonnie drove off with the sheriff as hostage.

Another account has the sheriff stopping the trio as they are driving through Carlsbad (buying the ice, I guess) and wanting to check out the number on the motor in Clyde's car. The boys get the drop on him, force him in their car, and they all take off.

What actually happened out there at Bonnie's aunt's farm was far from an almost accidental run-in between Clyde and a lawman. The contact between Clyde and Deputy Joe Johns was deliberately instigated by Bonnie's aunt. She always denied that she informed the local police. After Clyde and Bonnie were killed, the lawman who was involved began talking to the press and he told exactly what happened between the kids and himself.

I don't know where Clyde, Bonnie, and Raymond were for the five days between August 6, when they left Dallas after the tragedy in Atoka, and the following Thursday, August 11, when they dropped in on Bonnie's aunt. They were probably hiding out somewhere, trying to stay as inconspicuous as possible, living on the rather meager proceeds of the two Dallas-area holdups. Clyde rarely ever had enough money while he was out on the road. I am sure many people think of the bandit life as one of speeding down the road in a new and fast car, counting the thousands of dollars from the most recent haul. The truth of the matter was that Clyde almost never saw even a thousand dollars and considered himself fortunate when he was able to get away with a few hundred dollars.

Clyde, Bonnie, and Raymond did definitely appear at Bonnie's aunt's farm near Carlsbad on August 11. They merely wanted to spend a few quiet days at the farm before returning to their life on the highway. Bonnie's aunt had a large garden, from which she supplied a popular roadside stand with vegetables to sell. This stand was located close to her house and was well-patronized by the locals.

The kids' visit out to Carlsbad started out well, as this aunt had not seen her niece Bonnie for quite some time. But just a couple days after they arrived, this aunt got suspicious about something and arranged a clandestine meeting with a local deputy named Joe Johns.

Bonnie's aunt talked with Deputy Johns about her suspicions about the two young men who were with Bonnie. She wanted Johns to come out and check around the boys' car. The deputy promised he would do so very soon.

Deputy Johns lived up to his promise and went out to the aunt's farm the next morning. That whole area of the southwest was on edge. There had been a particularly atrocious double murder in San Antonio just a few days previously and this crime was on everybody's mind. Possibly the Eddy County deputy thought that Bonnie's aunt figured that the boys might have been involved in that crime (they weren't). He came out to her farm alone and probably didn't figure on meeting any desperate characters.

Johns began to look around Clyde's Ford V-8. The kids saw him and asked someone in the house who he was. When told he was a deputy, Clyde sent Bonnie out to stall him while Clyde and Raymond figured out how to take him. The boys decided to approach him from different directions while Bonnie was talking to him. They went out the back door of the farmhouse, each taking a different route around the house. Bonnie had gone back inside the house by this time, but Johns was so intent on looking at their car that they got the drop on him and disarmed him.

While Raymond held his gun on the deputy, Clyde disabled the other cars around and forced Johns into their V-8. Clyde took off out of there. My brother was driving, as he always did, with the deputy sitting next to him. Bonnie was sitting on Raymond's lap on the right side of the front seat. Both Bonnie and Raymond were holding guns on Johns.

The kids kept Johns with them for almost a full day. That was a miserable trip for everyone involved. Clyde really didn't know exactly what to do with the lawman. My brother had no serious intentions of harming the deputy, as long as Johns cooperated with them and didn't try any heroics. Johns, who was level-headed, realized his predicament and went along with the circumstances.

The quartet drove out of New Mexico into Texas and then gravitated down towards San Antonio. Finally, on Monday morning, the trio released Johns near San Antonio and drove on. None of the four had anything to eat for a full day and had very little sleep. Clyde knew they had to have some sustenance and some rest, so they released Deputy Johns and drove off to get some badly needed refreshment.

Of course, the crowd at the vegetable stand saw what happened when the kids took off with the deputy. Although Clyde had disabled all of the autos he could before he left there, the alarm over Johns' "kidnapping" was spread immediately. That whole part of the southwest was in an uproar; impromptu posses set up roadblocks on all of the major highways. In fact, a headless corpse found in the area was initially identified as Deputy Johns. The body later turned out to be that of a hitchhiker who took a ride with the wrong driver.

The kids knew that they had to have another car. In Victoria, Texas, they stole a car, another Ford V-8. Raymond drove this new acquisition, with Clyde and Bonnie driving the original auto. The alarm was immediately spread concerning the Victoria car theft. Someone noticed both autos heading along the highway going towards Wharton. The marshal at Wharton decided to set a trap on the bridge over the Colorado River. Lawmen were positioned at both ends of the bridge. The two cars were sighted as they sped down the highway. Clyde and

Bonnie were in the lead, with Raymond right behind. Clyde actually drove past the first line of cops onto the bridge. The police at the other end leapt out and began to fire. Clyde turned his car around in the middle of the bridge and sped off. He passed Raymond, who saw what was going on at the bridge. Raymond got his auto turned around and followed after Clyde. All the cops could to do was to helplessly fire at the disappearing cars. Down the highway apiece, Clyde and Bonnie transferred their possessions to the car which Raymond was driving. Then the trio disappeared.

After the adventures in New Mexico and west Texas, the three kids headed back to Dallas and hid out at the Grand Prairie farmhouse for almost two weeks. They are credited with raiding a National Guard armory in Ft. Worth during this time. If they did make the Ft. Worth raid, it was the first time Clyde did anything like it and it certainly was a taste of things to come. The ambush at the Wharton bridge made Clyde realize the importance of firepower. From that point on, Clyde made sure he had as powerful a gun as the police carried.

After the heat from the New Mexico action died down, the kids decided to take to the road again. Raymond Hamilton felt it was time to go to a "cooler" climate, both in terms of temperature and police interest. He wanted to go to Michigan to pay a visit to his father. This time Clyde and Bonnie drove him up there. The trio left Texas around the first of September. Bonnie and Clyde spent some time up there in Michigan with Raymond and his father and then left Raymond and struck out on their own. They traveled around the Upper Midwest throughout the early fall of 1932, seeing the autumn sights, living off of the small robberies that Clyde committed. When they left Texas to go to the Midwest, we received anonymous postcards in the mail assuring us that the couple was doing fine.

During this time period, my mother was actively trying to get Buck released from prison. While Clyde was getting involved in some of the wildest action since the days of the James Boys, Buck was staying out of trouble and was patiently serving his time. My mother was visiting any and all people who would have any input in the process by which Buck could be released on either a parole or a pardon.

We kept Buck informed of what Clyde was involved in regarding the Carlsbad abduction and the Wharton bridge ambush. We would watch Buck's expression fall as he heard about the rough-and-tumble things with which Clyde was connected. Buck kept blaming himself for what was happening with his younger brother. He frequently spoke about his initial trouble with the police in 1922 over the "hot" brass had gotten the whole set of circumstances rolling. Buck very much wanted his own personal reformation to extend to his younger brother. But Clyde's situation was too far gone to be rescued. Buck made the resolution that once he got out of prison, he'd get together with Clyde and try to talk his younger brother into giving up his outlawry, even if it meant leaving the country and going to Mexico.

Clyde and Bonnie continued their travels around the Midwest. After they saw all they wanted to see around the Great Lakes, they gravitated down towards the Kansas City area. They lived off the proceeds of grocery store and filling station robberies. They never tried to join up with any bandit gangs, operating out of Kansas City. I've heard stories about them trying to get tied in with gangsters up there, but they're totally untrue. There was even a story by a reporter who claimed to have met Bonnie Parker at a speakeasy up in Chicago. She was allegedly sitting there by herself, puffing on a big black cigar (which gives the story away as a fabrication, right there, since Bonnie never smoked cigars but did smoke Camel cigarettes). This "tough gun moll" supposedly told the reporter that she and Clyde were in town to try to join up with the Capone gang. Clyde was off somewhere trying to make connections with the Chicago mob. This story, like so many others, is pure rubbish.

While Clyde and Bonnie were sightseeing around the Midwest, Raymond Hamilton made his way back to Dallas after visiting with his father for about a month. Hamilton was getting low on funds and returned to familiar territory to replenish his bankroll during the first week of October. On October 8, two robberies occurred, one in Abilene and the other in Cedar Hill, TX. The Abilene robbery was credited to Clyde and Raymond. However, this account is, like others, false. When this robbery happened, Bonnie and Clyde were still sight-seeing up North, and Raymond was in Cedar Hill robbing Guaranty State Bank. Raymond walked into the bank alone, brandished a small bottle claiming it contained nitroglycerine, and demanded money. The bank employees, believing in his total sincerity, handed over something like $1,400. He made a clean get away after stealing some vehicles.

Hamilton was hiding out in the hills in southwestern Dallas county. He closely followed the newspaper accounts of the Cedar Hill robbery, including the comments of the bank president that fast thinking of bank employees prevented the robber from making an even bigger haul. The bank employees swiftly hid several hundred dollars in some cubby-hole while the robber's back was turned. The remarks of the bank president would have future repercussions.

Three days after Raymond's Cedar Hill robbery, there occurred an atrocious robbery-murder in a neighborhood grocery store up in Sherman, Texas. A meat cutter named Howard Hall was shot and killed during a robbery. Afterwards, Dallas law enforcement officials traveled to Sherman and told the witnesses that Clyde Barrow was the culprit. Since Clyde's name was all over the papers, and since he had already been accused of the murder of one grocer (Bucher in Hillsboro) it made sense to tie him Hall's murder. So, on October 12, the day after the robbery, a $200 reward was issued for Clyde by the Grayson County authorities for Howard Hall's murder.

Clyde always vehemently denied being the murderer of Howard Hall. Our family always believed him. Like every other major occurrence connected with Clyde's name, there are different stories about what happened in that neighborhood grocery store in Sherman.

These stories follow one of two scenarios. The first scenario is that Clyde, Bonnie, and (sometimes) Raymond Hamilton pull up to the store in Sherman. Clyde gets out and the others either stay in the car at the front of the grocery or take off and start to circle the block. Clyde goes in and puts in an order for a few groceries. When Clyde sees the cashier open the cash register to make change, he demands all of the money. Howard Hall comes at Clyde with a meat cleaver, saying "You can't do that, young man!" Clyde slugs Mr. Hall with the barrel of his gun. Hall drops his cleaver and grabs a hold of Clyde with a bear hug. Clyde drags him to the front door and hits him again with his gun barrel. Hall drops in the doorway, and Clyde stands over him, firing into the prone meat-cutter three or four times. Clyde then flees to the waiting car.

The alternative version to the first scenario has Bonnie inside the store with Clyde. The two start to hold up the cashier and Howard Hall grabs Clyde in the bear hug. It's Bonnie who whacks Mr. Hall with the gun until he drops to the floor. Then she stands over the prone grocer and fires into him several times. These accounts state that Bonnie was identified from photographs and that her fingerprints were found in the store.

What really happened that evening was an automobile pulled to the curb a block away from that particular grocery store. Three men were in the car. One man got out and walked to the grocery store. He went in, made a few diversionary purchases to get the cash register open, and demanded money. Howard Hall came at him with a meat cleaver and was slugged with the gun barrel. Mr. Hall grabbed him and was dragged to the front door of the store. The robber shot Mr. Hall and then fled to the waiting car a block away. There was absolutely no woman in the store or waiting in the auto. It's been claimed that the two men waiting in the car were Hollis Hale and Frank Hardy, but Clyde had not teamed up with them yet. Their association was still three weeks down the road.

What is overlooked is the fact that the robber had to have some familiarity with the routine of the grocery store. This bandit struck at the time that the day's receipts were tallied and taken to the owner's home. However, the robber erred and missed getting several hundred dollars by just a very short time. The day's receipts had been removed just a few minutes early. The fact that this robber knew just when to strike indicates that he was familiar with the actions of the employees. He had to have been casing this job for a few days to learn when the most money would have been available. Clyde had no connection with this grocery or this neighborhood. Most accounts of his involvement indicate it was a spur-of-the-moment thing with Clyde. Besides, Clyde never robbed a grocery at this time of day; he usually struck at noontime when most people were off the streets eating lunch at home. Noon was a naturally sleepy, slow time of the day when the tactic of surprise could be best used to his advantage.

Another reason that has been used to place Clyde in the Sherman area on that October 11 was the fact that he was identified as a man who entered the Sherman jail that same day to visit with my other brother L.C., who was supposedly imprisoned there. Sherman was located halfway between Dallas and Atoka, and Clyde's experiences at both places had been well publicized there in Sherman. I find it hard to believe that my brother, already wanted in connection with two murders, numerous robberies, and an interstate abduction would nonchalantly walk into a police station and ask for his own brother like nothing was wrong. If Clyde had reservations about stopping at the dance in Atoka, there is no chance he would have walked right into a police station in an area where he was well known.

Nevertheless, the murder of Howard Hall was chalked up against my brother. This was the third killing in 1932 that he was connected with by the authorities. His connection with Hall's murder kept Clyde out of the area for another couple of weeks, but the kids did make a fast trip home on Halloween night. They had been away for almost two whole months, but the intense pressure by the newspapers, radio, and police limited their visit to only one of just a very short time with both families.

Clyde also came back into Dallas to pick up a couple of boys to go out on the road with them, Frank Hardy and Hollis Hale. Frank Hardy was a boy Clyde met in the days when he was running with Frank Clause. The fact that Clyde and Bonnie were picking up Frank and Hollis did not mean Clyde had big time plans to form something called the "Barrow Gang." Clyde never had any big-time plans to form a bank robbing gang. If anything, my brother and Bonnie welcomed the company to break up the monotony of always being on the run. Later on, my brother L.C. would go out with Clyde on the road, as would other members of the family and close friends.

After quickly visiting with their families and picking up the two boys, the kids took off again and drove back up north. They settled in Missouri and began to look around for places that could provide much needed funds.

Clyde's and Bonnie's time with Frank and Hollis represents a series of adventures that had more in common with the Keystone Kops than with the James Boys. There was the bank that the boys had tried to rob which had failed a few days previously and therefore had no money to be taken. The sole bank employee on duty had to explain that since there was no money to be taken; their raid was merely an exercise in futility. This particular affair really tickled Clyde's sense of humor. Even bank banditry had its moments of slapstick action.

Then, there was the bank in Oronogo, Missouri, which the Boys did rob on November 30, 1932. Bonnie had initially checked the bank out and found it to be robable, so Clyde, Frank, and Hollis raided it. The bank employees were made suspicious by Bonnie's initial visit, so there was an armed reception committee awaiting the boys when they attempted to clean it out. There was some shooting back and forth, with no one being injured on either side. All my brother could do was to make a hasty grab through one teller's cage, where he got just over $100. Then, the trio fled.

Frank and Hollis apparently had their appetites for banditry whetted by reading in the newspapers about the Barker Gang's $240,000 robbery of the Cloud County Bank in Concordia, Kansas, during the summer of 1932. Charles "Pretty Boy" Floyd and George Birdwell had been robbing banks throughout Oklahoma during that whole year; getting thousands of dollars in each robbery. I imagine Frank and Hollis thought that, once they hooked up with Clyde, they'd soon be rolling in tens of thousands of dollars. But what they found out was that the big, successful bank robbery was relatively rare, and the life of a bandit was a pretty hard row to hoe.

Therefore, Frank and Hollis proceeded to back off from a life of "big-time" outlawry. One day, the two of them made some kind of excuse to separate themselves from Clyde and Bonnie. Frank and Hollis headed back for Texas, taking most of the loot from the Oronogo bank robbery with them. Clyde really didn't seem to be too perturbed by the fact that they went their own way; in fact, he later wrote an alibi letter for Frank.

Maybe Frank and Hollis were disillusioned about a life of bank robberies because of what happened up in Oklahoma eight days before they robbed the Oronogo bank. George Birdwell, Pretty Boy Floyd's partner, went ahead and tried to rob a bank with two other men. Floyd had a bad feeling about this particular excursion and backed out. Birdwell and the other two went ahead with the bank robbery in Boley, Oklahoma, on November 22, 1932. It turned out to be a wild shoot-em-up, with Birdwell, another bandit, and the bank president getting killed. The third bandit was pretty badly shot up also, but he lived - and swore off a life of crime afterward.

On the other hand, just three days after the Boley disaster, Raymond Hamilton made a successful strike at the same Cedar Hill bank he'd robbed about six weeks earlier. Between the two Cedar Hill holdups, Raymond had robbed another bank in LaGrange, over in east Texas. He needed money, and he remembered what the bank president had said about outfoxing the robber out of several hundred dollars in October. Raymond looked up Les Stewart, another west Dallas boy, and they marched back into the Cedar Hill Guaranty Bank on November 25, 1932. This time they got all of the money that was available, using sawed-off shotguns as persuasive influences. Both boys made a successful escape, getting away with well over $1,800 altogether.

This Cedar Hill bank robbery had an interesting aftermath, which took place in May, 1988. The town of Cedar Hill incorporated a re-enactment of the November, 1932, holdup as part of a town festival. The re-enactment was very well received by the townspeople. Time certainly works changes.

Chapter 10

After the comical interlude in Missouri, Clyde and Bonnie gravitated back towards Texas. They had been away from the area since early September, except for the one quick dash back home on Halloween. They missed being in regular contact with their families in general and their mothers in particular. Both kids were extraordinarily close to their mothers, and it was extremely hard for them to be separated from their mothers for any length of time. Clyde and Bonnie stayed around the Dallas area for a few weeks.

Another former associate of theirs was also headed back towards Dallas at the same time. Raymond Hamilton was escorted back to north-central Texas, against his will, of course. He had been arrested up in Michigan.

Just after Raymond had robbed the Cedar Hill bank the second time, he felt he had acquired enough money for awhile. Just for good measure, Raymond robbed the bank in LaGrange, Texas, with a friend of his named Gene O'Dare. After Raymond and Les Stewart held up the Cedar Hill bank, Raymond and O'Dare headed back north for another visit with Raymond's father. They were staying at the town of Bay City, Michigan, when Raymond thought he found himself a girlfriend at a certain restaurant. This girl was a waitress at this establishment. She resisted all of Raymond's advances and dismissed him as just one more blow-hard.

Raymond tried one last desperate ploy to get her attention: he told her that he was a thoroughly bad man and was wanted in Texas for all kinds of bank robberies and gunplay. This ploy definitely aroused the girl's attention, but not in the way Raymond would've wanted: this girl's steady boyfriend was a policeman. This policeman was definitely interested in getting involved with Raymond, if only for a short time.

This policeman advised his girlfriend to go ahead and set up a date with Raymond and to even fix up Gene O'Dare with a date. The girl was instructed to make it a roller-skating party for the four of them. So, on December 6, 1932, Raymond and Gene O'Dare went roller-skating with their sweeties. The affair turned out to be a surprise party, with a party of Michigan cops waiting at the roller rink as a surprise to Raymond and O'Dare. The boys couldn't escape while wearing roller-skates, and they were easily arrested. Both were returned to the Dallas area to face the music on several outstanding charges.

Hillsboro wanted Raymond very badly in connection with the Bucher slaying. In short order, Raymond was taken down to the Hill County jail to stand trial at the big courthouse in Hillsboro. It was the only murder charge Raymond had against him at this time.

Clyde had been with many different people so far this year: Ralph Fults, Frank Clause, Raymond Hamilton, Hollis Hale, and Frank Hardy. Bonnie Parker was the one constant in his life and the one associate with whom he really wanted to stay. Most of Clyde's "professional" associates were boys that he'd met in connection with his criminal activities. But now Clyde was about to ride with a boy from his early years in west Dallas.

One of Clyde's closest friends from his teenaged years in west Dallas was another boy named Clyde: Clyde Jones. In fact, the Jones family and the Barrow family were friends from back in the 1920s. Mrs. Jones and the Jones boys accompanied our family when we made the horse-and-wagon trip down to San Antonio in 1928. The three Jones boys and we three youngest Barrow kids paired off back in those days. The two Clydes ran together, while L.C. associated with William Daniel, who we always called W.D. I ran with the youngest Jones boy, Leroy. The Jones kids' ages paralleled our ages. So it was a natural that we'd pair off in this fashion.

It wasn't Clyde Jones that expressed a desire to ride with Clyde Barrow, though. It was L.C.'s friend W.D. All of west Dallas followed Clyde's experiences throughout 1932. What was to our family heartbreak seemed like an exciting adventure to the west Dallas kids who were emotionally removed from what Clyde was doing. Many of the west Dallas kids were still being picked up by the police all of the time, just as Buck and Clyde were back in the 1920s. Many of the youngsters vicariously lived through Clyde's battle with the law. W.D. was one of these kids.

Like L.C. and I, W.D. really looked up to his older brother and to our Clyde as well. The older boys were the ones who set the trends and standards for we younger kids. It was in late 1932 when W.D. began expressing a desire to go on the road with Clyde and Bonnie.

Most popular accounts treat Clyde's association with W.D. as a spur-of-the-moment incident. It supposedly occurs at some west Dallas service station, where Clyde casually asks W.D., who is pumping gas, whether he'd like to join up with them. The overwhelmed youngster immediately jumps at the chance and hops into the car with Clyde and Bonnie.

In his so-called memoirs, W.D. claimed he was almost shanghaied by Clyde and Bonnie. According to his account, he and my brother L.C. were driving along the Eagle Ford Road late one night when Clyde and Bonnie drove up to them. It was right before Christmas. Clyde told W.D. that he and Bonnie needed some rest, which involved someone else doing the driving when needed. W.D. was conscripted for that purpose. He got into the car right then and there and they took off.

It was W.D. who expressed the strong desire to go on the road with Clyde. If Clyde needed rest and had the choice of asking either L.C. Barrow or W.D. Jones, he would've asked his brother L.C. He wouldn't have asked a relatively unknown and untested quantity like W.D. My brother L.C. did go out on the road with Clyde on occasion when Clyde asked him to do so.

W.D. Jones kept hanging around my father's service station, hoping to make contact with Clyde there. The other place where W.D. also tried to make contact with my brother was the Fish Trap Dance Hall. That was a popular hang out in west Dallas and was just what the name implies: a dance hall. It was not an underworld hangout, but Clyde always liked going there. Clyde always enjoyed the dancing and the bands that played there. Sooner or later, anyone who wanted to get a message to my brother could make contact at the Fish Trap Dance Hall.

W.D. was not running from any serious trouble in west Dallas. He still had every chance to avoid any involvement with big-time criminality. W.D. just wanted to go out with Clyde and Bonnie because he thought it would be an adventure. Clyde figured that he'd humor W.D. for awhile and then bring him back to west Dallas when W.D. found out what the outlaw life was really like. W.D. would get sick and disillusioned and would want to be brought back home in short order. Clyde would then bring him back and W.D. would have learned a lesson about reality.

Tragically, W.D. learned the hard reality of the outlaw life on Christmas Day, 1932. Clyde figured the police may be watching for him to come to west Dallas during the holiday, so he got his visiting done a bit earlier. The holiest day of the year found Clyde, Bonnie, and W.D. down in the city of Temple, Texas. Clyde felt that they needed to switch cars. The three saw several autos parked in front of a house at which a holiday celebration was obviously being celebrated. Clyde saw a car he liked and sent W.D. out to take it. They'd drive both autos off and then would switch their possessions to the new car. They'd also switch license plates and then drive off somewhere to lay low.

Things went drastically wrong this time, though. W.D. jumped into the desired auto and tried to start it up. He tried to get it going several times, but it wouldn't turn over for some reason. W.D. still kept trying to fiddle with it. Clyde knew someone would soon notice what was going on, so he hurried over to give W.D. some assistance. The car still wouldn't start - and then someone saw what was going on and began to yell out. Other people began corning out of their houses at the sound of the ruckus and began to yell also.

Clyde realized it was a lost cause and began to drag W.D. out of the car. W.D. was still trying to get the thing started when Clyde grabbed a hold of him. The owner of the car, a young man named Doyle Johnson, finally ran out of one of the houses. He had been eating Christmas dinner at a family get-together and still had a napkin tucked into his collar. It turned out that it was his car Clyde and W.D. were trying to steal.

Johnson ran down to the street to where his car was parked. He yelled for his family to call for the police. Johnson jumped on the man on the outside of the car, which happened to be Clyde. The auto owner grabbed Clyde around the throat and yelled again for the police. Clyde pulled a gun and told Johnson two or three times to get back or he'd shoot him. Johnson began to hit Clyde and kept screaming for the police. By now the scene was one of total pandemonium. Clyde and Doyle Johnson were locked up on one side of Johnson's car. Bonnie was in their car screaming for Clyde to turn him loose and get back to their auto. Several people were running around and yelling several yards away from the struggle. By now W.D. had managed to pile out of the car and was close to Clyde and Doyle Johnson.

Clyde would've happily followed Bonnie's advice and turned Doyle Johnson loose, if he could've done so. But Johnson had him by the throat with one hand and was hitting him with the other. By then, W.D. had made it back to their original car and had started to get inside. But then he grabbed a gun out of the backseat and ran back over to where Johnson and Clyde were struggling.

My brother now expected the police to show up at any minute and knew it was now or never. If the cops showed up and he was caught, he knew it was the electric chair in either Texas or Oklahoma. Clyde squeezed the trigger on his pistol and fired. At the same time, a second gun fired from another direction. It was W.D. who fired this second shot almost at the same time Clyde fired. Whichever gun fired the fatal bullet, the end result was the same: Doyle Johnson released his hold on Clyde's neck and crumpled to the ground.

Both Clyde and W.D. piled into their initial car and Bonnie hit the accelerator. Just a few blocks away, Clyde took over the wheel and sped off. Both Clyde and W.D. have been credited with shooting Doyle Johnson, a lumber salesman who left behind a wife and a small child. It could've been either one of them; both were there with guns in their hands. But it would be Clyde who was charged with the killing, as it was with the slayings of John Bucher, Eugene Moore, and Howard Hall no matter who else was there shooting. Clyde, Bonnie, and W.D. went into hiding after the shooting in Temple. However, they were not immediately associated with this tragedy. In fact, it would not be until the autumn of 1933 that Clyde would be positively connected with the Johnson murder and then that would be through the confession of W.D. Jones. W.D. would say that Clyde fired the only shots during that trouble in Temple on Christmas Day.

The year of 1932 was finally coming to an end and it was none too soon for the Barrow family. It had been an extremely bad year. 1932 had begun with such high hopes and bright notes. Buck had committed himself to his personal reformation and was supported by Blanche, our family, and (seemingly) the officials in the prison system. Throughout the year, Buck had lived up to his commitment and had behaved himself as a model prisoner should have done. Our family hoped that his good behavior would result in his earlier release from prison, and my mother and Blanche were both working towards that end.

The beginning of 1932 appeared to have begun on a brighter note for Clyde also. He was finally released from prison just a few weeks into the year. Our family had hoped that he would commit himself to his personal reformation in the same way that Buck had done. All of us wished that Bonnie would have the same effect on

Clyde that Blanche had had on Buck. But the Caldwells were different people than the Parkers in terms of benevolent influence. Blanche and her pastor father were really much more positive influences on Buck than were Bonnie and Emma Parker on Clyde. Pastor Caldwell never looked disparagingly on Buck concerning his previous conflicts with the law and actively tried to influence my older brother towards the right path in life. There was a lot of positive reinforcement with him that just wasn't there with Emma Parker.

The end of 1932 saw Buck struggling in prison to turn his fortunes around for the better. Clyde, on the other hand, seemed to have left a trail of non-stop carnage behind him. It was too late for him to ever hope to get his fortunes turned around. All Clyde could now look forward towards was an unspecified amount of borrowed time until a peace officer's bullet brought it to a sudden end.

Yet, even in the waning days of 1932, there were events going on that would carry over into 1933 and would create more tragedy for Clyde and the rest of our family. Just a couple of days before the year ended, a bank in Grapevine, Texas was robbed by a couple of west Dallas boys. These two boys were named Les Stewart and Odell Chambless. Les was a pal of Raymond Hamilton's who helped Raymond rob the Cedar Hill bank in November. Odell's father Joe Chambless lived in west Dallas. Odell also had a sister named Mary who was married to Gene O'Dare, Raymond's associate in the LaGrange, Texas, bank robbery in November. It was Gene who was arrested with Raymond up in Michigan. But they were separated when they were returned back to Texas; Raymond was sent down to Hillsboro for the Bucher killing, and Gene was put on trial for his role in the LaGrange holdup.

These two Hamilton buddies went out on their own to take this Grapevine bank just before New Year's. They got away with almost $3,000, but Les was arrested during the pursuit just a few hours after the robbery. The two boys' getaway car had slid off the road and wrecked. At this point they separated, Les going one way and Odell another. Odell made his way back to west Dallas, where he went to one of Raymond Hamilton's sisters for assistance, which he received. Les wasn't so lucky, but then he tried to reverse his flow of luck by telling the authorities everything they wanted to know, including his and Odell's connections with the Hamilton family. The police, not realizing that Odell was long gone from the area, started keeping a watch on Raymond's female siblings, especially his sister Lillie

Hamilton McBride.

Other members of the Hamilton clan were trying to establish connections with certain parties during this period, especially Raymond, whose message was direct and clear: help me escape. Raymond was now in dire straits, going to trial on a murder charge in connection with the death of John Bucher, a crime with which he had nothing to do. Raymond was sending SOS's to Clyde for assistance. Clyde sent word back that he would provide what assistance he could.

Raymond was trying to pull off the same stunt that he did the first time he was in jail. When he made his first ever jailbreak from the McKinney, Texas jail in late January, 1932, he got himself a large radio. The jail authorities figured that this would do no harm, so they allowed him to keep it and eventually got used to Raymond's frequent and loud use of the radio. Raymond said he played the radio loudly so the other prisoners could hear it. The other prisoners supported this, so the jailers went along with it, figuring anything that would help keep everyone quiet and content was highly desirable.

But the loudness of the radio was for more than the edification of the other prisoners. While it did keep the others entertained, it also nicely covered the sound of the hacksaw blades cutting the jail bars. The blades had been smuggled into the McKinney jail inside the radio for Raymond's behalf. Raymond eventually cut a hole in the bars big enough for him to wriggle through. He made his way out of the cell-block and through the front of the jail and then out the front door to the street and freedom.

Raymond wanted to do this again. He asked that Clyde get him a big radio and to make sure that there were some hacksaw blades hidden inside. Clyde did so and delivered the items to Raymond's sister Lillie. This was the first time Clyde had ever had any close connection with any of the Hamilton girls. My brother promised Lillie that he would follow up with her to make sure that Raymond got the items.

The situation was now such that there were two conflicting forces focusing their attention on the Hamilton's. The forces of the law were trying to capture Odell Chambless and the forces of the lawless were trying to get Raymond out of jail. These forces accidentally crossed paths on the evening of January 6, 1933.

I remember that evening very well myself. Earlier that night, I had been palling around with Audrey Hamilton. We had not been at Lillie Hamilton's that day, but had been elsewhere by nightfall. That evening, I was pedaling along on the bicycle that Clyde had bought me a few weeks earlier. It was the first bike that I had ever owned and I was quite proud of it. No matter what Clyde may have done in regard to other people, he was always a generous older brother to both L.C. and myself. Even while he was in prison from 1930 to 1932, he was always making things for our family. He made me several things which I've kept for over 60 years. For example, there was a little colorful necklace that was composed of red, yellow, black, and turquoise-colored beads. Some of these beads spelled out "Marie." Clyde also made me a nice leather belt, and he made our mother a small pair of cowboy-type boots that said "Mom" on them. When he was out on the road after his time in prison, he was always giving us money and gifts. Clyde knew that I really wanted a nice bicycle and, in late 1932, he got me one. I was riding it back home from Audrey Hamilton's on the night of January 6.

It was close to midnight and I was riding east on Eagle Ford Road. I was pedaling back towards our service station. There was suddenly the sound of a police siren and I looked up to see what was going on. I saw Clyde, speeding down Eagle Ford Road lickety-split and cranking away on a police siren. His car zipped by and disappeared down the street.

I knew something pretty unusual had happened. Clyde wouldn't have done anything like that as a prank. It would have been extremely foolish for him to call attention to himself like that. But I hadn't heard anything like the sound of gunfire that whole evening. I pedaled on home to check with my parents as to just what had transpired.

My parents, however, had heard plenty of gunshots that evening. In fact, some of the shells had come dangerously close to hitting our service station and house. The action occurred over at Lillie Hamilton's house, which was just a couple of blocks away. Lillie lived over on County Avenue (now known as Winnetka Street). There were big, open fields between our filling station and that group of houses where she lived. There was nothing between our house and her house to stop any of the bullets. There were plenty of bullets flying around that particular night.

It turned out that there had been a posse of policemen over at Lillie's that evening. They were waiting in anticipation for an expected visit from Odell Chambless. There were police from two different counties. Since the Grapevine bank robbery had taken place over in Tarrant County, there were some Tarrant County officers, including a deputy named Malcolm Davis. Since west Dallas was still county land, there were Dallas County officers there also. They were all armed, but they didn't have any machine guns or the like. Odell Chambless wasn't noted as a violent gunman and he had no murder charges against him. The police figured that Odell would just meekly surrender to their superior forces. The trouble was that Clyde was the person who showed up there at Lillie's house, and the words "meekly surrender" were not part of his vocabulary.

Clyde, Bonnie, and W.D. had come into town earlier that evening. My brother had allowed Bonnie a visit of a few minutes duration with her mother over on Lamar Street. Then they drove over to Lillie's house. They pulled up in front of the house and Clyde got out to go up to the front porch. He was wearing an overcoat with a shotgun strapped underneath his arm beneath the coat. Bonnie and W.D. remained inside the car. Clyde was on the front porch and knocked on the door. Maggie Hamilton, another Hamilton sister, answered.

There have been differing accounts about what happened from this point on, but I'll tell the story that our family was told. We knew that there was at least five officers in the trap for Chambless: two out front, two out back, and at least one officer inside the house, watching out from the front window. Maggie Hamilton apparently gave Clyde some kind of verbal tip, telling him not to shoot and to think of her baby. At the same time, Clyde saw the officer inside the house make a motion. This inside officer also saw that it was not Odell Chambless outside, but Clyde Barrow, and brought his gun upward. The two fired at each other, both missing. The other officers began firing, as did W.D. from the car out on the street.

Clyde's shotgun jammed, and he crouched down low to try to dislodge the jammed shell with his fingers and to stay out of the heavy line of fire. Deputy Malcolm Davis ran around from the back of Lillie's house and jumped up on the front porch, demanding that Clyde surrender. Unfortunately, Deputy Davis jumped up right into the line of fire and was hit immediately after his call for surrender. The deputy was fatally wounded. Clyde finally got his gun unjammed and then ran for the street.

While running from the house, Clyde exchanged shots with one officer who had taken cover underneath a neighboring house. My brother looked up to see Bonnie driving down the block towards Eagle Ford Road. Bonnie had driven down the block to stop W.D. from firing at anything and everything that was moving. W.D. wasn't too particular about targets during a firefight.

Clyde saw the car heading down County Avenue, and then, he changed his direction, running down the alley in back of Lillie's house. He met Bonnie's car just as she turned right on Eagle Ford Road. My brother climbed behind the wheel and started cranking on that old police siren to clear any traffic for his getaway. It was just a few blocks down the street that the three of them tore past me on my bike.

Clyde headed west on Eagle Ford Road and then turned north heading towards the town of Grapevine. The trio drove along some of the same country roads that Odell Chambless had driven along just over a week earlier. They had the same misfortune Odell and Les Stewart had gone through; they skidded off the road. They were only about a mile from Grapevine when Clyde overshot a curve in the road and slid about 100 feet out into a farm field. Their car bogged down to the axles in the mud. Clyde knew he couldn't wait until morning to be pulled out by a wrecker and that police forces in both Dallas and Tarrant counties were starting to mobilize in the wake of the Davis killing. Clyde managed to find a farmer who was willing to pull them out via a team of horses, despite it being the middle of the night. The handsome bit of money Clyde offered the farmer was a big inducement. Once they had been delivered from the miry field, the three of them drove up through Oklahoma and up into Missouri.

Our family hoped that Clyde and Bonnie would lie low for awhile and not have any more close encounters with the police. Yet, it was around three weeks later that Clyde had his next up-close-and-personal dealings with the police. Mercifully, this action had no lethal consequences. Compared to the carnage connected with the County Avenue affair, it was almost comical.

What happened was as Clyde, Bonnie, and W.D. were driving along a highway near Springfield, Missouri, they were accosted by a highway patrolman on a motorcycle. The officer finally got even with them as they were crossing a bridge and told my brother to pull over. Clyde didn't want to get caught on a bridge, so he kept edging the car ahead slowly. This patrolman kept telling Clyde to pull over and to stop, but Clyde kept edging the car slowly forward. Clyde politely and smilingly kept telling the officer that he'd stop in just a moment.

Finally, my brother's car made it off of the bridge and Clyde pulled over on a part of the road that he felt was safe. The patrolman marched up to the car and was ready to give Clyde "what for" concerning his forward movements with the car. But Clyde had his own version of "what for" to give to patrolman Thomas Persell.

Just as the officer stormed up to their car, Clyde told W.D. to "take him." W.D. knew just what that meant and hopped out of the car, covering the patrolman with a gun while Clyde had his shotgun pointed at Officer Persell. Persell thought discretion would be the better part of valor in this situation, and he gave up. W.D. hustled the officer into their back seat, and their car took off.

Clyde's dealing with Officer Persell was much more relaxed than was the kidnapping of Joe Johns almost five months earlier. Clyde didn't quite know what to do in that situation back in August, 1932. He had no intentions of harming or killing the officer as long as the officer didn't try to be some kind of a hero. With the Joe Johns situation, Clyde had established his procedure for handling this kind of situation: just keep the officer with them until they reached a point where they found a spot that was isolated enough to afford them a head start before the cop could get to a phone.

Then something unexpected happened; their car developed trouble, and my brother determined that a new battery was needed. Clyde sent W.D. and Persell out to get a new one. Officer Persell was so cooperative during this venture, even helping W.D. by taking turns in carrying the heavy battery, that Clyde wouldn't consider dumping the patrol man out in some isolated area. My brother gave the man some money and let him go right then and there after the new battery was installed. Compared to the mayhem which accompanied the Atoka and west Dallas conflicts, this conclusion was a welcome relief to all involved.

Chapter 11

After the west Dallas gunfight and the Persell abduction, Clyde, Bonnie, and W.D. dropped out of sight for several weeks. They weren't accused in the newspapers of any new crimes. The three of them were lying low up in the Ozark mountain area of eastern Oklahoma, western Arkansas, and southwestern Missouri. This region was one of Clyde's preferred areas in which to hide. Our family didn't know exactly where Clyde's Ozark hideout was located, but we did know that he had one especially preferred place in which he holed up when the situation required. We knew that the kids spent quite a lot of time around the tourist camps in the vicinities of both Joplin, Missouri and Ft. Smith, Arkansas.

This tri-state area had been a traditional hideout for outlaws since the 1870s. Belle Starr's cabin at Younger's Bend on the Canadian River was about 50 miles west of Ft. Smith. Jesse James was accused of participation in a gun battle with officers in Joplin. Many of the most famous bandits between the James-Starr era and Clyde's time, out-laws like Henry Starr and Al Spencer, operated in this same region. In the early 1930s, however, the best known "favorite son" of this region was Charles "Pretty Boy" Floyd from Akins, Oklahoma. Akins was located just across the state line from Ft. Smith.

In fact, Floyd's name was drawn into the investigation of the slaying of Malcolm Davis. The newspapers were wildly casting about trying to identify the man who fired from Clyde's car there on County Avenue. Pretty Boy Floyd was the best known outlaw in the country at that time, so the Dallas newspapers tied him into the shooting. The press surmised that Floyd and many other bandits were hiding out at a "Robber's Roost" location between Dallas and Ft. Worth. It was supposed to be close to the town of Arlington. The police raided this area after the Davis slaying, hoping to capture Clyde, Pretty Boy, and other outlaws. Of course, the police came up empty handed.

Clyde, Pretty Boy, and others hid out in the Ozarks because of both its tradition and the good quality of the roads. My brother hid out in this area often, but he'd never had any contact with Floyd or any other of the Ozark gangs up through this time period. Clyde, Bonnie, and W.D. kept to themselves. They continued with their robberies of groceries and service stations. They also continued to send us the usual anonymous post cards. Clyde would sign his name "Bud" while Bonnie would be "Sis." W.D. used the name "Jack." These postcards were just to let us know that all was well.

Of course, all was not well with Clyde and it never again would be. Our family knew, but we tried to bear as well as possible under this knowledge. There was nothing that we could do about Clyde's situation except worry, but our efforts concerning Buck's predicament were just about to bear fruit. Mother and Buck's wife Blanche were working to try to get him released from prison. Blanche has been credited with the maneuver that may have finally gotten her husband released.

According to some stories, Blanche made her way down to Austin to speak with Governor Miriam "Ma" Ferguson with three kids in tow and pregnant with a fourth. These children of hers are described as being products of a previous marriage and the one she was carrying was Buck's. The first problem with this scene is that Blanche had never been married before she and Buck got together. The second problem is that Buck had been in prison for over a year already, so it is quite unlikely that the child was his offspring. The third problem is that Blanche never had any children from any marriage. Of course, Blanche could've borrowed three kids from someone, and she could've built herself up to look like she was pregnant. If Blanche did do this to play on Ma Ferguson's sympathies, it sure worked. Buck got a full and free pardon. Then again, it could've been the result of my mother's efforts. There were no lengths through which my mother would not have gone to help any of her kids.

Buck was released from prison and immediately returned to our place in west Dallas. We were all overjoyed to have him and Blanche back home. Not only was he no longer in jail, but the full pardon meant that no crime from the past could come back to haunt him. Buck felt that he had been given a new lease on life. He was equipped with a good, supportive wife and the knowledge that nothing from the past could be held against him. Buck's pardon was a bright spot in a very dark time for our family.

Despite the happiness concerning his freedom, our family could see that there was one circumstance that overshadowed Buck's attitude. He still felt guilty about the situation that Clyde was in, and his thoughts turned towards his younger brother. Buck wanted to extend his newfound freedom to Clyde and he talked about getting Clyde to quit his life of crime. But Clyde's surrender was an impossibility; there were already three counts of "murder one" lodged against him. Any of these counts could land him in the electric chair. But Buck just couldn't see this fact though. He just knew that there had to be a way to get Clyde to quit what he was doing.

Most popular accounts have Buck and Blanche planning to go up to Missouri and live with Blanche's parents on their farm. The trouble with this scenario is that her parents were separated with her father pastoring in Oklahoma. There was no Missouri farm on which to go and live.

Somehow, word got to Clyde that Buck had been released from prison. Naturally, Clyde wanted to visit with his brother. They hadn't seen each other for a substantial amount of time. Contact was made between my brothers and it was agreed that Buck and Blanche would spend some time with Clyde and Bonnie. However, Blanche was against this idea of visiting with Clyde. She had spent the year of 1932 seeing firsthand what Clyde was facing. Blanche knew that when the law finally caught up with Clyde there would be no quarter asked or given by either side. Blanche didn't want either she or Buck to be there if the cops did try to jump Clyde. She knew that it would be open season on anyone with Clyde and Bonnie. Blanche tried to persuade Buck that Clyde could never be pardoned as Ma Ferguson pardoned him.

But Buck wouldn't give up the idea of trying to redeem his brother. So about two weeks after Buck was pardoned and released, a car was arranged for him and Blanche to use. In early April, 1933, Buck, Blanche, and Snowball (Blanche's little white dog) met Clyde, Bonnie, and W.D. at a tourist camp near Ft. Smith. To further ensure that no trouble with the law would occur, the five of them drove further north to Joplin. There were no murder charges against Clyde up in Missouri as there were in Oklahoma and Texas.

The five of them found a nice apartment in a quiet residential part of Joplin. The apartment had four rooms and was over a double garage. This flat had a commanding view of the neighborhood and was made of stone, which suited Clyde. Another advantage was that since the living quarters were on the second story, no casual passersby could look inside.

Buck got down to business with Clyde after they got settled in. He talked to his younger brother and asked him to quit the outlaw life by either surrendering and taking his chances in the courts or leaving Texas altogether for Mexico. Buck pointed to what was happening with Raymond Hamilton in Texas at that time.

Raymond was being shuttled around from court to court and trial to trial. He had been put on nonstop trial for the crimes that he and Clyde had been accused of committing. Raymond had been given a 25 year sentence for the Neuhoff Packing Company robbery and 30 years for the Cedar Hill bank robberies. He was sentenced to 10 years for a couple of car thefts. There was also a 99 year sentence for the LaGrange bank robbery. Finally, there was a 99 year sentence for the Bucher killing in Hillsboro. These sentences totaled 263 years.

Buck admitted that this was an appalling number of years, but he emphasized that Raymond had not gotten any death sentences as a habitual criminal for any of these crimes. Raymond also didn't get the death penalty for the Bucher killing. Buck also pointed out that there were no plans to turn Raymond over to the state of Oklahoma to be tried on the Moore murder. Buck agreed that many years in prison were bad, but not nearly as bad as death by either the electric chair or by police bullet, which would be the inevitable end for Clyde, if he continued in the way he was going.

Clyde listened to Buck's reasoning, but he told his older brother that there was no chance for him, despite what Raymond was getting away with in Texas. Clyde said that he now had more on him than what Raymond had against himself. There was also the Howard Hall murder in Sherman, with which Clyde had nothing to do, and the Doyle Johnson and Malcolm Davis killings, with which Clyde did have involvement.

My two brothers discussed this subject every day for a week. Clyde resisted any ideas of surrender or exile. Clyde was starting to get restless, and not just because of the topic of conversation; the five of them had enjoyed a nice week of peace and quiet together, but Clyde didn't want to press his luck for too much longer. He felt that Buck and Blanche should pack up and head back to Texas and that he, Bonnie, and W.D. should hit the road.

But Buck refused to be denied. He kept asking for one more day in which to talk to Clyde. He told Buck that everyone ought to get out of Joplin while they were all well-rested. Buck would agree, but would ask for just one day more. Clyde told Buck that he and Blanche should get out to a Joplin-area tourist court and live there for the rest of the visit. Clyde didn't want his brother to be around in case there was a conflict at the apartment. Buck was afraid that Clyde would fly the coop while he was away, so he refused to move out to a tourist camp.

Printed accounts of their time in Joplin have stated that Clyde, Buck, and W.D. were the terrors of both their neighborhood and the Joplin area during their visit. My brothers were credited with burglarizing a lot of area businesses at night. They were accused of daylight jewelry store and bank robberies, as well as a National Guard armory raid to acquire more guns. Clyde had no intentions of instigating a crime wave in Missouri, using Joplin as their base. He absolutely did not want to get Buck and Blanche involved in what he was doing. Buck had a brand new lease on life due to his pardon and Blanche had never been in any criminal trouble in her life. They were poor candidates for initiation into a life of banditry.

Clyde had no trouble with any of his neighbors in that part of Joplin. The grocer from whom they purchased their food every day remembered them as nice customers and ordinary people. The kids didn't have that much to do with their immediate neighbors, though, and they didn't go out of their way to make anyone's acquaintance, due to their status as wanted people. But the kids did treat other people in the neighborhood with consideration when their paths crossed in everyday life. For example, there was a little girl named Bethy who made friends with Bonnie. The little girl was in their apartment several times and even had an evening supper of pork chops with my brothers one night. Then there was a law enforcement officer selling protective service to all of the residents of the neighborhood. For a dollar, he would make frequent patrols of the area and watch out for any potential trouble. This patrolman visited Clyde and Buck in their apartment. The boys paid him a dollar for his services.

But Clyde and Bonnie had to exercise some caution. Either Bonnie or Blanche would meet the grocery and laundry delivery boys at the door and would not let them inside. The girls would assume the whole burden of the grocery bags and laundry bundles and would not let the delivery boys help them carry the items. One day, the laundry boy was met by Blanche, who was upset by something that day. He noticed her emotional state, but did not attach any sinister connotations to it.

It may have been Clyde that made the initial mistake that later led to disaster in Joplin. One day while down in the garage, Clyde was messing with his guns. He let one of the machine guns go off. Clyde did not use the well-known Thompson submachine gun, despite what the movies portray. He preferred the World War I Browning Automatic Rifle. It was one of those BARs that cut loose that day in the garage.

Unfortunately, the sound of the BAR was heard by a man in the neighborhood - probably the only person who did hear it. But he turned out to be one person too many. This man began to keep a close watch on the residents of the garage apartment, and to pay close notice to their activities. Their constant odd behavior became sinister to him. He decided they were trying to hide something and he took his suspicions to the police. The concerned citizen described their movements as those of frightened animals. The police decided to keep a watch on the occupants of the garage apartment and to check them out.

The police watched the laundry company make their daily pickup and delivery. They talked with the laundry boy about these particular customers. The laundry boy noticed that it was always the women who received the goods, and the women would never let them carry the bundles into the apartment. The boy remembered that one particular woman seemed to be more and more nervous as the days went by. That must have been Blanche, who was getting more and more stressed by Buck's continued insistence on trying to talk to Clyde. She wanted to take Clyde's advice and go to the tourist court outside of Joplin. Clyde's uneasiness about staying there at the garage apartment was starting to affect Blanche and everyone else. Clyde's financial reserves were starting to run low and he felt jinxed because of the accidental burst of machine gun fire. But Buck still hung on, trying to talk Clyde into either surrendering or fleeing the country.

On the morning of April 13, Buck finally gave up and agreed to go back to Texas. But he wanted a day for him and Blanche to pack and to get their car ready for the return trip. Blanche eagerly began to pack their things; she was happy for the first time in several days. Blanche would've left immediately, but she was satisfied with Buck's promise to leave Joplin on the morning of April 14.

Clyde began to make his own plans to leave the Joplin area. He wanted a new car with which to go out on the road and asked W.D. to go out and get them one. W.D. went out that morning of April 13 and stole another Ford V-8. He drove the stolen car back to their apartment.

Clyde's accidental burst of automatic gunfire was the first mistake: it instigated police interest. The theft of the Ford V-8 was the second mistake: it instigated police action. The stolen car was immediately reported to the police, of course. When the officers who were keeping the garage apartment under surveillance saw the new acquisition being driven back up to the garage apartment, it was reported immediately to their superiors. The Joplin police then figured they "had the goods" on this gang of car thieves. The cops already figured they were either a bunch of bootleggers or petty criminals. Either way, with the purloined vehicle on the premises, the police figured now was the time to act. They organized a small raiding party consisting of two Joplin detectives, a constable, and two Missouri state highway patrolmen.

Then the police who were providing surveillance reported that two men (Clyde and W.D.) had driven off in the stolen Ford. Their observations over the previous couple of days had led them to believe that there were at least two couples in residence there. They figured the women were alone in the garage apartment. The police decided to set a trap for when the two men returned. The five men who made up the raiding party went out to the neighborhood where the kids were staying. Two of the officers walked up to the garage apartment and quietly slipped into the double garage, which was not locked. One of the cops hid in a corner behind the other car in the garage and the other hid at the opposite end of the auto by the other garage door.

The three other officers were waiting in a car a block away from the garage apartment. The plan was for the three officers in the auto to follow the stolen Ford when it passed them going back to the apartment. When the stolen car re-entered the garage, the two officers would arrest the car thieves while the other three officers would block the garage door with their auto, which would prohibit any of the thieves' cars from leaving. Once the two men were arrested in the garage, then the police would raid the upstairs apartment for the bootleg booze or the stolen goods or whatever they expected to find.

The police trap was set and the police settled back to wait for Clyde and W.D. to return. I would like to point out that the police were not expecting serious trouble. They had no riot guns, machine guns, or bulletproof vests. All they had were their basic small arms and their one non-armored police car.

Meanwhile, up in the apartment, the three B's (Buck, Blanche, and Bonnie) were unaware what was taking place outside. Their guard was let down. After all, they were all planning to leave the next day. Their time in Joplin had been seemingly quiet and uneventful, and there was no reason to suspect any police interest. All three of them were preoccupied with packing up and other normal household activities.

It was about five o'clock in the afternoon when Clyde and W.D. made their way back to the garage apartment. The three policemen in the car saw them pass and pulled out into the street behind them, keeping several yards back in order to eliminate suspicion. Clyde and W.D. pulled up to the double car doors. One of them got out to pull the garage door open and then the Ford V-8 was driven inside. Then, everything began to happen.

The officer who was hiding in the corner at the front of the other car jumped out and yelled "Get 'em up!" Clyde and W.D. opened up with shotguns, killing the officer. The other lawman who was at the back of the auto by the other garage door fled outside through the open garage door. At this point, the police pulled up to the front of the double garage in order to block it. The three cops piled out. One of them stood by their car. Clyde shot this man down, and he fell by the wheels of the police car. The other two officers took cover and began to open fire on the garage. Neither seriously wounded, Clyde was hit above his heart and W.D. in his stomach.

When the fireworks started in the garage, the three B's upstairs initially thought that it was another accidental burst of gunfire on the part of Clyde. But when the three kids heard the return fire, they realized that they had a real situation on their hands. Bonnie grabbed a gun and looked out the window down at the area immediately in front of the garage. She saw the police car parked there and saw one of the officers behind it firing into the garage. Bonnie fired at him but missed. The officers saw that gunfire was now coming from the upstairs and took different cover.

Buck didn't do any firing from the upstairs, but immediately ran downstairs to see what was happening with his younger brother in the garage. W.D. retreated from his position in the garage and headed upstairs. They passed each other on the stairs, but said nothing. W.D. was doubled over, holding his stomach. Buck made it down into the garage. A policeman started to fire at him and Buck grabbed W.D.'s shotgun and fired back.

Bonnie was the next one to come downstairs and then W.D. came back down. They began to try to move the officers' car from in front of the garage, which would enable them to flee in their own auto. The other three cops had taken defensive positions away from their car and the front of the garage. They were firing from behind trees. But the one injured officer was still lying by the police car. Buck wouldn't let the others attempt to move the car until he had pulled this injured man out from under it. Buck drug the fatally wounded man off to one side. Buck later said that doing this was one of the hardest things he ever had to do in his life, but he wasn't about to let them run over the man, even if he was already shot. They got the officers' car moving after shoving it. It rolled down the incline of the street for about 200 feet and then crashed into a tree on the other side of the road.

Blanche now came downstairs into the garage. But she didn't stop at their car or at the officers' car. Blanche dashed past the other kids, through the garage and then headed down the street with "Snowball" running ahead of her. The other four got into their car and went after her. They caught up with Blanche a ways down the street and Buck pulled her inside the car. They made a quick search for Snowball, but Blanche's little white dog had disappeared in all of the uproar. It had kept running when Buck grabbed Blanche and was gone.

While the boys were moving the police car out from in front of the garage, one the three surviving officers ran into a neighboring house to call for reinforcements. By the time the rest of the lawmen got there, my brothers were long gone. The rest of the policemen cautiously invaded the now empty apartment upstairs.

The kids' quick and unexpected departure had caused them to leave their half-packed belongings there in the apartment. Much of what they had to leave made identification of the occupants extremely easy. There was Buck and Blanche's marriage license, and Buck's pardon from the state of Texas, which was now meaningless. There was the registration for the car that Buck and Blanche had driven from Texas to Missouri. There was some of Bonnie's poetry, including the latest revision of "Suicide Sal," the poem which she'd started almost a year earlier in the Kaufman jail. And then there were the photographs.

The police found some undeveloped rolls of film there in the apartment. Hoping to aid in the identification of the occupants of the residence, the Joplin police had them developed immediately. It was these photographs that propelled both of my brothers to national prominence. Copies of these pictures appeared in every major newspaper in the country in connection with articles dealing with the

Joplin gun battle. The photos themselves were sensational in and of themselves and have become well-known symbols of the outlawry of the 1930s.

Everyone has seen them: the picture of Bonnie playing the "tough gun moll," with gun in hand, cigar in mouth, wearing her trademark beret and striking a burlesque pose on the fender of their car, and the picture of Bonnie disarming Clyde of Officer Persell's handgun while she is holding a shotgun on him with both of them unsuccessfully trying to keep straight faces. These were gag photos, but the American public took them seriously.

Chapter 12

Our family found out that both Clyde and Buck were involved in some trouble up in Missouri on the evening of April 13, but at that time the details were still sketchy. We were informed of the news by both the police and the press. But it wasn't until the next day that the full impact of what happened up there in Joplin finally hit us.

The Daily Times Herald, an evening newspaper in Dallas, ran its account of the trouble in Joplin under the screaming headline "BULLETS AWAIT BARROW BOYS IN TEXAS." and "*SHOOT TO KILL* Orders Issued For Desperadoes." Mug shots of both Clyde and Buck were prominently featured under the headlines. The boys were believed to have been headed back to their home turf and all north-central Texas peace officers were awaiting them with a hot lead welcome. The article said Clyde stated he would never be taken alive and that officers were more than willing to oblige.

The article said that their auto was seen in Seneca, Missouri, heading towards the south. Clyde was headed south all right, but Texas was not his destination. He figured that police were waiting for him down here. My brothers and their women headed deep into the Ozarks to hide out at Clyde's special place.

The boys laid low for about a week in the Ozark wilderness. Then, they made a dash back to Dallas in order to bring W.D. back to his mother's house. Although Clyde, Buck, Blanche, and Bonnie were identified by their personal effects, W.D. had not yet been identified by the authorities. Clyde made it a point to see that he wouldn't be identified and brought him back to west Dallas. Clyde told W.D. to get out of this situation while he was still able to do so. He brought W. D. back home and told him to "go straight."

Clyde tried to make three points clear to W.D.: (1) that nobody knew he was with the Barrow brothers in Joplin; (2) nobody knew of anything else that W.D. had been involved in with Clyde, such as the Doyle Johnson and Malcolm Davis killings; and (3) neither Clyde nor any of the others would snitch on him concerning these crimes if W.D. would just get out of the outlaw life.

However, W.D. did not want to come back home, despite all of the trouble with which he had been involved. W.D. hung around west Dallas for about a month after my brothers returned him to his mother's house. During these few weeks, W.D. was arrested for a minor crime that was totally unrelated to anything concerning Clyde. W.D. was sentenced to the "pea patch," but escaped from there and returned to west Dallas to get back in touch with Clyde. W.D. got a big kick out of his association with Clyde due to my brother's notoriety.

While W.D. was getting in and out of jail, my brothers made the newspapers again for something they were actually involved with. Of course, anytime they were "sighted" anywhere it made huge headlines. There was one occurrence just a few days after the Joplin gunfight where it was believed that two men who were involved in a car wreck up in Missouri were Clyde and Buck. It proved to be a false alarm, but the mistake still inspired huge headlines in the *Daily Times Herald*: *INJURED MEN ARE NOT BARROW BROTHERS.* Had anyone else been involved, the occurrence would've been buried deep in the paper, but since it involved Clyde and Buck, the story was front page headliners.

The headlines concerning the latest activity of Buck and Clyde read "BARROW BROTHERS KIDNAP COUPLE." This was not a kidnapping-for-ransom, but was an accidental abduction, much like that of Joe Johns in New Mexico and Thomas Persell in Missouri. After dropping W.D. off in west Dallas, Clyde and Buck found a third man to join their group. The need arose for them to acquire a new car, and they found just what they were looking for in the town of Ruston, Louisiana. The third man stole the car of an undertaker named Dillard Darby, who witnessed the theft. A friend of his, named Sophie Stone, offered the use of her car in which to pursue the thief. Miss Stone was merely an acquaintance of Mr. Darby and was not his girlfriend, despite what has been portrayed. They never did catch up with Darby's stolen auto, but they did meet up with Clyde and Buck during the chase. My brothers knew if they released Mr. Darby and Miss Stone, they would alert the police, which was definitely not in the best interest of Clyde and Buck. So they abducted Mr. Darby and Miss Stone and took the couple across the state line into Arkansas. They were released in the early hours of the following morning in an area where the boys would be given a head start before the couple could contact the authorities.

There was much speculation as to who actually stole Darby's car.

Newspapers surmised that it was Pretty Boy Floyd, but he wasn't with Clyde that day. W.D. was generally identified as the friend with Clyde, but he was still in west Dallas at the time.

After his revolving-door experience with incarceration, W.D. began to hang around Clyde's west Dallas haunts, which meant our service station and the Fish Trap Dance Hall. Both of our families tried to talk him into staying at home, but he refused to listen. We tried to point out that there would be no happy ending in store for either Clyde or Buck. The only thing awaiting them at the end of their trail was a violent death. We told W.D. that he could expect the same thing if he kept wanting to run with Clyde. But none of our reasoning seemed to have any impact on W.D., and he kept roaming up and down Eagle Ford Road, hoping to get back with Clyde.

One evening while W.D. was elsewhere on Eagle Ford Road trying to find Clyde, he showed up at our service station to pay a quick visit. Of course, Buck, Blanche, and Bonnie were with him. They pulled up into our driveway and stayed in the car while we talked. They never got out to visit, because they knew a quick getaway might be needed at any time. So my parents and I stood on the driveway and talked with them, all of us keeping an eye out for any passing policemen. The police were making it a point to frequently drive by our service station during this time.

My mother tried to talk Buck into staying with them and surrendering to the law. She thought that Buck could prove that he was in Joplin only on a visit and that he wasn't an active participant in the battle. Buck told my mother that there was no chance that he could get anything but the electric chair. Clyde was now talking to Buck like Buck had talked to Clyde before the Joplin fight. Clyde thought that Buck should surrender, with Clyde signing a statement to the effect that Clyde and W.D. had done all of the shooting at the garage apartment. Buck thought about it, but figured that he had no chance. After their all too short visit, they hit the road again. It was during this time that my brothers were credited with robbing a bank in the small town of Lucerne, Indiana. There was a gunfight with law officers and townspeople in connection with the bank robbery. A couple of women were injured by the gunfire, but, mercifully, their injuries were minor. It very well could have been Clyde and Buck, as Buck later said that hardly a week passed without their being involved in one gun battle or another.

There were several other robberies that occurred in late April and early May in which my brothers were identified as the perpetrators. They may have been responsible for some of these actions, but there were others that they definitely had nothing to do with. Amongst the latter category was a service station robbery in Broken Bow, Oklahoma, just a couple of days after the Darby-Stone abduction. Whoever held up this service station only got a few dollars and they brutally beat up the attendant in their chagrin at such a small haul. My brothers were accused of this piece of thuggery, but Clyde and Buck always denied any involvement. I believe them. They did not assault or abuse anyone who cooperated with their demands during their robberies. Clyde and Buck would've accepted the small amount of money seized as an occasional occurrence in their line of work and wouldn't have slugged the station attendant because his place of business was low on cash.

There was a robbery a few days later for which my brothers may have been responsible. This occurred in Ft. Dodge, Iowa, when a lone bandit entered a filing station and held up the attendant. The robber got what money he could and fled. This attendant later identified Buck as the bandit.

A few days after the Ft. Dodge holdup, there occurred a bank robbery in which my brothers were very definitely involved. It happened in the town of Okabena, Minnesota. The boys were credited with getting somewhere between $1,500 and $2,500. Actually they got $1,600, with $700 of it being in the form of silver dollars. Like the Lucerne holdup, there was an exchange of gunfire with the townspeople and the local police. No one was killed or seriously hurt. Clyde and Buck always tried to fire over the heads of such opposition. My brothers did this to drive such non-shootists back towards cover. While the local resident pistoleros were retreating with their squirrel rifles from my brothers' BAR warning shots, Clyde and Buck could make their escape. I remember very well this Okabena bank robbery because of all of the silver dollars the boys brought back to Texas afterwards. Before I relate the following story concerning those silver dollars, let me first describe how Clyde and Bonnie were kept in new clothing. My brother L.C. and I used to do the shopping for our brother and his girlfriend.

When they needed new apparel, they would give L.C. and I the money to go to downtown Dallas and get what they desired. I was the exact same size as Bonnie in terms of dress size, so anything I could try on she would be able to wear. L.C. always purchased Clyde's clothes. He would always go to a haberdashery near the courthouse in downtown Dallas. This clothing store was owned by a man named Harry. All of Clyde's clothes came from Harry the Haberdasher's.

Let me also point out that when Clyde gave us money for his and Bonnie's clothes, he'd give us additional money for our own clothing needs. Clyde was always giving our family money. L.C. would always buy himself clothes when he got things for Clyde. I'd always get myself dresses when I'd purchase things for Bonnie. L.C.'s wife Audrey Fay would go with me on these shopping excursions.

Anyhow, this particular time Clyde gave us money for clothes from the Okabena robbery loot. Naturally, it was all in silver dollars. L.C. and I took a lot of those silver dollars to our respective clothing stores and purchased garments for both Clyde and Bonnie and ourselves. I found a blue suit that I especially liked and bought it for myself.

I wore this blue suit out to meet Clyde and Buck the next time they came back to Dallas. When we met them, Bonnie took one look at my blue suit and fell in love with it. She wanted one just like it, but, unfortunately, there wasn't another one available. I gave her the suit she wanted, changing into one of her outfits in a discreet place out of sight of our family get-together.

Let me point out now that Bonnie had no particular preference for any color. I've seen it in print quite a few times that Bonnie always wore red dresses and hats, and would wear nothing but red. Like so much else about this girl, her alleged preference for red is pure poppycock. Bonnie liked clothing of all colors. I suppose this legend of her clothing preference derives from the fact that she was wearing a red dress and hat when she and Clyde were killed. It was just happenstance that she was wearing red that day, nothing more.

During one of these family meetings in this time period, both Clyde and Buck asked our mother to try to get their things back that had been left in their Joplin apartment. Clyde was especially wanting his guitar, which had been left behind in their unanticipated exit. She did write the Joplin police department concerning the return of my brothers' things. The letter she got in response said that all of the items that the police didn't confiscate were turned over to charitable organizations and distributed to people who were on public relief. There was nothing to return to the Barrow family: no personal belongings, no clothing, and no guitar.

I remember the month of May in 1933 very well, due to another example of Clyde's generosity towards his loved ones. My 15th birthday occurred about this time. As a birthday gift, Clyde gave me my first bedroom suit. Up to this time, I had slept on those big old iron beds and had no furniture to call my own. This bedroom suit consisted of a bed, a chest of drawers, and a dresser. I used this set of furniture for many years afterward. It was many years later that I loaned this bedroom suit to my sister Artie for use in her boarding house. The bed and chest of drawers were given to other relatives for use, but Artie returned the dresser. I finally gave the dresser to my nephew in 1996, 63 years after Clyde gave it to me in 1933. No matter what he did while he was out on the road, Clyde was always a first-class brother to me and to our family.

It was during the spring of 1933 that I was harassed by one of my teachers at school concerning what my brothers were doing while they were out living on the road. This particular teacher greeted me every morning as I entered the school building with the cheery question: "Well, have they caught your brothers yet?" Our family knew it was inevitable that Clyde and Buck were going to get trapped and killed sooner or later and so did this schoolteacher. Of course, nowadays this person would not be able to say things like this, but, back then, she could not be stopped. So everyday I had to put up with the same asinine question. I grew to despise the teacher's attitude and looked forward to the day when I was no longer responsible to that school. When the day arrived, I was planning on coming back and paying her a visit. The visit would not be with the best of intentions: I was going to whup her up one side and down the other. But I never followed through on my resolution; in fact, I cannot even remember her name.

This teacher wasn't the only one who thought about Buck and Clyde frequently. Since August of 1932, they were well-known in the southwestern states. Since the Joplin gun battle, my brothers had become nationally known desperadoes. They joined Pretty Boy Floyd in national notoriety. There was a third party which was about to become well-known along with Clyde, Buck, and Floyd: the Kansas prison escapees. On May 30, 1933, a group of convicts made a break from the State Prison at Lansing, Kansas. Various members of this group, especially Wilbur Underhill and Harvey Bailey, would become nationally recognized as public enemies. All of this action would keep the newspaper reporters and the detective magazine writers hopping all summer. The great "crime wave" of 1933 was underway.

It was also about this time that Frank Hardy and Hollis Hale were arrested at Waco. Those boys were apprehended through a woman friend of theirs who was under police surveillance. After their arrest, Frank and Hollis were separated to face different charges. Frank was taken to Temple to stand trial for the murder of Doyle Johnson. Hollis was transferred up to Missouri to stand trial for the Oronogo bank robbery. He was found guilty of the Oronogo job and got 20 years in the state pen at Jefferson City. Hollis attempted to mollify his sentence by stating that he separated from Clyde because my brother was "too ruthless." Actually, nothing that remotely resembled anything ruthless occurred while Frank and Hollis were with Clyde and Bonnie. But Hollis figured that if he disassociated himself from "the notorious Clyde Barrow," the court might give him a break. Hollis' strategy didn't work; despite his "good intentions" in deserting my brother, he still got the book thrown at him.

Clyde felt neither gladness nor sadness at the arrest of Frank and Hollis. Neither one of them especially impressed him. Besides, now Clyde was roaming the road with his older brother. Clyde deeply regretted the circumstances which caused Buck and Blanche to become publicly associated with him. Despite their differences in temperament, they got along well out on the highway. I've seen some accounts of Clyde's life which state that Clyde was the definite leader of the group and that Buck was merely a near-alcoholic, weak-minded, slavish follower of his younger brother.

But nothing could be farther from the truth. The fact is that the personality differences between my two older brothers made it impossible for one to docilely follow the other. Reference has already been made to the fact that Buck was much more impulsive, instantaneous, and quick to anger than was Clyde. Clyde may have been able to dominate the likes of W.D. Jones and Raymond Hamilton, but Buck Barrow was made up of different stuff. If anything, Clyde's primary concern in his life on the road with Buck was about keeping Buck's temper in check. Mercifully, Buck's change for the better in his final year in prison and Blanche's influence seemed to cool off his hot temper. It seemed that both of my brothers' attitudes had been changed in prison, with Buck's change being for the better and Clyde's for the worse. But it really didn't matter; both of them realized that their current circumstances in life were totally based on borrowed time.

This realization eliminated any flare-ups that might have occurred due to differing temperaments.

If there was anyone in that little group who could be characterized as the "odd person out" in the so-called "Barrow Gang" at this time, it was Bonnie Parker. Our family realized that Emma Parker looked askance at both Clyde and Buck because of their time in prison and their past troubles with the law. Mrs. Parker's attitude was especially curious due to the fact that the husbands of both of her daughters were in trouble with the law. In fact, Roy Thornton (Bonnie's husband) and Fred Mace (Billie Jean's husband) broke out of the jail in Waxahachie, Texas, together in March of 1933. Roy Thornton's stated purpose in making this break was to hunt down Clyde Barrow and get his wife back. It never occurred to Roy that Bonnie was totally through with him and was completely dedicated to Clyde. Thornton made his threats towards my brother from afar; "Mr. Bonnie Parker" never made any serious attempts to catch up with Clyde. In fact, he was soon recaptured and returned to jail. Bonnie may have realized this state of subtle tension and made efforts to compensate for it. She always tried to encourage our family to like her, even to the point of using self-deprecating humor, making herself the butt of her own jokes. I believe Mrs. Parker blamed Bonnie's love for Clyde, and Clyde himself, for her daughter's status as a wanted criminal. But the fact of the matter is that both Parker girls were already familiar with the rougher side of life before Clyde had ever met Bonnie.

For almost two months, Clyde and Buck had roamed the highways of the southwest and the Midwest as nationally notorious outlaws. They came and went into west Dallas with seeming impunity. They had been involved with several armed conflicts with the forces of the law throughout the spring of 1933, but they had neither killed anyone since Joplin nor were either of my brothers killed or seriously injured. But neither one of my brothers was foolish enough to believe that he was living any kind of a charmed life and could avoid what was waiting for him at the end of the road. All of us knew that violent death would visit their little group sooner or later. When we visited with Clyde, Buck, Blanche, and Bonnie, we did not deliver any hot lectures about the weed of crime bearing bitter fruit. Both the fugitives and we home folks were very familiar with the bitterness that my brothers' circumstances brought to everyone.

Chapter 13

Clyde and Buck had been relatively lucky during the spring of 1933, but their good luck was to disappear that summer due to a series of tragedies. The first of these tragedies was prefaced by a visit by Clyde and Bonnie into west Dallas in early June. Buck and Blanche were not with them at this time due to the fact that they were up in Oklahoma visiting with Blanche's father. While Buck was visiting with his in-laws, Clyde decided to make a quick dash into Dallas.

It was during this particular visit that W.D. Jones finally caught up with Clyde and begged my brother to let him go back out on the road with them. Clyde initially resisted W.D.'s entreaties, but he finally gave into his pleadings. When Clyde and Bonnie left Dallas this time, W.D. was riding with them.

The kids usually headed northeast when they left Dallas, but this time they drove northwest in order to meet with Buck and Blanche in far western Oklahoma. Clyde had driven all of the way to Collingsworth County, Texas, when disaster struck. Clyde, Bonnie, and W.D. were driving on the highway going north out of Wellington where the highway crossed the Salt Fork of the Red River. Clyde wasn't aware that the bridge was out until it was too late. His car went off the highway and tumbled into the dry and sandy river bed. Their car overturned several times before coming to a stop, and it landed upside down.

Clyde was thrown clear as their car rolled down the embankment. He crawled back to the overturned vehicle to assist Bonnie and W.D. Neither Clyde nor W.D. had been hurt, but Bonnie was trapped beneath the auto. The two boys were trying to get the car turned rightside-up to free Bonnie when their car caught on fire. Clyde and W.D. worked furiously, but they were unable to lift up the car by themselves. But just then unexpected help arrived in the form of two men who lived in a nearby farmhouse and who had witnessed the wreck. Between the four of them, they got Bonnie out from underneath the car. But she had already been severely burned by the flames and her right leg was in extremely serious condition.

The two men carried Bonnie back up to their farmhouse while

Clyde and W.D. followed along. The kids were still trying to shake off the effects of the accident and the fire. The two men got Bonnie inside the house and laid her down on a bed, where the farmer's wife immediately began to treat her burns.

Now that Bonnie was as well-situated as she could have been under the circumstances, Clyde's attention reverted back to their wrecked car. He told W.D. to stay up at the farmhouse with Bonnie while he went back down to the river bed to get their guns and possessions out of the car. Clyde wanted to stash these items some where until another car could be arranged. My brother left W.D. up there at the house while he attended to their things.

But without Clyde to keep him in check, W.D. began to play the role of tough gunman. He had been unable to do so for almost six weeks and he figured that this farmhouse was as good a place to start as any. W.D. pulled a pistol from out of a pocket and began to enforce his orders with the gun. There was no need to resort to any threats or intimidation; the residents of the farmhouse were already totally focused on providing Bonnie with whatever medical attention and assistance they could.

W.D.'s resorting to threats of violence immediately changed the complexion of the situation. Seeing the turn events were taking, one of the men slipped outside. He had already been gone several minutes when W.D. finally caught on to his absence. W.D.'s attitude then took another turn for the worse and he began to threaten the other man. Both of them realized that the other fellow was going to go for the police.

When W.D. realized that he had given them away as probable outlaws and then had compounded his mistake by letting one of the men get away, he began to panic. He realized what Clyde might say or do when my brother would see what had happened on account of W.D.'s trigger-happy tendencies. W.D.'s nervous tension became stretched to the breaking point and he was ready to shoot at anything that moved. And then something moved at the back door of the house.

One of the men's daughter-in-law lived nearby. She saw that there was a lot of activity over at his farmhouse and decided to go see what was going on. As she opened the door, W.D. fired, figuring it was the cops. She screamed in pain as W.D.'s bullet hit her hand.

Clyde was down at the wrecked car when he heard the sound of the gunshot. He immediately grabbed some rifles and sped back up to the farmhouse, not knowing what to expect. My brother knew he had to be ready for anything. For all he knew, somebody recognized Bonnie and shot her for some imagined reward money.

Clyde was greeted by pure pandemonium upon entering the residence. The daughter-in-law was down on the floor, holding her injured hand and screaming. The husband and wife were trying to give her what assistance they could. Bonnie had staggered out of the bedroom at the sound of the shot and stood there helplessly. W.D. was just standing there, mesmerized by the whole incident.

Clyde saw the gun in W.D.'s hand and the injured woman and put two and two together. My brother came close to using one of his rifles on W.D. right then and there, but he figured there were enough wounded and injured on the scene already. Clyde did a quick count of those present and came up one man short. He asked W.D. about where this missing man had gone. W.D. then told Clyde that the man had given him the slip.

Clyde knew the police were undoubtedly on their way out to the farmhouse. He knew he could not let himself, Bonnie, and W.D. be trapped and surrounded by an undetermined number of officers. Clyde saw he had a real situation on his hands and took control. Clyde herded everyone out of the house and into the front yard. My brother made everyone settle down and stay still in the shadowed, unlit front yard. All six of them waited for the law to arrive.

Just a short time after the group settled down in front of the house, a car containing only two law men (a sheriff and a town marshal) drove towards the place. It didn't stop in front of the house, but pulled around to the back. Both men got out with their guns drawn and carefully entered the back door. They went slowly through the house, surprised at finding nobody there. They worked their way towards the front of the building.

After going through the house, the officers' initial tension decreased, leaving them more puzzled than jittery. They went through the front door onto the front porch and stood there peering out into the darkness, trying to see some sign of movement. Their relaxed state was just what Clyde and W.D. were hoping for and anticipating. The two boys crept alongside the front porch and then sprang out of the darkness at the two officers. Both lawmen were immediately disarmed. Clyde grabbed the handcuffs from the marshal and manacled the two together.

Clyde's mind was still working fast. Not only had the lawmen been disarmed with no harm to anyone, but their automobile would provide a means of escape. They were marched back to the sheriff's car, which was still parked in back of the farmhouse. Clyde told both of them to get in the back seat. Bonnie was brought around from the front yard and placed in the laps of the two officers.

Clyde grabbed his rifles and threw them into the car. My brother apologized to the residents of the farmhouse about the woman's injured hand. Clyde then took the wheel with W.D. riding in the front seat, keeping an eye on the officers in the back. The carload of people sped off from the farmhouse.

After the kids had gone, the injured daughter-in-law was taken to a hospital while her father-in-law spread the alarm concerning the abduction of the two officers. But, by the time the posses were raised and the searchers were organized, Clyde was already well into Oklahoma on his way to meet up with Buck.

The two officers who held Bonnie on their laps in the back seat were extremely gentle and considerate with her. Bonnie later spoke about one of them, the one on whose lap her head was placed. She was impressed and touched with how he nursed her just like she was a baby, trying to protect her from the bumps of the road and the jolts from Clyde's extremely fast driving. He asked Bonnie where Clyde was taking them and if he was going to kill them. Bonnie reassured him that she wouldn't let Clyde and W.D. shoot either one of them.

Unlike the situation with New Mexico deputy Joe Johns, who wasn't released until a day after his abduction, Clyde released the two Collingsworth County officers a mere three hours after leaving the farmhouse. They were able to return to their loved ones safe and sound. Clyde sped straight over to where Buck and Blanche had been awaiting them. Clyde filled his older brother in on what had caused the delay: the wreck, the shooting at the farmhouse, and the abduction of the two officers.

Buck knew Clyde felt the same as he did about killing people, but Buck still asked his younger brother about what he was going to do with the two officers and asked if he was going to "bump them off." Clyde laughed at the notion and said both officers had been with him so long that he began to like them. I know Clyde developed some respect and consideration for them: he'd noticed their gentle behavior towards Bonnie. But they were still peace officers, and Clyde knew their duty was to spread the word about being with the Barrow brothers as soon as possible. So he had to insure that he had an adequate head start. Clyde and W.D. took the two officers out into a field to where an oak tree was standing. My brother intended to tie them up to the tree, but Clyde discovered that there was no rope in either the sheriff's car or in Buck's car. The boys tore some barbed wire from a nearby fence and bound the two officers to the oak tree. Then, my brothers and the others took off in the two cars.

Just as soon as they got out of sight of the two officers, Clyde ditched the sheriff's car. He knew it would be the auto for which all of the authorities would be looking. The five of them were riding in Buck's car with Clyde at the wheel. He drove back towards Ft. Smith, Arkansas, where he hid out so many times in the past. They rented cabins in a tourist court there. Clyde told the manager of the tourist court his wife had been injured the previous evening by the explosion of an oil stove.

Clyde's first order of business was to get some professional medical care for Bonnie. They contacted a local doctor to come out to the tourist cabin and examine the burned girl. Clyde gave the doctor the same story concerning the oil stove. The doctor told my brothers Bonnie should be put into a hospital. At the least, she needed a full-time nurse to regularly dress her burns. The doctor made a second trip out there to examine her and told Clyde the same thing again. Clyde said he would see about getting the full-time nurse; entering Bonnie into a hospital was out of the question.

Now that the group was settled down, my brothers evaluated their situation to determine their next course of action. Clyde knew Bonnie needed someone who would clean her burns. They also had to have the medicine and supplies with which to treat the injuries. Hiring a registered nurse to stay with them full-time ran the risk of them being recognized as outlaws. Continuing to depend on legally prescribed drugs also increased the chances that they could be recognized; they could be identified during the regular visits to the drugstore and in their dealings with the pharmacist.

Clyde's first priority was to supply full time care for Bonnie. So, after getting the doctor's directions on how exactly to treat Bonnie's bums, Clyde drove from Ft. Smith to Dallas in order to get assistance from his and Bonnie's families. My brother simply had no one else to turn to; he really wasn't a career criminal, who had the "fix" in some safe city where he could get a "sawbones" to treat Bonnie. Both our family and the Parkers had read the newspaper accounts of the Collingsworth county auto wreck, the shooting of the daughter-in-law at the farmhouse, and the abduction of the two officers. We were already extremely upset and concerned over this news. Clyde came into west Dallas and contacted both families with his request for assistance. Both my mother and I offered to return to Ft. Smith with him to provide for Bonnie's needs. Mrs. Parker desperately wanted to go back with Clyde. But my brother had already decided that Bonnie's younger sister Billie Jean was the best person to provide a nurse's care. The law was already keeping a watch on the actions of both my mother and Mrs. Parker. Bonnie was close to her sister and Clyde figured that this sisterly closeness would translate into both physical and emotional support.

So Clyde and Bil1ie Jean returned to the Ft. Smith tourist camp. Billie Jean acted as primary nurse with Clyde and Blanche supporting her. With Clyde focused solely on Bonnie's recovery, it was up to Buck and W.D. to monitor the money situation. Buck felt they had enough funds on hand to last for several days, so there was no immediate need to go back out on the road. My brothers and the rest of their group settled down in their tourist cabins to deal with Bonnie's injuries.

This period of quiet lasted just over a week. During this time of relative tranquility, Clyde and Buck made several trips over to Sequoyah county, Oklahoma, which was just over the state line from Ft. Smith.

My brothers wanted to make contact with Charley "Pretty Boy" Floyd and they knew that the best way to do this was to get in touch with Pretty Boy's family members who lived in the vicinity of Sallisaw and Akins. Clyde and Buck were hoping Charley Floyd would provide directions towards a safe place in which they could hide until Bonnie got better. Clyde knew they couldn't spend too long in the Ft. Smith tourist court; he remembered very well what happened in Joplin when they stayed a couple of days too many.

My brothers went to the home of Pretty Boy's younger brother E.W. Floyd several times during that June week. E.W said his older brother hadn't been by there for quite some time. But he did give my brothers some food and other supplies. Clyde and Buck asked the Floyd family how they could get in touch with their fugitive relative. A family member told them he would see that Pretty Boy write a letter to our parents at their service station in west Dallas and would sign Clyde's name to it.

In this letter, Charley would establish a day, time, and location for the three of them to meet. Shortly afterward, my mother indeed got a letter as described above mailed to her from Pretty Boy Floyd, stating when Floyd would be back in the Sallisaw-Akins area and when Clyde and Buck could get with him. However, it was several days before Clyde was informed of the arrival of this message. By the time Clyde learned of the proposed meeting and made it up to Sallisaw, Pretty Boy Floyd had come and gone.

Clyde and Charley Floyd did meet later that year, but they never pulled any jobs together. Clyde told us about the get-together, saying Pretty Boy had what Clyde described as a "foreigner" with him. The "foreigner" had to be Adam Richetti, who was captured in Ohio when Charley Floyd was slain there in the autumn of 1934. Actually, Richetti himself was American-born, but his parents were immigrants from Italy. Richetti was raised in the town of Lehigh in south-central Oklahoma.

Pretty Boy Floyd had been relatively low-key since the death of his partner George Birdwell during the Boley, Oklahoma, bank robbery in late November, 1932. Unfortunately, that status was about to change. At the same time Clyde and Buck were trying to make connections with him, a series of three unrelated events was occurring that would blast Floyd's name back into the headlines.

The first of these events was a bank robbery in the town of Mexico, Missouri, on June 14, 1933. Shortly afterward, two officers operating a roadblock in an attempt to catch the Mexico bank bandits were shot and killed. The murders were committed by the occupants of an automobile the two cops had stopped. Floyd and Richetti were later blamed for the bank robbery and the double killing. However, years afterward, another man confessed his part in these crimes. Pretty Boy Floyd had nothing to do with them.

Two days after the Mexico robbery, the second event took place and this time Floyd and Richetti were definitely involved. This second event also took place in Missouri, but in the town of Bolivar. The car in which Floyd and Richetti were traveling developed mechanical trouble. Fortunately, their auto broke down near Bolivar, where Richetti's brother worked at a garage. Floyd's car was towed into the garage. While their car was being repaired, the county sheriff dropped in on a purely social visit. Adam Richetti pulled a WD-type maneuver by panicking and grabbing a gun. Pretty Boy Floyd managed to keep everything under control, but they immediately commandeered another auto in which to get away. They took the sheriff as a hostage, much as Clyde did so many times. With the state of Missouri still in an uproar over the crimes in Mexico two days earlier, immediate pursuit was instigated and posses were organized. Even an airplane was sent out to try to find Floyd's auto from the air.

Floyd and Richetti were heading towards Kansas City. Missouri, a favorite stomping grounds for Pretty Boy. Since the forces of the law knew what car they were looking for. Floyd commandeered another auto and took its driver along as hostage. With this new car, Floyd and Richetti made it safely into Kansas City late that evening. Pretty Boy released his two hostages unharmed, much as Clyde always did Pretty Boy Floyd's bad luck in being in the wrong place at the wrong time was about to get worse. If his presence in Missouri at the same time as the Mexico atrocity was unfortunate, his arrival in Kansas City on the night of June 16/17 was an absolute disaster.

The very next morning after Floyd and Richetti made their much publicized arrival, the third event in the trio of disasters occurred at Kansas City's Union Station, a gang-related shooting in which four law officers and their prisoner were killed by machine-gunners. One of the murdered lawmen was a federal agent, one was an Oklahoma Chief of police , and two were Kansas City detectives. Their prisoner, a 1920s train robber and 1930's associate of Ma Barker's boys named Frank Nash, may have been shot and killed by one of the officers before the officer himself was cut down by the machine guns.

Law enforcement authorities immediately blamed the most notorious outlaws of the region, which meant the convicts who had escaped from the state prison at Lansing, Kansas, almost three weeks previously and also Pretty Boy Floyd. Some of the Kansas prison escapees, especially Harvey Bailey, were known as one-time criminal associates of Frank Nash. Surprisingly, Clyde and Buck were never officially connected with the so-called "Kansas City Massacre," despite their notoriety that spring. Of course, neither one of my brothers had ever had any previous contact with either Harvey Bailey or Frank Nash.

It was these three events that drove Pretty Boy Floyd into deep cover and prevented his meeting with Clyde and Buck, which in turn prevented my brothers from finding a safe place to sequester Bonnie for the duration of her recuperation. Clyde knew their group would have to be leaving Ft. Smith pretty soon, so he and Buck inventoried their cash. My brothers didn't like the small amount they had on hand. It was becoming rapidly apparent that the costs of Bonnie's medical needs, as well as the food and lodging requirements for six people, were consuming their financial resources at a much faster rate than was initially anticipated. It was increasingly obvious that at least two of the men would have to go out on the road and score some cash. Since Clyde felt the obligation to stay close to Bonnie, Buck and W.D. offered to go out. Clyde agreed to the arrangement, but offered a couple of conditions to his brother: (1) Buck and W.D. should not commit any robberies anywhere close to the Ft. Smith area, and (2) they should not hit any major targets, like banks. Clyde knew the tourist courts would be one of the major investigation areas for the police. Either a local holdup or a big-time robbery would cause the police to give all of the area tourist courts a thorough check-up.

Buck and W.D. decided Fayetteville would be far enough away that any grocery store or filling station holdups would not create a state-wide dragnet. On June 22, the boys drove up to Fayetteville and checked out the town for potential targets. They found a grocery store where they figured they could get a desirable quantity of cash. The next day Buck and W. D. hit the target. There wasn't much to this robbery. Buck just walked into the place, told the people there that he was broke and said that he would have to have their money. Of course, the pistol he was carrying acted as a powerful inducement towards cooperation. W.D. waited outside in their car, which also contained a couple of Clyde's rifles that he'd salvaged from the wreck near Wellington. The rifles were taken in case the boys ran into any unexpected resistance from the police. But there were no unanticipated events; the robberies went smoothly. Buck and W.D. got only a very few dollars from this grocery store, much to their chagrin. Buck figured it wasn't worth the drive they made up there and they decided to return to their tourist camp. The two boys turned their car back towards Ft. Smith and sped down highway 71.

Buck and W.D. followed Clyde's advice in not committing any major crimes around the Ft. Smith area. Unfortunately, there were other people around who had their eyes on that particular area, which included the town of Alma. Alma was just a few miles east of Ft. smith. On June 22, the same day Buck and W.D. were checking out the Fayetteville area, two men robbed the bank in Alma. They committed this robbery in a fairly conspicuous manner. These two robbers grabbed Alma Marshal Henry Humphrey right off of the main street and carried him bodily into the bank. They tied the town marshal to one of the pillars in the bank. After he was secured, the bandits got the bank's safe and put it on a wheeled contraption. The robbers rolled the safe across the bank's interior and out the front door. They had a truck parked just outside the bank and wheeled the safe across the sidewalk and lifted it into the bed of their truck. Then the crooks fled in their truck, leaving Marshal Humphrey still tied to the pillar inside. He was finally freed when passersby noticed his predicament and freed him. Marshal Humphrey was embarrassed by the manhandling he had undergone, although no one blamed him. He was both out-numbered and out-gunned; both of the Alma bandits had been heavily armed. Nevertheless, he resolved he would personally bring these two robbers to justice. The Alma marshal was eagerly anticipating meeting these two men again.

The following day was the day that Buck and W.D. held up the grocery store in Fayetteville and then headed back south towards Ft. Smith. The fact that the Fayetteville bandits were last seen speeding south was telephoned to all towns along U.S. 71, including Alma. Marshal Humphrey and a deputy sheriff named Salyars received the tip. The two men got into a car and headed north on 71 out of Alma, hoping to intercept the two Fayetteville robbers. Marshal Humphrey may have felt that these were the same two men who had robbed the Alma bank. Even if they were not the same two men, Humphrey still might have felt that his apprehending these criminals might remove some of the embarrassment he felt after being manhandled the previous day.

Just a short distance north of Alma, Humphrey recognized a friend of his approaching from the north. This friend also recognized the Alma marshal and the deputy. Both cars stopped in the middle of U.S. 71 while the occupants rolled down their windows and spoke. The officers' car was facing north and the other car was facing south. As fate would have it, it was this precise moment that Buck and W.D. came speeding down from the north. Buck was driving at the same breakneck speed that he'd seen Clyde driving. The boys' car came over the crest of a hill, with the two Alma vehicles parked at the bottom. Humphrey yelled at his friend to move out of the way. Buck couldn't stop his car in time and it plowed into the back-end of the Alma vehicle. Humphrey had moved his auto out of the way just in time to avoid being involved in the accident. The other two cars went flying different ways from the impact.

The marshal's friend was furious at being rear-ended.He got out of his car after it skidded to a halt and grabbed a couple of sizable rocks from the side of the road, probably to do some additional damage to the other vehicle. Then again, he may have intended to do some damage to the occupants of the car. Buck and W.D. saw this very angry man coming towards them. They doubted the large rocks he was carrying were intended as peace offerings, so they grabbed a couple of Clyde's rifles off of the back seat, intending to scare this fellow off. The rifles had their intended effect: the other driver took one look at the artillery and immediately fled the other way.

Humphrey and Salyars had pulled down the highway a ways, far enough from the scene of the collision that they were unable to stop their friend from using his hand-held rocks. They were surprised to see their friend suddenly stop and flee. Both lawmen began to look back towards Buck's car to investigate what happened.

Buck and W.D. saw the two Alma officers coming towards them. The two boys hoped they could get the drop on the two officers as Clyde and W.D. had done over near Wellington. They directed the points of the rifles at the officers, who saw the action and pulled their own arms. Then someone fired and the other three joined in.

Humphrey went down almost immediately at the beginning of the battle. Buck had jumped out of the boys' auto, firing one of the rifles. W.D. raised up on his side of the car and started shooting. Whoever actually shot the Alma marshal was never actually determined, but Buck always assumed responsibility for the crime. Buck and W.D. later argued about exactly who fatally wounded Humphrey. Buck told my mother that, during their argument, W.D. admitted to Buck that he had actually shot down Humphrey.

Deputy Salyars was putting up a magnificent resistance against the combined fire of Buck and W.D. The deputy darted around, firing his rifle as he ran. He never gave Buck and W.D. any kind of a stationary target. As the deputy used up the shots in his rifle, he was backing towards a nearby barn at the side of the road. His intent was to use the barn as cover while he quickly reloaded his gun. Deputy Salyars finally fired his final shot and then darted behind the barn to reload and rejoin the battle.

Buck and W.D. had no further intentions to continue the gunfight with Deputy Salyars. The officer had shot well enough that the boys did not want any more conflict with him. When the deputy disappeared behind a building to reload, Buck and W.D. grabbed whatever they could get out of their disabled auto and ran over to the Humphrey-Salyars car, which was the only one of the three autos that was able to be driven. The boys had to hurry up and get out of there: the gunbattle had only taken a few minutes, but traffic along U.S. 71 was starting to back up in both directions with drivers remaining a safe distance away from the action.

Buck and W.D. threw their guns and other things into the officers' vehicle and got it started. It was still pointed towards the north and that's the direction in which the boys headed. Seemingly, Buck and W.D. were headed away from the Ft. Smith/Alma area, which would draw the pursuing forces away from the tourist camp where Clyde and the three women were still situated. If the boys would've headed straight into Ft. Smith, the hotels, motels, and tourist courts would be the first places checked for suspicious characters. With Bonnie still too sick to be moved and with Billie Jean Parker still there, Buck and W.D. wanted to draw police interest away from Ft. Smith.

The boys knew everyone would be looking for the Humphrey-Salyars automobile, so they got rid of it as soon as possible. They hijacked another auto shortly after they left the scene of the battle. But they kept this car only a short while until they ditched it. Buck and W.D. kept running into roadblocks around the area, so they decided to return to their tourist camp on foot. They walked along the railroad tracks until they were close to their home base and then made their way back to the cabin on foot.

The Alma bank robbery and the shooting of Marshal Humphrey had the whole area in an uproar. Roadblocks were set up everywhere and posses were roaming all around. Buck and W. D. told Clyde of all of the police action around the area. They made a decision to clear out of their cabin just after nightfall. All six of them hurriedly packed their things. They had only one car now to provide for their transportation. Clyde first took Bonnie, Billie Jean, and Blanche to a relatively safe and secluded area. Buck and W.D. continued to pack things at their cabin. Clyde returned to the tourist camp and picked them up. The group kept using this "leap frog" method of transportation until they had gotten well into eastern Oklahoma.

It was popularly believed by everyone in the area that the same people were responsible for both the Alma bank robbery and the Humphrey shooting, and the big manhunt was continuing in the Alma/Ft. Smith area. The day after the battle on U.S. 71, the focus of the manhunt suddenly swung northward to the hills between Ft. Smith and Fayetteville. A woman who lived in that mountainous area reported that her home had been invaded by two men who had demanded the use of her car. When she refused to let them take her vehicle, she said one of the men began to hit her with a chain in order to force her to give them the keys. These men were frightened off by the sound of one of the posses which were combing the woods for the two men who had shot Marshal Humphrey. These two men fled on foot. The woman informed the posse members of what had occurred with the two intruders. The authorities focused their activities on this area, while Clyde. Buck, and the others were slowly making their way westward.

In just about every published account of my brothers' life, either Clyde or Buck (or sometimes both) has been blamed for the assault on this woman in the Arkansas mountains. Afterwards, a charge of rape was added to the long list of crimes already connected to my brothers' names. While Clyde and Buck had already been involved in enough crimes to guarantee either of them the electric chair, they were not involved in the attack on this woman. The Barrow brothers were certainly not the only outlaws that hid around the Ft. Smith area. The intense manhunt that followed the Alma robbery and the Humphrey shooting wound up flushing many wanted men from cover in the Ft. Smith area. The identity of the two men who tried to take the woman's car has never been established, but both of my brothers were heading west from Ft. Smith and not north.

Although the physical assault in the Arkansas hills turned the attention of the police towards that particular area, Clyde still had several things to worry about. Bonnie was still in no condition to do any traveling. My brothers wanted to get Billie Jean Parker back down to Dallas as soon as possible. They desperately needed another automobile that could transport six people. Buck and W.D. left behind many of their guns in their wrecked car back on U.S. 71, and Clyde felt that another raid on a National Guard armory would have to be made as soon as possible.

In terms of priorities, Clyde felt it was necessary to get Billie Jean out of harm's way. With the southwest in a state of siege over the outlaw situation in late June of 1933, anybody seen in the company of bandits could expect to get the same medicine the police planned on giving to the desperadoes themselves. "Shoot to kill" orders towards any and all public enemies were given to all police officers, according to the newspapers. In those days, the newspapers themselves convicted and condemned many people of crimes they actually had not committed, especially if these people were already on the run. When these outlaws were finally run down and slain, many communities could "close the books" on many untried killings and robberies, which was frequently to the relief of the actual guilty parties.

The fever pitch of the "crime wave" of summer, 1933, did make it extremely dangerous for anyone to be in the company of wanted people. At that time, Billie Jean had not been in any trouble with the law herself and Clyde meant to keep it that way. The Barrow, Parker, and Caldwell families already had enough sorrow and grief attached to their names due to the situations of Clyde, Buck, Blanche, and Bonnie. Clyde wanted to get Billie Jean away from them before tragedy could strike again, or before she unintentionally became involved in something that would make her become as badly wanted as the others. Clyde drove her down to the town of Sherman, Texas, and put her on the Interurban to get her back into west Dallas. Clyde didn't want a repetition of the scenario which had caused Buck and Blanche to become involved in the outlaw life with Clyde and Bonnie.

Once Billie Jean was safely on the Interurban, Clyde and Buck took stock of their situation and decided what had to be done next. They inventoried their needs in terms of priority. First and foremost, they needed to get Bonnie to a safe place where she could get rest and the proper medical treatment. Second, they needed to replenish their arsenal. Between the Wellington accident and the Alma manhunt, Clyde had lost most of the arsenal that he had accumulated during the spring of 1933. Clyde knew of a place where both of these objectives could be met, and where they could get themselves another badly needed car.

My brothers drove to the north-central part of Oklahoma. Clyde knew that the town of Enid had an armory, from which he anticipated getting Browning Automatic Rifles and automatic pistols. Clyde also figured he could get medical supplies and a new car from that area also.

The medical supplies and the new auto were acquired first. Clyde killed two birds with one stone by stealing the car of an Enid doctor, thereby getting transportation and the doctor's medical bag. Then my brothers rebuilt their firearms inventory by raiding the National Guard Armory. They got guns - lots and lots of guns. My brothers got so many guns that Clyde later told us they didn't know what to do with all of them. They were staying in another tourist camp in the Enid area. The boys brought the guns back to the camp and had so many that a tub wasn't big enough to hold all of them. All they could do was to dump them out in the middle of the floor and let each one pick out the gun they wanted. It was a limited choice: neither Bonnie nor Blanche liked guns. The two girls let the three men pick and choose. Buck didn't particularly like guns, although he used them when he felt he had to defend himself. Only Clyde and W.D. were enthusiastic about a whole new supply.

Clyde knew guns, and he knew a good gun when he saw one. My brother preferred automatics and he wouldn't use any thing else unless he had no other choice. Other outlaws of the period didn't care for automatics. In fact, John Dillinger Sr. told me his son—bank robber John Herbert Dillinger—told him once that he didn't trust an automatic pistol or a district attorney's promise. Clyde also liked semiautomatic shotguns, which he would saw off at both ends, so the shorter shotguns could be easily handled in the interior of a car.

But Clyde never stole any shotguns from any National Guard Armories. He only took the weapons he could get at no other place: automatic pistols and the Browning Automatic Rifles (BARs). These BARS were manufactured for use during World War I. The ones that were not used by the armed forces were stored around the country in these armories. Clyde liked the BAR because of its heavy fire power. Clyde called these rifles "submachine guns." Most people, when they think of the machine guns of the so-called gangster era, think of the Thompson submachine gun. Despite what the movies and TV programs show, Clyde never used the Tommy gun, nor did he want to.

Buck told us one time that they would go out and practice in a secluded part of the country for a whole day at a time. Clyde would tryout all of the guns he'd taken from a National Guard Armory. He would also break in the shotguns he'd purchased. Clyde would never steal shotguns when these hunting-type guns could be purchased at hardware stores. Clyde would also purchase what ammunition he could through legal means, but the ammo for the BARs and the automatic pistols were taken at the same time as these guns. Clyde one time told me that there were some days when they'd use up $500 worth of ammo during these practice sessions.

After getting the doctor's car, medical kit, and the guns from the armory, the kids took to the road again and headed further north. They drove from Enid up into Kansas and found another tourist camp at which they felt they would be safe. Here they were able to settle down and to attend to Bonnie's recovery. It was at this Kansas tourist court that Bonnie's burns began to mend somewhat, and they were able to enjoy two or three weeks of quiet time.

Circa 1910 (taken near Corsicana in Navarro county, Texas): Artie, Buck, and Nell attend public school. In those earlier years, the Barrow kids were regarded as no different as any of the other children of their time and place. They had no inkling of the trouble yet to come. Photo courtesy of the author

Circa 1933 (Barrow filling station): Henry Barrow constructed his small home (the right part of the building) at the West Dallas campgrounds and then moved it to the site of Eagle Ford road while Clyde was in prison. He built the "oil room" (the left part of the building) when he made it into a filling station. The cars in the picture belong to L.C. Barrow and Joe Bill Francis (who was courting Marie at the time). Courtesy of Texas/ Dallas History and Archives Division, Dallas Public Library, image PA76-1-33018A.

Circa 1923 (taken in West Dallas): Nell, Clyde, and L.C. are sitting with a group from their neighborhood. Clyde and L.C. are seated between a neighborhood chum named Walter Bennett Howard. The two Barrow brothers are beginning to find out that life in the big city was different than that of their bucolic years in Ellis and Navarro counties. Photo courtesy of the author.

Overleaf: Circa 1926 (Clyde's mug shot): This picture from Clyde's extended use of the rental car and the truckload of turkeys, which he and Buck purchased. No charges were filed against Clyde in either case, but police interest continued to grow. The officers began to pick up both Buck and Clyde in the round-up of "usual suspects" whenever a crime was committed in Dallas. Courtesy of Texas/Dallas History and Archives Division, Dallas Public Library, image MA83-7-MB-B-33.

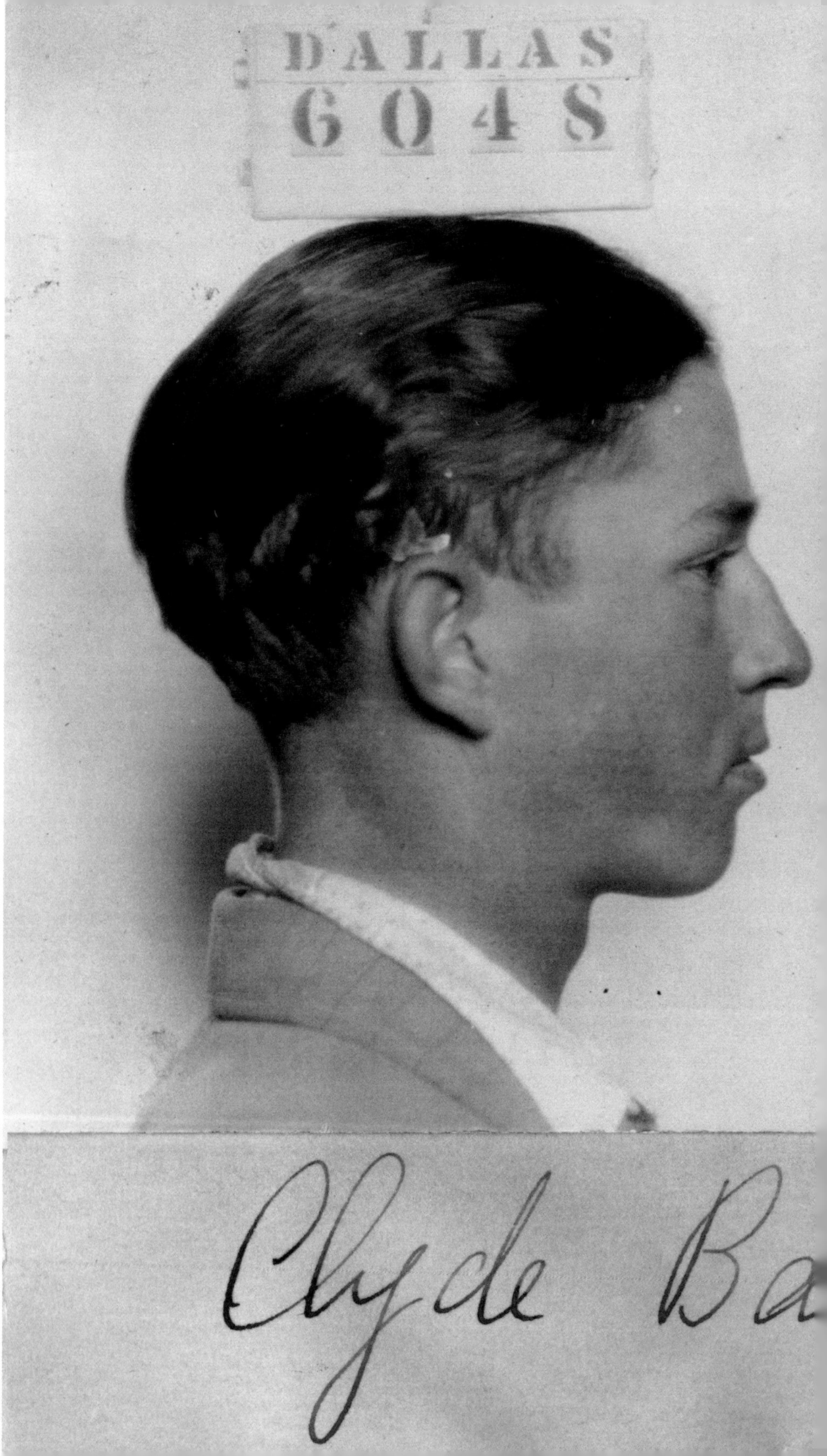
DALLAS
6048
Clyde Ba

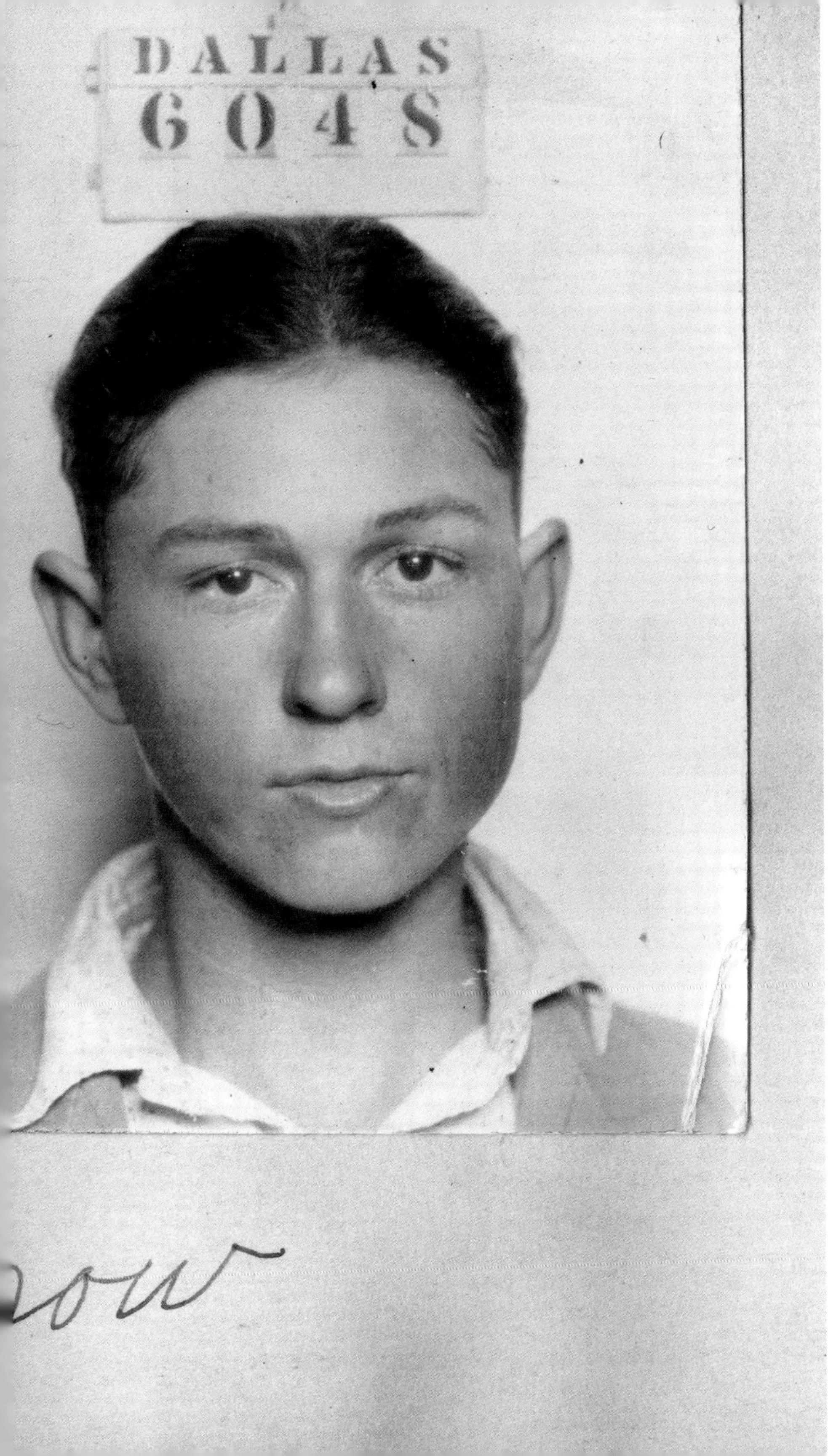
DALLAS
6048

Above: Circa 1926 (Bonnie's glamour shot): At the same time Clyde was being photographed by the Dallas police, Bonnie Parker had a more formal studio portrait made. She was on the verge of marriage to Roy Thornton, a West Dallas boy. She would not meet Clyde Barrow for another four years. Courtesy of Texas/ Dallas History and Archives Division, Dallas Public Library, image PA76-1-33005.

Right: Circa 1925 (Buck's mug shot): In West Dallas, Buck continued his involvement with fighting dogs, cockfights and gambling in general. Buck's interest in such activities were a source of serious concern to his parents. Courtesy of Texas/ Dallas History and Archives Division, Dallas Public Library, image MA83-7-MB-B-28.

Right: Circa 1933 (Blanche Barrow's mug shot): Cumie Barrow had such high hopes for Buck after he met and married Blanche Caldwell of Oklahoma. Buck's concern for Clyde, which resulted in the disastrous trip to Joplin, ruined the lives of both Buck and Blanche. Courtesy of Texas/ Dallas History and Archives Division, Dallas Public Library, image MA83-7-MB-B-5.

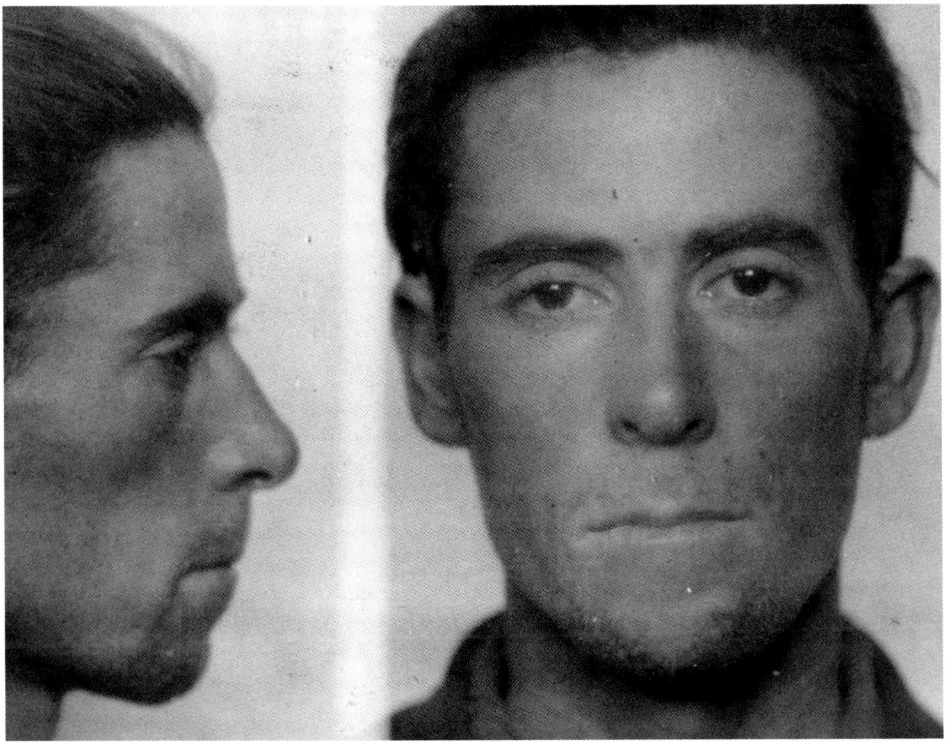

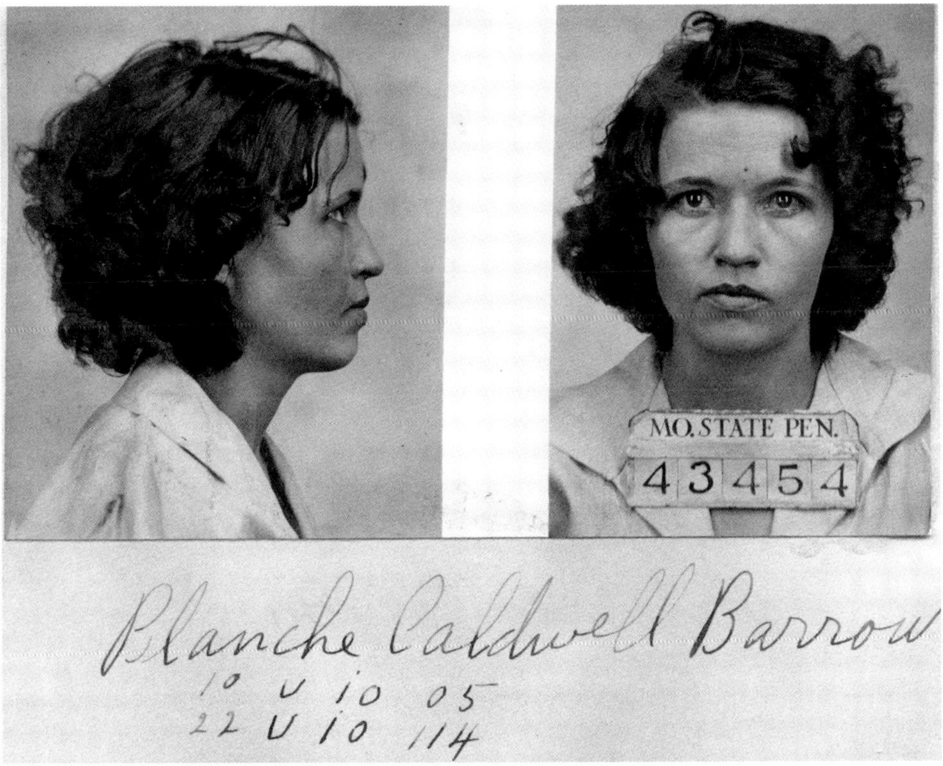
MO. STATE PEN.
43454
Blanche Caldwell Barrow
10 U 10 05
22 U 10 114

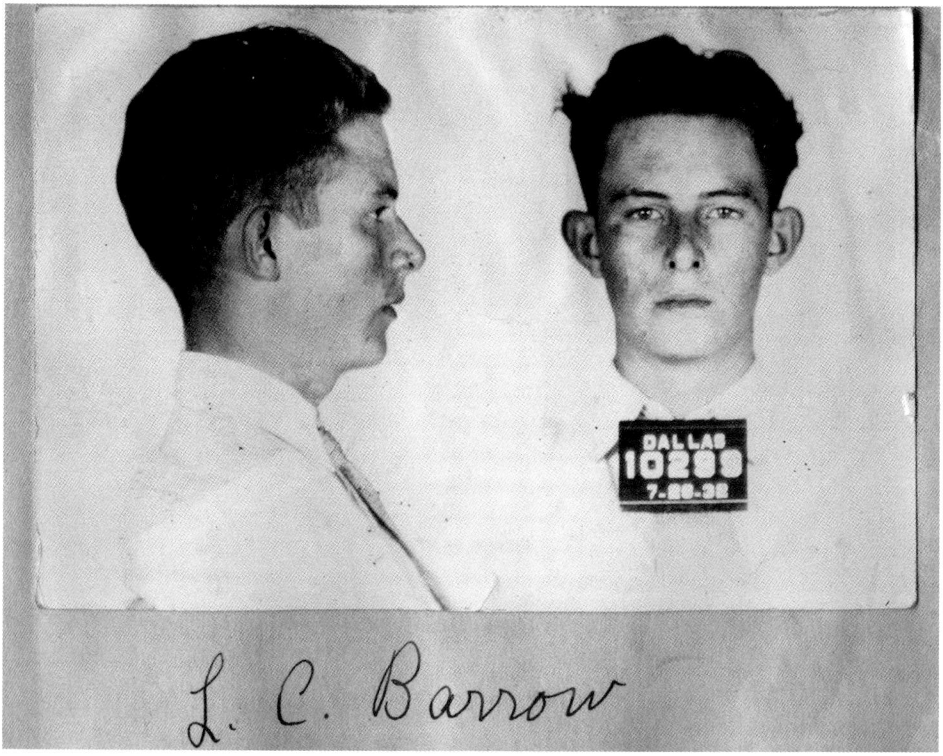
DALLAS
L. C. Barrow

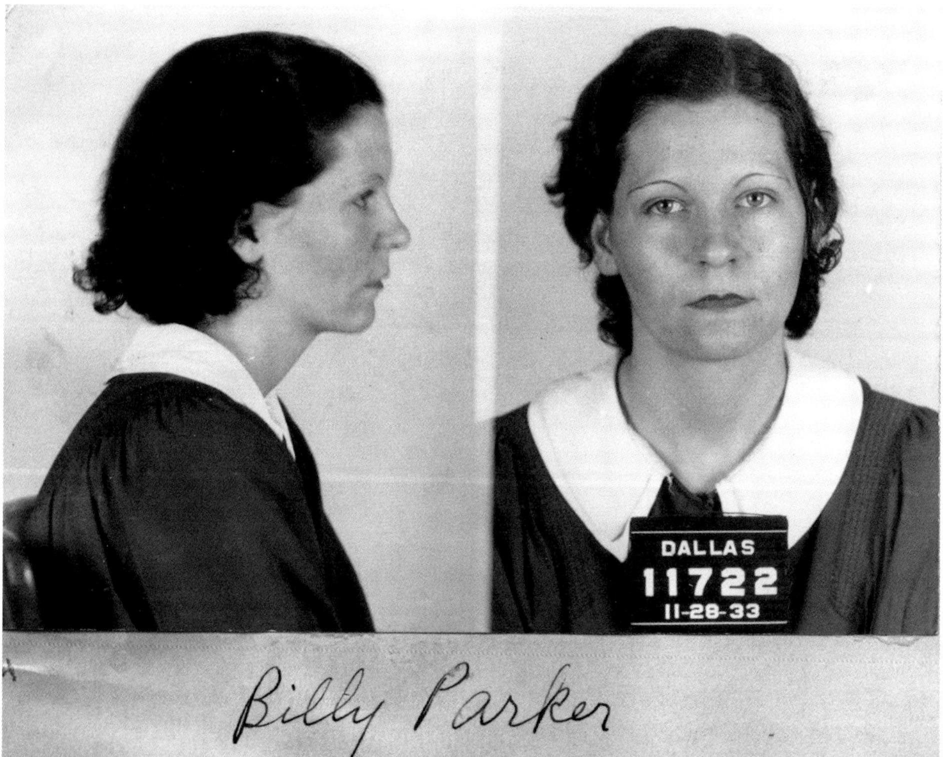
DALLAS
11722
11-28-33
Billy Parker

Circa 1933 (Lillie McBride house): Officers position themselves where both officer Malcolm Davis and Clyde Barrow were standing when a shoot out took place in January, 1933. Marie Barrow and Audrey Hamilton had visited with Lillie Hamilton McBride a few hours before the gunfight. Courtesy of Texas/ Dallas History and Archives Division, Dallas Public Library, image PA76-1-33024.

Left: Circa 1932 (L.C. Barrow's mug shot): Police would pick up L.C. Barrow as they did his two older brothers during the 1920s. L.C. was now regarded as one of the "Barrow Boys" of West Dallas. Courtesy of Texas/ Dallas History and Archives Division, Dallas Public Library, image MA83-7-MB-B-22.

Left: Circa 1933 (Billie Parker): Billie Parker was picked up by the police after anything connected with the Barrow gang occurred. This photograph was taken about the time of the Sowers ambush, where Billie was waiting with the Barrows and her mother to meet Bonnie and Clyde. Courtesy of Texas/ Dallas History and Archives Division, Dallas Public Library, image MA83-7-MB-P-4

Circa 1933 Barrow and Parker November Reunion. Standing left to right are Billie Jean Mace, Clyde Barrow, Cumie Barrow, and LC Barrow. In front, Left to right, are Marie Barrow, Emma Parker (Bonnie's mother), and Bonnie Parker. Photo courtesy of Buddy Barrow.

Circa 1933 Clyde Barrow with his arm around his mother, Cumie Barrow. Courtesy of Texas/ Dallas History and Archives Division, Dallas Public Library, image PA76-1-33008.

May 1934 (ambush posse): The Barrow and Parker families had differing opinions on the members of the posse that killed Bonnie and Clyde. They were sympathetic toward Ted Hinton and Bob Alcorn because the two Dallas county officers were just doing their job. Their attitudes toward the two former Texas Rangers and the two Louisiana officers were totally different. The Barrow family never forgave Frank Hamer for not returning much of Clyde and Bonnie's possessions to their families. Courtesy of Texas/ Dallas History and Archives Division, Dallas Public Library, image PA96-5-7.

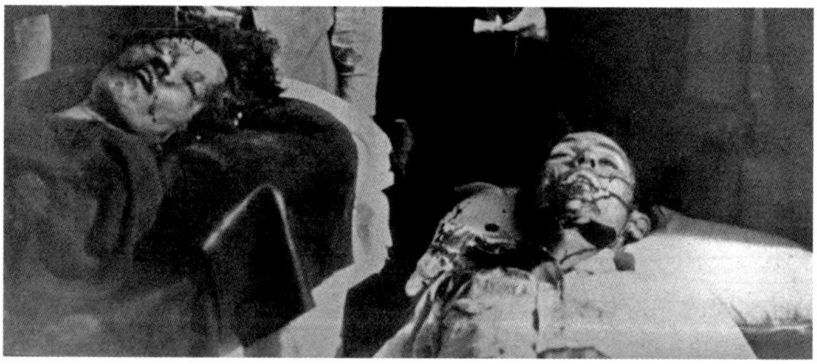

Right: May 1934 (Clyde's body): On the morning of May 23, 1934, Marie visited her parents and was headed back to her home when she stopped by a service station and heard the news of Clyde's assassination on the radio. She immediately turned around and went back to her parents' house to share the family's grief. Courtesy of Texas/ Dallas History and Archives Division, Dallas Public Library, image PA76-1-33010.

Right: May 1934 (Bonnie's body): Marie was also greatly grieved by Bonnie's death. While Clyde was in prison, Bonnie initially spent a lot of time at the Barrow service station and she and Marie became very close. Whenever she was asked what Bonnie was really like, Marie would respond that she was "just a li'l old girl." Courtesy of Texas/ Dallas History and Archives Division, Dallas Public Library, image PA76-1-33020.

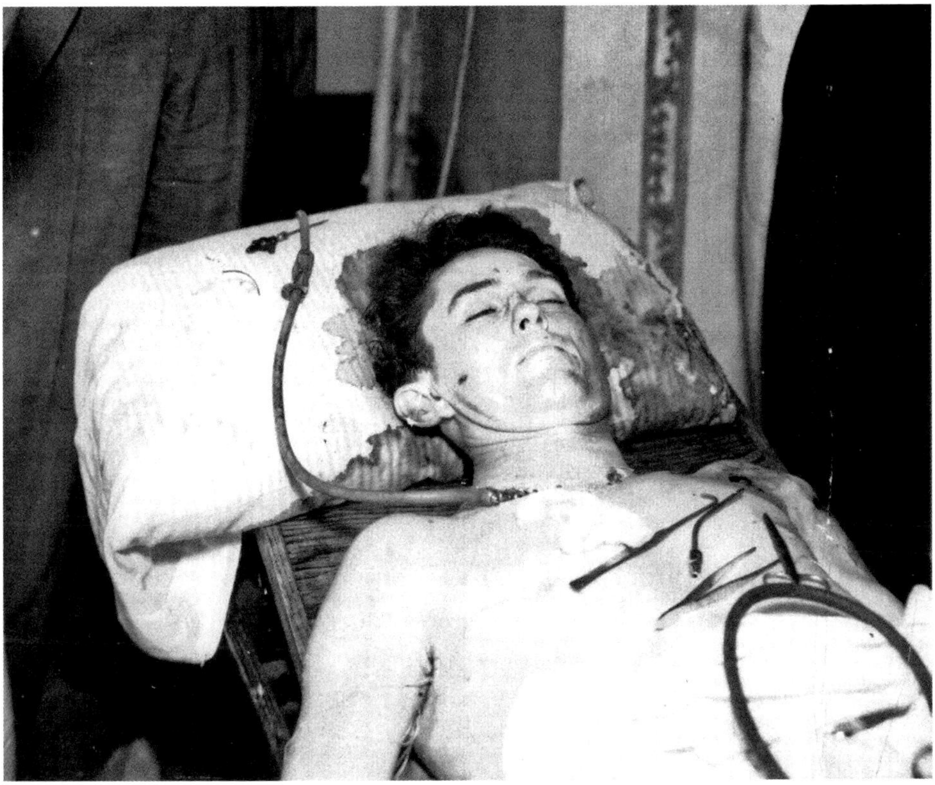

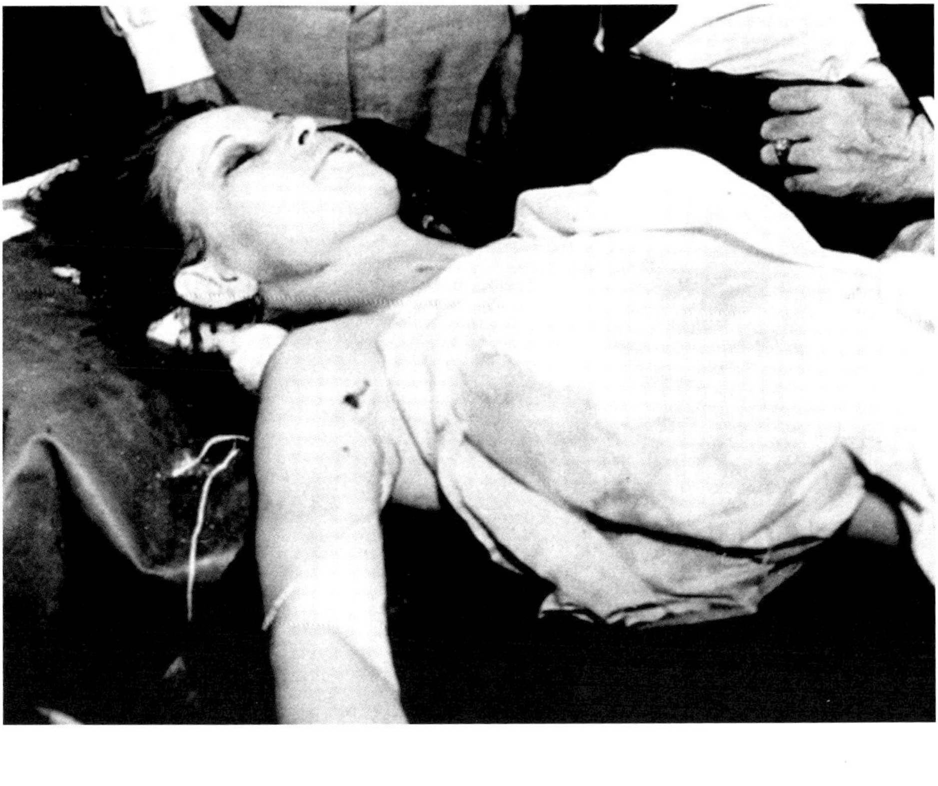

May 1934 (Bonnie's casket being carried out of funeral home): The visitation and funeral service for Bonnie Parker was almost as raucous as that for Clyde. Crowds lined up out into the street to see Bonnie's body. She was placed in the hallway of the funeral home where people could enter in at the front door, go down the main hallway where she lay, and were immediately ushered out the back. This photograph shows the Parker family following behind Bonnie's casket. Courtesy of Texas/ Dallas History and Archives Division, Dallas Public Library, image PA78-2-513.

May 1934 (close up of Parker family members): Emma Parker is seen being supported by family members as Bonnie's casket is placed in the hearse. Son Hubert "Buster" Parker is partially seen on Emma's other side. Courtesy of Texas/ Dallas History and Archives Division, Dallas Public Library, image PA76-1-33014.

Right: May 1934 (back door of the funeral home): Great crowds of people tried to get into the funeral home to see Clyde's body any way they could. Courtesy of Texas/ Dallas History and Archives Division, Dallas Public Library, image PA76-1-33015.

lay 1934 (Clyde's funeral): Thursday, May 24, and Friday, May 25, was an additional nightmare for the Barrow
ımily because of the never-ending line of morbid curiosity seekers that came through the funeral home on those
ays. Most were respectful toward the situation and the family, but some of the curiosity seekers tried to provoke the
arrow family members. This photograph shows the hearse being positioned and the funeral procession starting to
ɔrm. Courtesy of Texas/ Dallas History and Archives Division, Dallas Public Library, image PA78-2-502.

1936 (Cumie Barrow being carried into court): Even after the 1935 trial, Cumie Barrow's trials did not cease. In 1936, Cumie was shot by a waiting gunman outside the Barrow service station. The assailant fired at Joe Bill and Marie Barrow-Francis, but one of the bullets entered the window and hit Cumie in one of her eyes, which caused her to lose sight in that eye. Courtesy of Texas/ Dallas History and Archives Division, Dallas Public Library, image PA76-1-33011.

February 1935 (seated courtroom of harboring trial women): Marie thought that the filing of harboring charges against the Barrow and Parker families was very unfair, since no such charges were ever filed against the families of other noted fugitives like John Dillinger and Pretty Boy Floyd. Marie was sentenced to one hour in custody of a federal marshal. Cumie Barrow and Emma and Billie Parker received harsher sentences. Courtesy of Texas/ Dallas History and Archives Division, Dallas Public Library, image PA76-1-37313-1.

February 1935 (women in Barrow-Parker harboring trial): The federal government filed charges concerning the harboring of wanted fugitives against many West Dallas people who were related to Bonnie and Clyde, including Cumie and Marie Barrow, as well as Billie and Emma Parker. Courtesy of Texas/ Dallas History and Archives Division, Dallas Public Library, image PA76-1-37204-2.

Chapter 14

Bonnie's injuries began to heal during the few weeks the kids spent at the tourist camp in central Kansas. My brothers were laying low for awhile. This was a welcome relief for all of them after the tumultuous occurrences near Wellington, Texas, and Alma, Arkansas. They spent their time in Kansas quietly, taking care of Bonnie and just taking it easy. They lived off the money that Buck and W.D. had gotten in robberies committed away from their current Kansas hideout.

Those of us living at the service station in west Dallas continued to get the notes and postcards signed "Bud," Clyde's code name. These messages contained the usual generic news that all was fine and that they were enjoying themselves. Some of these notes would state that "Sis's" condition was improving. Of course, that veiled reference dealt with Bonnie's health.

The activities of the Barrow brothers were so quiet during late June and early July that the newspapers decided to create some Barrow-related news. Our family was greatly surprised to see articles concerning an alleged plot by Clyde and Buck to raid Leavenworth Prison in Kansas and free a third brother who was supposedly held in there. I did a quick inventory of all of my male siblings to see who this additional brother could possibly be: Buck and Clyde were out on the road; Jack was still living over on Forest Avenue in south Dallas, raising his family and working at his garage; and L.C. was living in west Dallas with his wife Audrey Faye. With the whereabouts of all of my brothers accounted for, I could only assume that this Barrow boy in Leavenworth Prison must be that eighth Barrow child that everyone says exists but that no one can identify.

This three week period of relative tranquility was about to come to an end. The time finally came when Clyde thought they should move on. He never liked to stay in one place for any length of time. Bonnie's burns had improved to the point that she could now travel with a lesser degree of discomfort.

The kids' financial resources were getting low again and they felt the need to replenish their money supply. This situation was remedied when the group traveled over to Ft. Dodge, Iowa, in mid-July. On July

18, they made a series of service station raids. Clyde and Buck had been in Ft. Dodge two months previously when Buck robbed a service station. Apparently Ft. Dodge was noted for its prosperous gas stations by my brothers.

These service station robberies seemed to have become a specialty for my brother Buck. He had the ability to pull them off with no violence or shooting. Buck would just mosey in and tell the service station attendant he was broke and needed money and would take their business' proceeds. He would then clean out the cash register and leave on foot, meeting the rest of the group just down the street in the car. Of course, the fact that Buck was carrying a pistol during these holdups reinforced his sincerity.

After the relatively successful Ft. Dodge raids, my brothers undoubtedly felt that it was time to gravitate back towards Texas and they headed south from Iowa. The Ft. Dodge robberies were committed earlier in the day of July 18, so they drove all afternoon and into the early evening hours. The group approached the Kansas City area and figured that it would be a good place to stop over for a short time. Bonnie still hadn't recovered to the point that she could easily undergo long stretches of driving. She still had to be assisted in her movements.

The boys knew of a place called the Red Crown Cabin Camp, which was located at the junction of U.S. Highway 71 and Missouri Highway 59. This establishment had both tourist cabins and a nightclub-restaurant to meet the needs of travelers. The cabins were located out in back of the nightclub. Clyde particularly liked these cabins because they were made of stone and brick, which, of course, were resistant to gunfire. But this was one time Clyde didn't anticipate any trouble; all the kids wanted to do was just to get a couple of nights' sleep and a full day of rest for Bonnie. Buck and Clyde pulled in to the Red Crown Cabin Camp at about 6 o'clock on the evening of July 18. They planned to resume their trip back to Texas early on the morning of July 20.

Blanche got out of the car and went into the nightclub to make arrangements to rent the cabins. They were renting a double cabin arrangement. The two cabins were connected by a garage area. The cost for the five of them for both cabins was $4.00 a night. Blanche paid this amount and rejoined the others in the car. They pulled up to the cabins and Clyde backed their car into the garage. Buck and

Blanche were to take one cabin and Clyde, Bonnie, and W.D. took the other.

After they got themselves situated, Blanche went over to the restaurant and purchased food and drink for all of them. She paid for the edibles with small change, as she had paid the rent with small change also. The employees there thought this was a little odd, but money was money and the small change was accepted. The five of them spent a quiet night in the cabins.

The following day, July 19, Blanche arranged for the second night's rent and again purchased some food and drink. Again, she paid for everything with small change, which was again noticed. The others stayed in the cabins and never came outside. The doors were left closed and the window shades were rolled down. I've heard that W.D. may have went over to the restaurant during the day. I know neither Clyde nor Buck ventured outside of their cabins. The newspapers were always printing front-page stories about the boys, giving their pictures in connection with these articles. They were called the "Bloody Barrows" in all kind of sensational and untrue accounts. So much awful publicity made it almost impossible for them to go out in public together. For that matter, they rarely went out individually by themselves: Buck and Blanche went out together, as did Clyde and Bonnie.

The whole state of Missouri was on edge that summer, due to all of the prominent crime news. The newspapers were always featuring page-one headline stories about Pretty Boy Floyd, the Kansas Prison escapees, and the investigation of the Kansas City Union Depot Massacre of June 17. Because of the tragedy in Joplin during April, any reported activity of Buck and Clyde was also given wide play in the papers.

The morning and afternoon of July 19 came and went in a quiet fashion. Clyde and Blanche attended to Bonnie's burns and all of them ate the food Blanche had bought at the restaurant. Towards the late afternoon and early evening hours, they began to pack up their things in order to resume the trip towards Texas the following morning. Clyde and Blanche inventoried Bonnie's medical supplies and they noticed some items were in short supply. Since Platte City was close by, they knew these supplies could be acquired in any drugstore there. The day had gone by so quietly that Clyde was feeling relaxed about their situation. He offered to go into town himself and buy these things, as he had not been out of the cabins and felt the need to get out and stretch his legs. But he did not take the only car they had with them. He walked out to the highway and hitchhiked into Platte City. By the time he got into the Platte City drugstore, it was about 8:00 p.m.

It was at this point that Clyde's relaxed mood suddenly ended. While he was at the counter buying Bonnie's medical supplies, he overheard a conversation between two men concerning a lot of police activity out near the junction of highways 59 and 71 - and that location meant the area of the Red Crown Cabin Camp. Clyde completed his purchase and hastened out of the drugstore. He knew he had to get back and see what had happened; the police activity he heard about may very well have involved Buck and the others. But it took a little while for him to get back out there.

There was indeed a lot of police activity going on out near the Red Crown Tourist Cabins. The interest of the police had been generated by several small factors which had been noticed by the Red Crown employees: the fact that Clyde's group always kept to themselves, the closed doors and curtains around the cabins, the fact that both rent and foodstuffs was paid for with small change, and the fact that someone had noticed the heavily-bandaged Bonnie entering her cabin the night they arrived. The Red Crown people went and talked to the Missouri State Highway Patrol on the afternoon of July 19. The highway patrol then talked to the Platte county officials. The Platte county officials then called the Jackson county officials and asked for help. Kansas City was in Jackson county. All of these law enforcement groups were putting together a massive raiding party. An armored car, tear gas, Tommy guns, and steel shields were being brought up from Kansas City.

Of course, Clyde didn't realize the extent of these preparations, but he sensed something was wrong and that his people should leave the Platte City area immediately. What he overheard in the drugstore was enough to send him speeding back towards Buck, Bonnie, and the others. Clyde managed to make it back to the Red Crown Cabin Camp and slip back into his cabin without being noticed. It was now after dark. No one was in bed at that time and he quickly informed the others that something was up and that they should all pack up and get out as soon as possible. Buck and Blanche went back to their cabin and began to get their things together. Clyde, Bonnie, and W.D. were doing the same in their area.

Clyde kept looking out the front window every few seconds as they threw their things together. He was looking for any unusual activity outside. About 10 p.m. he noticed several cars turning into the Red Crown area and told W.D. and Bonnie "There's the law." The other two looked at Clyde for direction and he told them to douse the lights. By now Buck and Blanche had turned off their lights also.

A policeman came up to one of the cabins and knocked. He exclaimed "This is the law. We want to speak to the men." There was a momentary stillness inside the cabin and then Clyde grabbed one of the BARs they had gotten from the Enid armory. Buck and W.D. did the same and all three men opened up through the doors and windows on the officers outside. These rifles were so powerful that they were chewing up everything the police had with them, including the steel shields. The officers with the shields began to retreat. The policemen had pulled their armored car up to the garage to block in Clyde's car. While Clyde and W.D. were forcing the police back, Buck was firing as much as both of them put together.

Even though Clyde's attention was primarily directed at the officers outside, he was still surprised at the amazing amount of gunfire coming from Buck's cabin. When he later told us about the Platte City battle, he said he figured he and W.D. must have fired about 200 times and Buck must have fired that many times on his own.

Bonnie was the first one to make it out to their car. Clyde covered W.D. as he ran out to the car and got it started. Clyde yelled out at the others and asked if Buck and Blanche were out there. W.D. said that they were not out there yet. Clyde continued to fire, but he knew he had to be getting out to the car himself. He finally ran out into the garage, but Buck and Blanche were still not out there.

Clyde now turned his attention towards the armored car, which was still marked directly in front of their garage. He unleashed his BAR on the armored car, firing from the inside of the garage through the doors. The armored car didn't hold up any better against Clyde's fire than did the steel shields. The officers inside the armored car knew they were in trouble and they backed the car away from in front of the garage. Clyde's way was now clear.

But Buck and Blanche were still not out there. Clyde opened the garage door and unleashed another barrage against the police. Finally, he saw Buck and Blanche heading towards the car from their cabin. But just as they reached the auto, Buck was shot in the head and went down. W.D. covered Clyde as Clyde ran over to assist his brother.

Clyde and Blanche got Buck into the car and then Clyde got behind the wheel. Blanche had to hold her fingers to Buck's head injury in order to try to stop the flow of blood.

Bullets were flying every which way. Clyde later told us that W.D. was hit in the head from the police gunfire, but the wound was very minor. As their car started to pick up speed as it headed away from the tourist cabin, a police bullet shattered one of the windows in their car, sending splinters of glass into Blanche's eyes. Clyde did outrun the range of the officers' gunfire and their car disappeared into the night.

Clyde headed back north towards Iowa. He felt that he was still too far away from the Ozarks to make a run for that hideout. My brother had no particular destination up in Iowa. Clyde could tell at a glance that Buck was severely wounded. Buck had been shot in the forehead, with the bullet tearing away part of his brain. Clyde knew that he had to get away to somewhere quiet where the wounded and injured in their little group could be treated. Buck's head wound was the worst injury suffered on either side of the combatants at Platte City. A few members of the police attack force were taken to various hospitals in both Platte City and Kansas City for non-critical wounds. But the fighting instincts of the officers were aroused by the big gun battle and they were not going to let the matter end with my brothers fleeing the scene.

In addition to the local, county, and state officers of Missouri who were now after Clyde and Buck, federal agents joined the manhunt. It turned out that Clyde's raid on the National Guard armory in Enid, Oklahoma, gave the G-men the opening they needed to initiate their pursuit of the so-called "Barrow Gang." The Feds were going to all hospitals in northwest Missouri and asking them to report any people who appeared with gunshot wounds desiring medical assistance. The agents also went to all of the regional radio stations and asked them to frequently broadcast descriptions of my brothers and the women with them.

The newspapers across the country gave a great deal of publicity to the big shoot out at Platte City. Of course, the home folks in Dallas were extremely upset to hear about the severe head injury Buck sustained during the battle. It turned out that Buck's wound made their trail extremely easy to follow. The newspapers and radio frequently reported bulletins concerning the discovery of campsites at which blood-covered clothing and bandages were found. Many times these articles were half-burned in a campfire. The stories related the same continuous scenario of a small group of people who were seen burning items in a campfire and who fled in an auto when anyone approached them. The description of these people always included a heavily bandaged woman (Bonnie) and a man with a head bandage (Buck).

This trail of campfires and bloody bandages finally led into central Iowa. Another such campsite was found in a park located several miles west of Des Moines. The park was named Dexfield Park because of its proximity to the small towns of Dexter and Redfield.

Ironically, the county in which this park and these towns were located was Dallas County, the same as the kids' home turf in Texas. Maybe Clyde thought that an area with the same name as his home town might be a good place in which to hide out, but their reception there did not resemble anything like hometown hospitality due to the discovery of their campfire and bloody bandages. They had also tried to burn at that same site one of the cars which they had stolen in making their way into Iowa. Even though this site was located in a remote area of Dexfield Park, it wasn't remote enough.

A man who was walking through the park came across the partially burnt bandages and car. Fortunately for this passerby, no one was present at the time he discovered the latest campsite. The newspapers in Iowa had been reporting the trail of campsites and this person realized that he'd found another one of them. This man immediately reported what he'd found to a member of the local law enforcement organization. There was a vigilante group in Dallas County, Iowa, which was a cooperative effort between the county sheriff and concerned citizens. Iowa was especially noted for such organizations by bank robbers in the early 1930s. These vigilante groups were formed as a reaction against the numerous bank holdups of the period in the small towns and rural areas of Iowa. Many local peace officers in these areas were frequently outnumbered and out-armed by the roving bandit gangs. These vigilante groups were not made up of imported hired guns, but consisted of local farmers and merchants who owned firearms and knew how to use them. These organizations were always factors to be considered in determining whether or not to select probable targets in the state of Iowa. Many bank robbers preferred to do their business elsewhere.

The vigilante to whom the news of the campsite was reported

went out to Dexfield Park to keep the site under surveillance. This surveillance was rewarded when Clyde and his group returned to this spot. They had been out to get another car to replace the one they'd tried to burn. Their mission was successful when they'd gotten a Ford sedan in the nearby town of Perry. My brothers and the rest of their little group brought this new acquisition and their other car back to the campsite.

By then the vigilante had seen all he figured he needed to see, and he discreetly left his observation post to put together a raiding party. He contacted several other local law enforcement officers and they organized their plan of attack. Another member of the vigilante group was sent out to keep an eye on the suspected campsite and campers. He reported the group seemed to be settling in for the night. The raiding party decided to make their move early the next morning at daylight; if they attempted a nighttime raid, the officers might wind up shooting at each other in the darkness. After all of the newspaper accounts of Clyde's and Buck's activities in the spring and early summer of 1933, some of the officers might have believed that Clyde and Buck had the ability to see in the dark. In any case, the officers resolved to wait until daylight.

As for Clyde and Buck themselves, the last few days had driven them all to the point of exhaustion. After they had returned with the stolen vehicle, they started up their campfire and attended to their wounded, which was the majority of the little group. Buck's head injury needed frequent cleaning and re-bandaging. Bonnie's burns still needed medication. Blanche's injured eyes prohibited her providing any great assistance to the others. It was primarily up to Clyde to care for those who needed medical treatment. He had learned his lessons well from his relatively limited exposure to the doctor in Ft. Smith. Clyde was doing a surprisingly good job with both Buck's and Bonnie's injuries. After Clyde had gotten everyone situated as well as possible, all of them drifted off to much needed sleep after nightfall.

The kids woke up at sunrise and started to stir around. They began to prepare whatever foods they had in order to make a semblance of breakfast. Eggs, wieners, and coffee were put on the campfire. Those who weren't involved with food preparation stood nearby and smoked cigarettes and watched the cookers. Then one of them looked up and saw the approaching posse and sounded the warning. Every one of them grabbed for a nearby gun and began to fire at the officers. The lawmen reciprocated and the battle was on.

The size of this posse was been estimated at anywhere from several dozen to several hundred. Actually, when the daylight attack was initiated, there were only a handful of actual police combatants. But there was a large crowd of spectators who had heard about the upcoming "fun" and wanted to watch the proceedings. These people were following the officers from a little ways back. When the cops and robbers began playing their game for real, real bullets began to fly awfully close to the spectators, who suddenly realized that they'd gotten more than they'd bargained for and hit the dirt.

Clyde, Buck, and the others saw this approaching large group of people and apparently believed that they were facing a literal army of officers. All five of them scrambled to one of the two cars at their camp in order to flee. The police riddled this car with bullets in order to disable it. Clyde's group spilled from the first car and headed for the second. The posse saw their intentions and began to concentrate their fire on this other car. All five of Clyde's group made it inside the car and attempted to flee in it. This car was also disabled when Clyde ran into a stump. The officers unleashed another volley into this auto and the kids piled out of it. My brothers and their group fled on foot into the underbrush.

The officers made their way to the campsite and the now-deserted cars. They found many bloodstains around the vehicles and figured their fire had wounded at least some of the bandits. Some of the spectators had fled at the first round of gunfire and had called for reinforcements, the first of which were now arriving, and many more were on the way.

After he pulled his group into the underbrush, Clyde sequestered everyone under the most adequate cover he could immediately locate. Buck and Blanche were situated behind a massive fallen log, and Bonnie and W.D. were hidden in nearby underbrush. Clyde then left to get the first available car in which to retrieve the others.

The officers knew they had hit at least some of the opposing party and did follow the trail of blood into the underbrush and the wooded areas. They found Buck and Blanche behind their fallen log and captured them. Buck had been hit in the body several more times by the police gunfire when they tried to escape in the cars and was certainly in no physical shape to resist arrest. He had to be supported by members of the posse as he and Blanche were escorted away. There is a famous photograph of the occurrence that day at Dexfield Park.

In the left side of the photograph, Blanche is seen struggling and screaming while being physically restrained by members of the posse. In the right side of the picture, a man always identified as Buck is seen kneeling while posse members surround him. There's two things that I'd like to point out about that photo. First is that Blanche was struggling because she saw someone pointing what she thought was a gun at her and thought a member of the posse was taking aim at her. With her eye injuries, Blanche was unable to recognize that it was only a cameraman taking the famous picture. Second is that the kneeling man always identified as Buck is actually not my brother. Buck was lying on the ground, curled up in a fetal position, behind this kneeling person. Buck was able to walk for awhile, but the wounds he received there at Dexfield Park caused him to periodically faint. It was during one of these fainting spells that the picture was taken.

While the posse was occupied with the apprehension of Buck and Blanche, Clyde crawled back through the underbrush to where Bonnie and W.D. were still hiding. He was unable to get a car. More and more lawmen and vigilantes were pouring into the area. Reinforcements were called for when Clyde and Buck resisted the posse's initial call to surrender. These reinforcements were arriving in a continuous stream. More and more roadblocks were being set up around the Dexfield Park area. Clyde told the others that they'd have to try to get away on foot and then try to get the first car they could outside the ring of posse men. Bonnie told Clyde that Buck and Blanche had been taken away by the officers. There was nothing the three of them could do to try and free the other two. Bonnie was still semi-crippled from her burns. Clyde himself had been painfully wounded in the volley of shots that seriously injured his older brother. They were in no physical shape to attempt to confront the dozens of officers that were now in the area. The three of them would be doing well enough to just avoid capture and get away.

Clyde, Bonnie, and W.D. began to crawl towards a nearby river. Clyde figured that the river would act as a natural obstacle to the pursuing posse, provided the three fugitives could get across first. The trio slowly began to cross the river. Some of the posse members that were scouring the underbrush saw them attempting to cross the river and opened fire on them. Bonnie was struck by one of the bullets, but was supported by W.D. until the three of them made it across. Then they disappeared in a cornfield which bordered the river. Posse members were already entering the river in order to continue the chase.

Clyde and the others passed through the cornfield and came to a farmhouse where several men were standing and listening to the gunfire coming from Dexfield Park. Clyde approached them from the cornfield and didn't mince words; he told the men that he had to have a car right now because he was being pursued by the law. Clyde's disheveled, blood-stained, water-soaked appearance, plus the pistol he was holding, inspired immediate cooperation: a nearby car was offered for his use. Clyde then ordered W.D., who was still supporting Bonnie, to bring her to the car. The three of them got in with Clyde behind the wheel and took off.

A few minutes later, several posse members arrived and heard about the commandeering of the car. The alarm was spread concerning the description of Clyde's auto. Airplanes were now brought into the chase in order to sight the fugitives' car from the air. Their auto was sighted by the pilot several times, and the plane would dip low over the car. The signal told the posses which direction to head towards. But Clyde outran both the planes and the posses. The three kids disappeared.

But the law still had Buck and Blanche. Our family in west Dallas was informed of their capture. We were told of Buck's serious injuries, and family members should soon leave for Iowa if they wanted to see him alive. My father couldn't afford to leave the responsibilities of his service station, so my mother and my brother L.C. started on the trip to central Iowa. They were accompanied by Bonnie's mother and sister. Mrs. Parker and Billie Jean were extremely concerned about the news that Bonnie had been injured by police gunfire. In fact, the people at the farm where Clyde took the car said that Bonnie appeared to be more dead than alive when she was placed in the car by W.D. Her mother and sister did indeed fear for her life, since she was shot after already being seriously burned.

But the families of Clyde, Buck, and Bonnie were not the only ones interested in what had happened up in Iowa. Police officers from both Missouri and Arkansas were also heading north into Iowa to talk to Buck and Blanche. The Missouri officers wanted to discuss the shootouts at both Joplin and Platte City. The Arkansas cops wanted to question Buck in connection with the shooting of Marshal Humphrey at Alma.

Mercifully, my mother made it up there before Buck died. She had a short time to talk with him. Our mother had made many trips in the past to provide personal support for her kids. She never supported a lot of what Buck had done in the past, but such was the bond between Cumie and her children that she never hesitated to respond when one of her offspring truly needed her. My parents had gone to great trouble and expense in 1928 when they made that horse- and-wagon trip from Dallas to San Antonio in order to support Buck during that trial. Now our mother was making her last trip for Buck's benefit.

My older brother Marvin Ivan "Buck" Barrow died on July 29, 1933, at the hospital in Perry, Iowa. He was 30 years old. Most accounts of the lives of my brothers claim that Buck passed away as a result of the fearsome head wound he received at Platte City, but that was really not the case. He was holding his own with the head injury,due to both Clyde's doctoring and the fact that the actual brain damage had occurred in a non-vital area. Buck was able to accompany the others when they stole the car in Perry, Iowa, and was able to shoot back at the posse when the battle in Dexfield Park began.

Over the years, I have been given many pieces of correspondence and information concerning my brothers Clyde and Buck. One of the more interesting of these bits of information is a copy of a 1974 letter from one of the doctors who treated Buck in the Perry hospital after he was captured. The doctor said that they had operated on Buck to remove a bullet that had lodged in his chest. After the operation, pneumonia (and possibly meningitis) set in, and it was the pneumonia that carried my brother off.

Buck's body was accompanied back to Dallas by those of our family and Bonnie's family who went to Iowa. His services were held at the Sparkman funeral home on Ross Avenue near downtown Dallas. Burial took place in the Western Heights Cemetery in west Dallas on July 31, 1933. There were widespread rumors that Clyde attended the funeral and burial, disguised in women's clothing.

CHAPTER 15

BUCK WAS NOW FOREVER beyond the jurisdiction of any earthly court, but Blanche was just beginning to deal with what would be a long series of legal activities. She was initially resistant to the interrogations of the prosecutors and the lawmen, and gave out either false information or no information at all concerning the identities of her companions and their activities during the spring and summer of 1933. Blanche maintained her defiant attitude during the week that Buck was fighting for his survival in a hospital bed in Perry, Iowa. She was also strengthened by the public rumor that Clyde and Bonnie were putting together a massive raiding party of desperadoes and were planning to storm the whole town of Perry to rescue her and her husband. Because of this rumor, the number of guards around the hospital were greatly increased. After the Kansas City Massacre of the previous month, the authorities were taking no chances with any outlaw rescue attempts.

But then Buck succumbed to his wounds. When my brother died, much of Blanche's defiance and resistance died also. It became readily apparent that no rescue attempt would be made by any army of outlaws, due to the extremely well-armed and numerous guards that were watching Buck and Blanche. Blanche finally faced the certainty that she would be put on trial and the possibility that she could serve time in prison.

It has been said by many that at this point Blanche became bitter towards Clyde and towards our family. This alleged bitterness came about due to what Blanche perceived as Clyde's "desertion" of his older brother at Dexfield Park. The prosecutors may have tried to trick Blanche into giving them information by instilling the notion that Clyde threw Buck to the wolves by letting him and Blanche get caught while he fled with Bonnie. The prosecutor might have then emphasized that Blanche owed Clyde no loyalties due to this "cowardly act" and would encourage her to inform on him. I have never seen any evidence of any such bitterness on Blanche's part towards our family. We did help Blanche in whatever ways we could during this time, but she was still firmly in the clutches of the law and nothing could allay that fact.

Blanche was transferred from the county jail where she was initially held to a much bigger jail in Des Moines. From there Blanche was extradited to the state of Missouri where she was put on trial in connection with the gunfight at Platte City. She was found guilty and received a sentence of 10 years at the women's penitentiary in Missouri. Our family was devastated by both Buck's death and Blanche's prison term.

We knew she never had any intentions of being involved in a life of crime and that her only real crime was her steadfast loyalty to her husband. Blanche was simply a fine young woman from a good family who accidentally became involved in a short career of outlawry due to her husband's desire to try to redeem his younger brother.

After outrunning the Iowa posses and airplanes, Clyde, Bonnie, and W.D. were looking for deep cover in which to hide. They were sighted all over the Midwest and southwest in the weeks following the Dexfield Park conflict. There were sightings of the trio in Missouri, Nebraska, New Mexico, Kansas, Colorado, and many other places as Clyde sought to throw off any pursuit by leaving a confusing trail.

The three of them stayed together during August, but W.D. told Clyde that he'd finally had enough of the outlaw life. My brother was glad to hear W.D. admit what Clyde had warned him of all along. W.D.'s second excursion with Clyde and Buck had been much rougher than his first time out with them.

This second road trip started off with Bonnie's severe burns in the car wreck near Wellington, Texas. Then W.D. was involved with Buck in the second car wreck just north of Alma, Arkansas, and the resulting gunfight in which Marshal Humphrey was killed. Shortly after that came the terrible conflicts in both Platte City, Missouri, and Dexter, Iowa. Bonnie's burns, Buck's death, and Blanche's arrest had struck too close to home for W.D. He had come to believe that Clyde and anybody riding with him were always going to be able to fend off tragedy and that death and injury would always happen to the other party. Clyde had always known better than that and many times had told W.D. to get out while he still had not been positively identified by the police. Now, W.D. was finally ready to follow my brother's good advice. But he agreed to stay on until both Clyde and Bonnie had sufficiently recovered from their wounds and injuries to be able to go it alone.

But Bonnie's health was not good at this time, nor would it ever be good again. She was never able to walk around normally after she was burned. Bonnie was burned deep in her knee and, as a result, her right leg was always drawn up. She was able to hop around in order to move, but Clyde generally had to help her. In addition to her burns, the gunshot wounds she suffered at Dexfield Park further complicated matters. As a result, when both her burns and bullet wounds began to hurt simultaneously, she often had to be kept still and quiet at a safe place with someone while Clyde went out to get needed supplies and to commit robberies at gas stations and grocery stores in order to keep them in funds.

There were times that Clyde and W.D. were seen around and about in various cities and towns. These sightings were usually made at diners and gas stations where the boys stopped fleetingly to get either food or fuel. People always gave them a substantial head start before reporting that they'd caught a glimpse of Clyde Barrow and an unidentified male companion. The three traveled about from location to location, keeping on the move until their trail seemed cold and all pursuit was lost.

By the end of August, Bonnie had recovered to the point that Clyde felt that the two of them were able to go it alone for awhile. Before they brought him back to west Dallas, Clyde began to drill into W.D. the alibis the younger man should use if he was ever arrested and connected with any of the activities of the so-called "Barrow Gang." When W.D. had finally memorized these alibis to Clyde's satisfaction, Clyde drove W.D. back to west Dallas. But, by this time, W.D.'s mother had moved from west Dallas to Houston, so W.D. followed her down there. He proceeded to maintain a low profile and tried to melt in with the common folk. At that time, the common folk were hiring out to pick cotton. W.D. became a contented and inconspicuous cotton picker along with his other family members.

Although W.D. was finally through with Clyde, there was still never a shortage of boys who wanted to ride with my brother. It was at this time that Clyde met up with Henry Massingale and another boy named Dock Potter. Henry had already been in trouble down in Hill County. He'd been sentenced for burglary twice during the 1920s. During his second stint in jail, Henry escaped and hooked up with Dock Potter, who had also escaped from jail.

Bonnie was having one of her bad spells due to her burns and gunshot wounds. She stayed put while Clyde went out on the road with Henry and Dock. The very short time my brother was out with these two boys turned out to be an almost slapstick affair, reminiscent of his month up in Missouri with Hollis Hale and Frank Hardy.

The three boys decided to head towards the Enid, Oklahoma, area. Although Clyde had been through Enid before, none of them had any real familiarity with the area around Enid. Therefore, Clyde stopped their car at a gas station to get a road map. My brother asked the attendant for a map of the area. Just after the attendant went inside the station to get the map, a carload of police officers pulled up next to the three boys' car. Clyde took off hurriedly without waiting for the road map.

The peace officers noticed this peculiar behavior exhibited by Clyde and decided to catch up with his car. The cops were interested in finding out why the trio had fled at their approach. At this time, all of Oklahoma was on edge. There had been a big prison break at the state penitentiary at McAlester just a few days earlier. A trio of convicts, consisting of "Blackie" Thompson, "Whitey" Walker, and Roy Johnson, had escaped. The police probably thought that the three men in Clyde's car could have been the three McAlester escapees.

The police officers caught up with Clyde's car and stayed close behind it. The boys were very much aware of the officers' interest and hurriedly talked about what course of action to take in response. Henry asked Clyde if he should start shooting back at the officers. My brother noted that they were still in the more populated section of Enid. Clyde told Henry not to start anything yet and to wait until they were out of populated areas. Somewhere along the way, Clyde raided another National Guard armory and took some more Browning Automatic Rifles and automatic pistols. Henry held one of the BARs in his hand.

The two cars finally cleared the populated areas of Enid. Henry cut loose with his machine gun on the following police car. He emptied one of the clips, but he missed. He didn't hit their car once, but his burst of gunfire did cause the officers to back off some from following Clyde's car at such a close distance.

Undaunted, Henry replaced the empty clip with a new one. He opened fire again and emptied the clip at the police car. Though missing his intended target, Henry forced the cops to further reduce their speed. But they still kept Clyde's car in sight. This second reduction in speed by the cops was exactly what Clyde was hoping would happen. My brother gunned his auto and lost the pursuing officers in the distance.

But the boys' luck was to take a turn for the worse: their car became mired in a mudhole on the highway. There had been a great deal of rain in that part of Oklahoma and the roads were in terrible shape due to the rainfall. The three boys tried and tried to extricate their car from the morass, but it wouldn't budge. They were stuck. To complicate matters further, the pursuing police car finally caught up with them. Cautious of the situation, the cops remained distant from the car. The police got out of their car and took cover behind it. They were waiting to see what move the machine gunners would make.

Neither Henry nor Dock had ever experienced an armed confrontation with the police. They didn't know what to do or how to act in that situation, and they looked to Clyde for guidance. My brother told them to stick the machine guns out of their car and fire at the police. The two novice shootists poked their rifles out of the windows and fired at the officers' car, again missing completely. But the police didn't venture out from behind their auto; they now realized that their best chance of safety remained in being a stationary target. Plus, they didn't have anything in terms of firepower to match several automatic rifles.

While they were indeed outgunned, the officers realized they had the advantage in terms of mobility and began to circle around towards Clyde's immobile car. My brother saw he would soon be at a disadvantage due to their strategy and he knew his group would have to desert their car before the police got into a superior position. So Clyde, Henry, and Dock grabbed what guns they could carry and left on foot. The trio began to walk across a field next to the highway, constantly keeping a wary eye on the officers. The police hung back and did not engage them as they crossed the field.

The three boys made it across the field and came to a farmhouse. They saw a car sitting there and decided the auto would have to do. In their current circumstances, they could not afford to be overly choosy. They loaded their guns into it, drove off, and proceeded to run right into the officers they had just left on the highway. The cops returned to their car after the boys walked across the field. When the trio emerged back on the highway, the officers were in the first car they met. Both groups recognized each other, and the chase was on again. Clyde, again, ditched the pursuing police.

Clyde headed north from Enid, but their luck on this trip continued to go downhill. Shortly after losing the cops the second time, Clyde didn't notice a washed out bridge and drove his car off the road into a gully. None of the boys were injured, but their car was too damaged to be drivable.

Clyde, Henry, and Dock saw a nearby farmhouse and walked over to it to commandeer yet another vehicle. They told the residents they had been involved in a wreck at the washed out bridge and a woman was injured. They said they needed a car with which to get her to a hospital. The farmer and some other men returned with the boys to the scene of the accident.

Clyde got the drop on these good Samaritans with one of the BARs. He told the group that, while he hated to take their car under such circumstances, his situation forced him to do so. Clyde added that his group would not go far with it and would leave it off just as soon as they could get another auto. My brother did not like to do anything to anyone who could not afford the loss. The three boys again loaded their guns and took off.

Just a short time after leaving the scene of the last accident, the trio was nearing an old bridge at a curve in the highway. Clyde saw a Plymouth automobile coming and he decided he was going to get that car. Henry didn't like the looks of it and told Clyde it could be the police. Clyde told him they needed the car anyway, police or no police. My brother proceeded to cut the oncoming Plymouth off right there on the highway, bringing both cars to a stop. Clyde stepped out of his car with a gun, just in case it was the police. The occupants of the Plymouth turned out to be a couple and several children, who took one look at the approaching Clyde and fled from the car into a field. The three boys again transferred their guns from one car to another, making this the fourth auto they commandeered on this trip.

The three boys continued to drive north into Kansas and came to the town of Meade. Once again, Clyde and the boys found themselves in a mud hole on the highway. This time it occurred in a populated area. The three boys were unable to get it out of the mud hole. They began to look around to find whatever they could to get them out of town. Then Henry remembered seeing a crowd of people at a residence they had passed a few blocks down the street. There were several cars parked nearby. Henry told Clyde and Dock that he'd go back there and get a car. Henry took two .45 automatic pistols and walked back toward to house. Clyde and Dock remained at the car and waited for Henry to return.

There was indeed a crowd at the house down the street; there was a big croquet game in progress in the front yard. Henry decided to take a car from one of the women, figuring it would be the path of least resistance. He inquired concerning the particular car he wanted and approached the owner. Henry then demanded the car keys and pulled out one of the .45s to reinforce his sincerity, which was a big mistake. Two of the elderly women players began to swing their croquet mallets and hit Henry on the head. The croquet game erupted into a riot, with several people fleeing at the sight of the pistol and other people screaming for help. At the sound of the ruckus, several neighbors ran over to see what was going on. Henry was quickly subdued after the initial clubbings. To his credit, Henry did not fire on any of the elderly woman who were whacking him in the head. The police were called, and Henry was taken away.

Meanwhile, Clyde and Dock were still waiting down at their mired car, unaware of the scuffle at the croquet game a few blocks away. They finally got so tired of waiting on Henry to return that they got some people to help get them out of the mudhole. The two boys then drove back towards the area where they last saw Henry. Clyde and Dock drove through the area twice, looking for Henry. They noticed the excited crowd where the croquet game had taken place and figured that Henry had made off with someone's car.

Clyde and Dock then drove out of Meade on the same road they'd come in on. About ten miles outside the city, Clyde pulled over to the side of the road and waited for Henry to appear. After about 15 minutes, they two boys decided they shouldn't wait any longer. They left Kansas and drove back towards Texas, robbing gas stations and grocery stores along the way for funds.

Back in Meade, Henry Massingale had been identified by his fingerprints and photographs. He initially told the Kansas authorities he was Dock Potter before his true identity was established. The other two men who were seen with Henry were still unknown, although many guesses were made. The farmer,whose car had been stolen at the washed out bridge identified Clyde as "Blackie" Thompson. Someone else gave the inevitable identification of Pretty Boy Floyd. The newspapers conjectured that Machine Gun Kelly could have been one of the bandits. It seemed that everyone except Clyde Barrow had been identified. Henry later admitted that he had been with Clyde and that my brother was indeed the mystery bandit no onc could recognize.

Henry Massingale was tried in both Oklahoma and Kansas for his short-lived alliance with Clyde. He was tried on a charge of robbery with firearms in Kansas and was sent to the state penitentiary at Lansing to serve his twenty year sentence.

Clyde and Dock returned to Texas from their misadventures in Oklahoma and Kansas. There, they parted company, and Clyde went back to stay with Bonnie, who had recovered somewhat from the latest bout with her injuries and wounds. After his latest activities, neither Clyde nor Bonnie ventured very far from their home area in Dallas. Living on the run had taken its toll on Clyde and Bonnie. It seemed they had aged substantially from the time they had left home in early June to their return two months later. I could see the effects of all of the events on both of my parents and Mrs. Parker as well. It was as if they aged years in a span of a few weeks.

Our family kept in frequent contact with the two fugitives after Clyde came back from the Midwest in early September. We assisted Clyde and Bonnie with what items we were able to give them. Our families supplied them with household goods like clothing, food, and medicine when we met with them out on some remote road. Both seemed to realize their dependency on their kinfolk.

Buck's death had an extremely severe effect on Clyde. For sometime after coming back home, he seemed extremely reluctant to venture any distance away from his family. He knew that the same thing that had happened to Buck was going to happen to him sooner or later. Any contact with his parents and siblings became all the more precious to Clyde.

Clyde became more than willing to drive his family anywhere any of us wanted to go. There were times he would take our mother and me over to see out Aunt Susie, who lived near Martinsville, Texas. Of course, the fact he was driving his mother and kid sister around did not influence his method of driving. Clyde still drove lickety-split both over the roads and through the fields when he decided to take a short-cut to his destination. My mother and I would bounce around on the car seats as Clyde hit the bumps and took the curves at high speed. Although these antics petrified my mother and me, Clyde seemed oblivious to our anxiety. He seemed to relish such uninhibited driving.

One of the things I particularly remember about these trips over to Aunt Susie's was one experience I had when I went horseback riding. All of the older Barrow kids had grown up around horses in Telico and out at Uncle Frank's farm. Clyde especially liked to ride horses, and I still remember him pretending like he was Jesse James riding his horse, Red Fox. All of us picked up this love of horses from my father. Aunt Susie had horses at her place, and I continued to ride horses during these trips to her house—until I came across one particular horse. This horse did not take a liking to me. After the saddle was readied, I got up on the animal, and we took off. Unfortunately, we didn't stay together very long. The horse galloped up to a fence at full speed and then came to a screeching stop right up against the fence. I was unable to stop with the horse, and I went sailing through the air, over both the horse and the fence, coming to a hard landing several feet away. I wasn't seriously hurt, but the experience stopped my career in horseback riding.

There was another occasion during his stay where Clyde himself had a bit of misfortune with another means of transportation—this one nonliving. While I came out on the losing end with a horse, Clyde came in second-best with a motorcycle. Our brother, L.C., had acquired himself a motorcycle and brought it out to one of our meetings to show it to Clyde. Clyde was very impressed with this new vehicle and he had to try it out himself. L.C. gave his older brother a quick crash course on motorcycle operation and then Clyde took it out for a spin. He drove off in the distance and finally disappeared from sight. Our family felt Clyde would be back after just a very few minutes, so we waited. The few minutes then stretched into many minutes and we became concerned. We organized into search parties in order to try to locate the missing cyclist. Then, we heard a gunshot and headed towards that direction, not knowing what we would find there. We found Clyde pinned underneath the motorcycle. My brother had lost control of the bike and went off the road. He was unable to get out from beneath the vehicle and had fired a shot to get our attention. Neither my brother nor the motorcycle were seriously damaged in this misadventure.

This same motorcycle figured in another escapade during this time, although Clyde was not involved this go-around. L.C.'s wife, Audrey Faye, and I ran around together. The two of us would sometimes "borrow" an auto which would be parked at my parents' gas station when it was not being used and we knew who owned it. Audrey Faye and I would take it out for a quick spin around west Dallas and would bring it back to the station afterwards. One day, we did this with L.C.'s car when he and Audrey Faye were over visiting. L. C. saw us take off in his car, and he took exception to it for some reason. He jumped on his motorcycle and gave chase. Both of us in the car could tell that he was not amused and Audrey Faye began to drive for her life. L.C. finally caught up with us on his motorcycle and forced the car over to the curb.

Audrey Faye was scared and didn't want to wait around to see why her husband was so upset. While L.C. was getting off of his motorcycle, Audrey Faye bolted out of the car and began running. L.C. started to go after her. She came to a wire fence, but that didn't hinder her in the slightest: she cleared that fence in a single bound, much like a runner would go over a hurdle in a track meet. That leap for life amazed both L.C. and myself. In fact, that forced display of athletic ability completely stopped my brother in his tracks, and he fell over on the ground laughing as hard as he could. When she was convinced that there was no wrathful husband to face, Audrey Faye came back. All three of us drove back to our parents' gas station, still chuckling over her remarkable athletic ability.

Chapter 16

Despite all of the family high-jinks and pratfalls, none of us ever forgot Clyde's status as the most wanted fugitive in the southwest in the early fall of 1933. Despite what meager help our family could provide, we knew that the robberies would continue. Therefore, we were not surprised to see articles in the newspaper connecting Clyde with grocery store robberies in the north central Texas area.

For example, on September 16, Clyde supposedly raided a Piggly Wiggly store on Lancaster Avenue in Ft. Worth. He was later identified as the robber by three people who were in the store at the time of the holdup. Then, just nine days later on September 25, both Clyde and Bonnie were accused of committing another grocery store robbery in McKinney, Texas.

Our family initially had some doubts about Clyde's participation in these banditries, but his presence at one of them was verified by one of his old west Dallas running buddies. This boy told us that Clyde told him that he did indeed commit the robbery in McKinney.

After the troubles up in Missouri and Iowa which resulted in Buck's death, Clyde and Bonnie went deep into hiding after they brought W.D. back to Dallas. But there was still no let-up in the newspapers concerning the "crime wave" of 1933.

On the same day that Buck was buried, a wealthy oilman from Oklahoma City who had been abducted on July 22 was released by his kidnappers. This oilman's name was Charles Urschel, and the people who abducted him were named Albert Bates, George R. Kelly, and Kathryn Kelly.

The Urschel kidnapping case dominated the front pages of the newspapers in the southwest in August, September, and October. There were in-laws mixed in with the outlaws in this case: Ora Shannon, Kathryn's mother, was involved also. Mrs. Shannon was married to named Robert G. Shannon, who lived just south of the small town of Paradise in Wise County, Texas. Urschel had been held captive near the Shannon farm.

Kathryn Kelly's husband was known as "Machine Gun" Kelly in

the newspapers. George Kelly's real name was George F. Barnes, Jr., originally from Memphis, Tennessee. George Barnes was a bootlegger during Prohibition, and he gravitated west from Memphis into Oklahoma City where he met Kathryn. Sparks flew, and George and Kathryn were married shortly thereafter. Kathryn was living in a house in Ft. Worth at the time. George Barnes had become George Kelly in his bootlegging days, and it was under the name of George Ramsey Kelly that he became associated with the north central Texas area. Neither Clyde nor Buck had ever had any association with Machine Gun Kelly, but other men of note in the underworld were affiliated with him. Machine Gun Kelly became associated with a team of bandits that included Eddie Bentz, Eddie Doll, and Albert Bates. This group had robbed banks all of the way across the country from Colfax, Washington, to Tupelo, Mississippi. Machine Gun Kelly was credited with involvement with several bank robberies in north central Texas, including a heist in Sherman in 1931 and holdups in Ponder and Blue Ridge in 1932. The Kellys and Bates decided to try the kidnapping racket, and it turned out to be their undoing. They targeted Charles Urschel and abducted him at his house late one evening while he and some other people were playing bridge. While the trio were negotiating the ransom conditions with the family, the oilman was held hostage at a farmhouse in rural Wise county. The kidnappers got $200,000 and then released Urschel unharmed near Norman, Oklahoma. The police were on the case immediately after Urschel was returned home. Kathryn had unwisely confided in two Ft. Worth detectives, believing they could be bought off. These detectives informed the G-men of what Kathryn told them, and the Kellys and Bates were immediately considered the prime suspects in the crime.

Albert Bates was arrested in Denver, Colorado on August 12 for charges unrelated to the Urschel kidnapping. On the same day, an Urschel-connected raid was made on the Shannon farm in Wise County, resulting in the arrest of several Shannon family members, including Ora Shannon. Also arrested in the raid was Harvey Bailey, one of the Memorial Day escapees from the Kansas State Prison in Lansing. Ironically, Bailey had no connection at all with the Urschel kidnapping itself, but had driven down to the Shannon farm to return a Tommy gun he borrowed from Machine Gun Kelly. The Shannon farm raid was carried out at sunrise. Harvey Bailey was planning to leave later that same morning. Bailey was brought down to the Dallas

County Jail.

On September 4, Labor Day, Harvey Bailey made an incredible jailbreak from the county jail. There had been many articles in the newspapers about how secure the jail was from an attacking army of gangsters. Bailey managed to bribe one of the jailers to smuggle a pistol into the jail to allow him to escape. The jailbreaker took along a hostage, stole a car in downtown Dallas, and headed into Oklahoma. But Bailey was arrested as he drove through Ardmore and was returned to the Dallas County Jail. Shortly after this escape, Bailey, Bates, and the Shannons were all taken to Oklahoma City to be put on trial in the federal courts for the Urschel kidnapping.

George and Kathryn Kelly had taken their share of the kidnapping ransom and drove into Mexico with no problems. Upon hearing about the arrest of Robert and Ora Shannon, George and Kathryn returned to the states and crisscrossed the country. They were betrayed by a dispossessed farm family who was hitchhiking across Texas and who Kathryn picked up and befriended. The family told the G-men where the Kellys were hiding in Memphis. George and Kathryn were arrested there on September 26 and were returned to Oklahoma City to stand trial. The Kellys, Bates, Bailey, and the Shannons all received life sentences and were hustled off to federal prisons to serve their time. The Urschel kidnapping case monopolized the front pages of the major newspapers in the southwest during August and September. Newspapers across Texas and Oklahoma insured wide coverage due to the location of Urschel's kidnapping in Oklahoma and Bailey's escape from Dallas.

Neither Clyde nor Bonnie felt neglected at all by the press given to the Urschel kidnapping. They were relieved to have been given a breather from the seemingly non-stop stories concerning the whereabouts of the so-called "Barrow Gang." Clyde and Bonnie were content to maintain a low profile around north central Texas and to frequently visit their loved ones. They were more than willing to let the Machine Gun Kellys and Pretty Boy Floyds have the headlines if it meant no additional police pressure on them.

The month of October passed without any major incidents involving Clyde and Bonnie. We continued to meet with them out in remote sites, well away from any populated areas or well-traveled thoroughfares. Both the Barrow and Parker families kept them supplied with what we were able to afford in terms of necessities. Clyde and

Bonnie were operating pretty much on their own at this time. All of their previous associates were either dead, in prison, or in hiding elsewhere.

No longer were we able to take the money Clyde would give us and go downtown to purchase them suits and dresses. Clyde's grocery store holdups were providing them with only a subsistence-level existence, and we were not able to supply much more than that. They were living totally in their car and in abandoned farm houses. The days of the big bank robberies were gone as were the days of living in tourist camp cabins. Any person who ever thought a life of outlawry was one of complete freedom and reckless prosperity had only to see Clyde and Bonnie in the autumn of 1933 to become totally disillusioned. It was a truly miserable existence, and it made living a humble life in west Dallas look good by comparison.

While Clyde and Bonnie were continuing to maintain a low profile, the newspapers continued to headline the continuing developments in the "crime wave." About the same time as the Urschel kidnappers were taken off to prison, the newspapers in the southwest began to feature front page stories about what was going on in the states of Indiana and Illinois concerning a group of escaped convicts who broken out of the Indiana State Prison at Michigan City on September 26, the same day Machine Gun Kelly was arrested in Memphis.

In the three weeks after this mid western jailbreak, one of the escaped convicts was slain in a gunfight with a posse of vigilantes, a couple of the escapees had been recaptured, and a bank in Ohio had been robbed by the others. Shortly after the Ohio robbery, the same escapees invaded a county jail in Lima, Ohio, to free an arrested associate. The sheriff was shot and killed during the raid. The group then raided a police station to get adequate weapons and supplies (Tommy guns, riot shotguns, bulletproof vests, police badges, and ammunition) to carry out their planned activities. The states of Indiana, Ohio, and Illinois were calling out the state militias, the county vigilante organizations, and even the WWI veterans groups to help combat what the newspapers were calling the "Terror Gang."

The individual who was freed from the Lima jail by the escapees would eventually become as well-known as Clyde and Bonnie, although they would always be popularly known by their first names while he would be recognized by his last name: Dillinger. I would later become acquainted with his father, a kindly old gentleman named

John Dillinger Sr.

While Dillinger and his cronies were causing an uproar in the Midwest, the Southwest was having its own troubles, even with Clyde and Bonnie lying low. There were still a few of the Lansing, Kansas Memorial Day jail breakers on the loose, including the notorious Wilbur Underhill. Pretty Boy Floyd was still occasionally sighted. The three escapees from the McAlester, Oklahoma prison were still being widely sought by officers.

In fact, a robbery was committed in East Texas that had peace officers disagreeing over who committed it: the so-called "Barrow Gang" or the "Whitey-Blackie Gang." The robbery was committed at an oil refinery in early November, and some policemen were blaming "Blackie" Thompson and Mr. and Mrs. "Whitey" Walker, while other officers were blaming Clyde, Bonnie, and an unidentified man.

I personally don't believe that Clyde and Bonnie had anything to do with the robbery at the oil refinery. Whoever held up the place got several thousand dollars, and Clyde never showed any signs of having a large bankroll. Also, Clyde and Bonnie were not taking on any running partners. There were plenty of boys in west Dallas who would've liked to have gone on the road with Clyde, but my brother would have none of it. There was no third person with them who could've assisted them in robbing the refinery.

Our suspicions were confirmed when the refinery workers who were present when the holdup took place identified the Walkers and "Blackie" Thompson. Also, the employees described both robbers as being tall men and my brother was only of medium height at five-foot-seven. But then, the man who helped in robbing the Bucher store in Hillsboro was about six feet tall, but he was still identified as the five-seven Clyde. Many accounts still credit my brother with the refinery holdup, but he wasn't there.

Clyde was content at this point in time to subsist on the money he accumulated from his grocery store and service station robberies. His motivation for his life of crime was anger over his prison experience, not avarice or ambition to accumulate a huge bankroll. My brother was in regular contact with the only people with whom he had any emotional involvement: his family and Bonnie's people. He was getting by with the proceeds from his holdups, the material assistance our family could give him, and the psychological support he got from being with his family members. But his attitude had changed from earlier that year, especially after Buck was slain. His perspective on everything was even more fatalistic than it had previously been after his initial release from Huntsville. Both Clyde and Bonnie had become preoccupied with their own mortality. They were not foolish enough to believe they could continue indefinitely in the way they were going. They both knew what their inevitable end was going to be; they just didn't know when or where it would happen.

Clyde's and Bonnie's fatalistic outlook was greatly reinforced by the sudden and unexpected passing of Billie Jean Parker's two young children. Despite what has been written in the past, neither Clyde nor myself ever had any contact with these children. The kids were the offspring of Billie and Fred Mace. Bonnie doted on the youngsters, of course; she was a noted baby-adorer.

It was in the mid-autumn of 1933 that the two children suddenly took ill and were stricken with food poisoning. Both of them became sick within a very few weeks of each other and died. This double tragedy pushed their aunt Bonnie deeper into a state of melancholy. Both the Barrow family and the Parker family had been stricken with the death of loved ones during 1933.

These tragedies made Clyde think about his own passing, and he began to decide on some of the particulars concerning his last rites. My brother had even decided on the type of marker, including the color, that would be placed on his final resting place. He told our mother that he wanted a dark colored stone with the motto "Gone, But Not Forgotten." Our parents had not yet put up a marker on Buck's plot, due to financial considerations. I am sure that they were waiting for the inevitable end concerning their other fugitive son. Then both of my brothers would be buried together, side by side, in our family plot.

Bonnie, on the other hand, began speaking to her mother about being buried side-by-side with Clyde. Bonnie knew that she and Clyde were going to go down together. She knew Clyde would never surrender, and she would never leave Clyde. There was no alternative for either Clyde or Bonnie. They knew Clyde had no chance of getting a long prison sentence like Raymond Hamilton had gotten. Clyde would get the electric chair for sure. There have been stories about Clyde offering to surrender if he was given a life sentence or if Bonnie would be allowed to go free. These stories are pure fiction. Both sides of the equation knew how the conflict would end between Clyde and the forces of the law.

Nevertheless, Bonnie's family, particularly her mother, did not seem to believe a violent death by police bullets was inevitable for their loved one. Both Mrs. Parker and Billie Jean were overheard on several occasions when they were talking to Bonnie during our clandestine visits, trying to influence Bonnie towards working out a deal in which Clyde would be turned in to the authorities, and Bonnie would get off with only a short-term or suspended sentence. Of course, Clyde would wind up getting the works. To her credit, Bonnie never even seriously considered the idea of assisting in a plot to turn Clyde over to the law. But I've always wondered if, on the night of November 22, 1933, someone tried to force the particular issue unilaterally.

By late November, roughly three months had passed since Clyde had dropped W.D. off back in Dallas, and he'd left to pick cotton with his family in Houston. There'd been no contact since then. It was common knowledge around west Dallas that W.D. was the "mystery man" with Clyde during early 1933, but no one ever informed the authorities. With the Jones family out of the picture, the Barrows and the Parkers were the only people who maintained any close contact with the fugitives. We were certainly the only people who were privy to the details of the secretive meetings with the couple in the remote areas of Dallas County. Yet, even with this tight web of secrecy and security stretched around the affairs of Clyde and Bonnie, a breach was made. Someone had talked to the authorities. As a result, we were almost killed on the evening of November 22.

That night, five of us were set to meet up with Clyde and Bonnie. We had agreed to meet on the highway near the small community of Sowers in west Dallas County. Five of us were driving towards Sowers: our mother, myself, Bonnie's mother, Billie Jean, and Joe Bill Francis, a fine young man from west Dallas with whom I was going steady (and would later marry). We were in Joe Bill's auto. He was driving, and my mother was in the front seat passenger area. I was seated in the back with the two Parker women. We drove towards the setting sun intending to meet with Clyde and Bonnie.

There have been all kinds of conjectures as to why we were meeting our fugitive family members at the site just a half mile from the little settlement of Sowers. I think the great mystery of the rendezvous point derives from the fact that we had met with Clyde and Bonnie at the same spot the previous evening. To keep authorities guessing, we generally did not meet at the same location on consecutive nights. If we would have used a very few sites on a regular basis, sooner or later someone nearby would have seen the regular meetings. If these observers recognized Clyde and Bonnie, the authorities would have been informed immediately. Sooner or later, an unfriendly reception committee, comprised of machine-gunning officers, would have been hidden at the site waiting for Clyde and Bonnie to show up. We were determined not to let that happen; we wanted to keep the two kids with us as long as possible.

The reason we agreed to meet with Clyde and Bonnie at the same location on the following evening was simply one of convenience. November 21, 1933, was our mother's birthday. The two fugitives had driven in from Oklahoma City. I don't know what Clyde was doing up there, but whatever it was, it wasn't important enough to prevent him from remembering his mother on her birthday, although the time factor didn't allow him to purchase her a present. Clyde told our mother that he was unable to give her a gift, but he would give her a present later. It didn't bother our mother at all. Just being able to visit with Clyde was good enough for her. My brother did indeed get our mother a nice birthday gift later as promised. Clyde never failed when he made a promise regarding any of his family members.

Our families spent almost the whole day with Clyde and Bonnie out there near Sowers on November 21. As always, a number of photographs were taken of all of us. The time we spent with the two kids went by all too rapidly, and finally, the inevitable hour to separate came at last. But before we left to go our opposite ways, Clyde said to our mother: "Mama, I am going to leave town and will drive around until tomorrow night and will meet you. I am leaving here for a while." Clyde had been visiting with us pretty regularly throughout the autumn. He apparently wanted to get just one more visit in before he and Bonnie left the Dallas area. Therefore, in the interest of convenience, we all agreed to meet here again at dusk on the following day.

Unbeknownst to us, at least the majority of us in the car, another party was already in the area awaiting the arrival of Clyde and Bonnie, but their intentions were not quite as friendly as ours. The not-so-friendly group hid themselves in a ditch near where the family meeting would take place. The concealed group consisted of the Dallas County Sheriff Richard Allen "Smoot" Schmid and three of his deputies, Bob Alcorn, Ted Hinton, and Ed Caster. This quartet had automatic weapons pointed towards the highway where they expected Clyde and

Bonnie to appear.

Of course, the police were not there by accident; someone had tipped them off as to when and where we were to meet up with Bonnie and Clyde. It had to be someone who was familiar with the Barrow and Parker families. Of the five travelling to meet Clyde and Bonnie, my mother and I were the only two who could be completely eliminated as the culprit. Even to this day, there are still debates between historians, researchers, and writers as to who the informant truly was. The county officers knew but never revealed the true identity.

It was just getting dark when Clyde's car appeared on the horizon. As they approached, we signaled with our headlights. The officers apparently saw this as a sign of recognition, because just as Clyde and Bonnie passed us in their car, the cops opened fire. We were all sitting in our car on the side of the road, waiting for Clyde. Our stationary status made us sitting ducks for the police gunfire when they began to shoot. There was no "halt," or "surrender," or even a plain "stick 'em up;" they just began firing. Clyde's quick instincts served him well. He saw the stream of bullets coming from the ditch and made a quick getaway, moving faster and faster away from us and the police.

Clyde had been almost even with the front of our car when the officers began to fire. No one in our car was hit by any stray bullets, nor was our vehicle struck by any. But the firing was close enough that just about everyone in our car ducked down to take cover. I was the only person who didn't head for the floorboard. My brother's safety was my only concern at that moment, and I wasn't conscious of the danger represented by gunfire. I saw Clyde and Bonnie turn off on a side road and disappear over the crest of a small hill, outrunning the range of the posse's barrage. I yelled out to the others in our car, "Yonder they go up the hill! They haven't got him!" When the gunfire ceased, I could hear my mother, who was still crouched down on the floorboard, praying for my brother's safety.

We didn't wait to see what was going to happen next. The hidden officers were not making any attempt to approach our vehicle, and we were not going to make ourselves available for them. Joe Bill whipped his car back out on the highway, and we headed back towards west Dallas. All of us were thoroughly shaken and upset by the experience. We were all rattled by the first-hand encounter of the law's determination to end Clyde's run for good.

Clyde and Bonnie headed south from the scene toward the town of

Grand Prairie. Clyde found the Ft. Worth road, which he had wanted to use, torn up. The road was not the only thing torn up: both Clyde and Bonnie had been hit by the police gunfire, and their car had been shredded in the barrage. They were having to travel on at least one flat tire. Clyde finally stopped his car on the highway by the government airfield. My brother knew he would have to commandeer another car and could not afford to be too choosy. The next drivable auto that came along would have to suffice at the moment.

Clyde saw approaching headlights on the highway and ran out onto the road in front of the oncoming vehicle. He pulled a gun on the occupants just in case they happened to be more policemen. My brother was unsure just how big the police ambush was in terms of numbers, but, after the huge posse that had chased him near Dexter, Iowa, he could not afford to take any chances. Clyde ordered the two men inside the now-stopped car to get out. They refused to do so.

Clyde demonstrated his sincerity by shooting off one man's hat, causing the two motorists to scramble out of the automobile. These men later claimed that Clyde had hijacked their car in a simple highway robbery and that he also cleaned out their wallets. What really happened was they immediately hid the money they were carrying in the side pockets of the car doors, thinking it was actually a highway holdup. Of course, both men were scared, and they didn't really realize just what was going on. When Clyde and Bonnie drove off in their car, their wallets went with the auto in the side pockets on the doors.

Due to the forced nature of their circumstances, they could not transfer their belongings to the new auto. Most of their possessions were left. Getting out of the Dallas area as fast as possible was the sole imperative now and they headed north into Oklahoma.

Clyde was heading back towards the Sallisaw area to try to approach the Floyd family for help in arranging a hideout somewhere in the Cookson hills. Both he and Bonnie had been shot in the knees. For Bonnie, the gunshot wounds were especially bad; one of the bullets had reinjured the right knee which had been severely burned in the auto accident near Wellington, Texas, five months prior. That leg had never really healed properly and the bullet wound would leave her leg permanently drawn limp.

Clyde first drove to the residence of one of Pretty Boy Floyd's brothers. The police had been watching this particular brother's house in the hopes that Charley Floyd would pay him a family visit. The first brother did not want to take the chance of Clyde Barrow getting into a gun battle with officers who were hoping to catch Pretty Boy Floyd. Clyde. Remembering what happened when he walked in on the police trap set for Odell Chambless, Clyde agreed and went over to the other Floyd brother's house to try to arrange for a temporary refuge. This may have been the only time Clyde and Pretty Boy Floyd might have actually met with each other. I do know they did meet sometime in late 1933, and this seems like the most likely occasion for them to make contact. I also believe this was the last time Clyde ever tried to make contact with Pretty Boy or any of his family members. In 1934, Clyde never showed any interest or concern with seeking assistance from the Floyds.

Meanwhile, the Sowers ambush was causing an immediate sensation in and around Dallas. It had been well over ten months since the west Dallas gun battle in which Malcolm Davis had been killed. Clyde's "adventures" had generated a lot of interest among the Dallas area newspaper reading public. His name was always a good circulation booster and the papers really took off with the Sowers conflict. The car Clyde and Bonnie had abandoned along the highway near the airfield was towed into downtown Dallas and publicly displayed. The men whose car was hijacked were interviewed. The sheriff and the three deputies who made up the ambush posse were photographed with the personal items which were left behind in Clyde's bullet-disabled auto.

Chapter 17

The Sowers ambush created a huge sensation in the media of Dallas during the era. But much of the publicity was not favorable to Smoot Schmid or the deputies who had accompanied him. The lawmen were ridiculed with comments concerning the fact Clyde had let them get away again or that my brother gave them only 24 hours in which to get out of town. Our family was not among those who were giving the sheriff's posse a hard time. Out at Sowers, we had come closer than we'd ever either intended or wanted to be to the conflict between the forces of the law and my brother. We figured that the Sowers ambush would be typical of the way the cops would eventually catch up with Clyde. Our family knew what was going to happen sooner or later, but we certainly did not want to be there when the inevitable happened.

Then the Dallas County sheriff's department dropped a bombshell of their own in response to the ragging they had gotten over Clyde's escape and their perceived ineffectiveness in dealing with the so-called "Barrow Gang." The lawmen announced they had already apprehended one of the primary members of Clyde's "gang" and had been holding him in jail until the others could be rounded up. Their mystery prisoner turned out to be none other than W.D. Jones.

Just a few days before the cops had set up the Sowers ambush, W.D. had been arrested down in Houston by the Dallas County officials. The officers had received a "confidential tip," obviously from one of W.D.'s fellow cotton pickers, concerning the identity of the mysterious third man who had accompanied Clyde and Buck during the spring and summer of 1933. The arrest was made without incident or resistance, and W.D. was brought up to the Dallas County Jail. There was no word to the press concerning the capture of one of Clyde's known associates.

The news W.D. had been apprehended and held in jail was a complete and total surprise to our family. We had not heard anything from any of the Joneses since Mrs. Jones had moved down to Houston. Our family had hoped W.D. had finally learned his lesson about the ultimate futility of going out on the road with my brother. Clyde himself was pleased that W.D. had finally found that the humblest honest labor was still superior to the life of an outlaw. But W.D.'s change for the better was made too late; he was in jail, charged with being an accessory to Clyde Barrow.

Clyde and Bonnie stayed away from Dallas for a full week after the Sowers ambush. They didn't return to their home area until November 29, after their attempt to make contact with Pretty Boy Floyd's family. It was at this time my mother began to keep track of the dates that Clyde would come back home to visit. She kept those dates marked on the wall of our house. After the incident at Sowers, she felt Clyde couldn't last much longer out on the road. Every visit he and Bonnie made to visit his family became more and more precious in my mother's eyes. Only the months and days were noted on the wall, as we were frequently being visited by reporters at this time. My mother did not want them to get any ideas concerning how frequently Clyde was coming home. The dates themselves could've signified anything to those who didn't know what they represented.

The ambush near Sowers was the first time Clyde had been involved in any significant armed conflict with the forces of the law in four months. My brother had not been shot at by the police since escaping the huge dragnet generated by the Dexfield Park firefight. The notion of the Sowers ambush especially infuriated my brother, particularly the fact that his family in general and his mother in particular had been used as unknowing bait in a plot to kill him. Clyde's anger toward law enforcement was driven to an even deeper level, leaving him bound and determined to seek retribution.

Clyde's rage had reached a dangerous point. Our family hoped his anger would subside over a period of time and that nothing would act as a spark to set off an explosive reaction. But then, the spark appeared; messages began coming from the Eastham prison farm near Huntsville. Raymond Hamilton, Clyde's old off-again, on-again partner from the summer of 1932, was wanting out of prison, and he was looking to my brother to break him out.

Hamilton was sent down to Eastham prison farm in late 1933

to serve his 200 years consecutive sentence for his crimes during the summer and autumn of 1932. Some of these holdups had been committed in association with Clyde; others, like the two Cedar Hill bank robberies, were committed with other people or by himself. Although he had accumulated well over 200 years of prison time, Raymond had no intentions of remaining behind bars.

Clyde Barrow had no real obligations toward Raymond Hamilton. They were neither old buddies nor did they run together back in the old west Dallas days. Clyde and Raymond were thrown together by the circumstances of their identification in connection with the John Bucher slaying in Hillsboro. The newspapers had both of them inside the store holding guns on Bucher; but, in reality, neither of them were in the store. Clyde was outside waiting in the car and Raymond wasn't even in Texas at the time. Yet, both of them were connected with the killing because one of the real killers resembled Raymond, and Clyde had been previously known to the Buchers back in the late 1920s due to his acquaintance with Bucher's son.

Raymond's charges and sentences were not a direct result of any action done on Clyde's behalf. In fact, Raymond had been separated from my brother for several months when he was apprehended. Raymond's desire to drink, dance, and socialize in public places led to his arrest. Clyde had warned him multiple times that wanted men and fugitives had no business in a public social scene.

It was not only the fact of how Raymond was arrested, but the fact that Raymond was arrested at all that differentiated his attitude from Clyde's outlook. My brother made no apologies about his intentions to never be taken alive. His family knew about his intentions in this regard, and I am sure Clyde impressed this certainty upon Raymond after the Eugene Moore killing at Atoka. Clyde had very little sympathy towards Raymond's arrest from the areas of both principle (don't let them take you alive-period) and practicality (don't get caught while wearing roller skates at a public place).

For some reason, maybe the chance to seek revenge on Eastham prison and on the law system, retrieving Raymond from prison appealed to Clyde. He despised Eastham prison during his incarceration, which he called a "burning hell." Helping Raymond would kill two birds with one stone. Our family was unaware Clyde was entertaining any notions towards freeing Raymond and that he was listening to Hamilton's entreaties.

Raymond Hamilton wasn't the only past associate communicating messages concerning my brother. W.D. Jones was talking nonstop to the police from his cell in the Dallas county jail. He was telling about his months on the highway with Clyde and Buck. W.D. was definitely "singing," but he was singing a song Clyde had taught him, note by note, verse by verse. The first verse Clyde wanted W.D. to memorize was the one concerning W.D.'s age. In reality, W.D. was 19 or 20 when he joined up with Clyde and Bonnie in December of 1932. Had he revealed his age, he'd have been tried as an adult. Therefore, when he was arrested, W. D. became a scared 16-year-old kid when he joined up with Clyde.

Verse two of the song my brother drilled into W.D. concerned the "scared" part of the "scared 16-year-old kid" charade. W.D. had went off with Clyde simply because he desired to, and he did it out of his own free will. But there was no way W.D. could've admitted that fact if he was arrested; it would have been the equivalent of signing his own execution warrant. So my brother told W.D. to tell the cops he was basically shanghaied into joining Clyde and Bonnie and doing the driving. W.D. was to say that he was so "intimidated" by the "ruthless" Clyde Barrow that he felt in fear of his life if he did not cooperate with my brother's demand for his driving services.

There was a third verse to W.D.'s song concerning his actions during the gunfights that occurred while with Buck and Clyde. W.D. had a lot to answer for in regards to the shootings. He was on scene, gun in hand, for each and every killing that had taken place. It would be very difficult for W.D. to try convincing the courts he was not involved in the conflicts, but that is exactly what he did. W.D. claimed he was physically incapacitated during each of the affairs. At the shooting in Alma, he swore he had blacked out due to the impact of the car crash. In actuality, he had shot at the officers when the city marshal was slain. In Joplin, he was allegedly hit by a bullet and was too shocked to return fire. But, of course, during the Joplin shoot out, W.D. was inside the garage rapidly returning fire. He continued similar state of shock excuses in the telling of the Wellington and Temple activity.

His claims to have been "conked" on the head each and every time someone was shot and killed were strictly his own creations. Clyde thought no one in their right mind would have taken such outlandish claims seriously, especially when there were so many eyewitnesses around who could contradict W.D.'s alibis. My brother always found W.D.'s version of events to be very funny and entertaining when he saw them in the newspaper.

Just before the calendar flipped from November to December, Clyde and Bonnie returned to Dallas. Still keeping track of his visits, my mother's handwritten records noted visits on December 8th, 10th, 14th, 20th, and 29th. Our mother was keeping track of the dates of Clyde's visits. The frequency of his visits dropped somewhat from the level of the previous autumn before the Sowers ambush. I began to get the impression something was "up," but I didn't know what was going to happen. We had no way of knowing that parties representing Raymond Hamilton were approaching my brother. Clyde certainly wasn't saying anything and we weren't asking any questions. We were still on "pins and needles" concerning Clyde's emotions over the Sowers trap. He never made any inquiries about exactly who tipped off the officers, and no one was admitting anything. All we could do was be more careful concerning our meetings with Clyde and Bonnie. Clyde would let our mother only know where the meetings would be, and she would tell the driver where to drive the car. As a result, all of the visits with the fugitives in December were quiet affairs, with no unpleasant surprises.

December of 1933 was a fairly quiet ending to the southwest's "crime wave" in that year, at least when compared to the spring, summer, and early autumn. There were no major occurrences like the Kansas City Massacre, the Urschel kidnapping, and the big jailbreaks from the penitentiaries at Lansing, Kansas, and McAlester, Oklahoma. Most of the activity related to famous fugitives was centered around the Upper Midwest, especially in Chicago. The Chicago police were involved in a struggle with what the newspapers called the "Terror Gang." John Dillinger was associated with this group, which consisted of the prisoners whom he helped to escape from the Indiana state prison. John

Hamilton, as old friend of Dillinger's, shot and killed a Chicago cop at a garage in mid-December. As a result, the Chicago police's "Dillinger Squad" was raiding hideouts where the "Terror Gang" could be hiding. Just a few days after the slaying by Hamilton, the "Dillinger Squad" raided a suspected hideout and killed three armed criminals.

Though none of the men killed were associated with Dillinger, the police counted the raid as a victory because the men had resisted arrest. December turned out to be the calm before the storm, even with all of the fireworks in Chicago. The month of January, 1934 started off fast and furious. The stage was set at the very end of December when a posse of local, state, and federal officers cornered Wilbur Underhill, one of the remaining escapees from the Kansas prison still not captured. Underhill had gotten married in the town of Coalgate, Oklahoma, a few weeks earlier. He used his real name during the ceremony, and this fact was relayed to the police. The officers were given a fresh start on Underhill's trail and they didn't lose it. He was traced to a small house in Shawnee, Oklahoma, where he was honeymooning with his new bride and two other people, Ralph Roe, one of Underhill's associates, and a local beautician from Shawnee that Roe had picked up. Both Underhill and the Shawnee beautician were mortally wounded in the resulting gunbattle.

Ralph Roe and the new Mrs. Underhill were arrested. Underhill was taken to the hospital at the state prison at McAlester where he died on January 6, 1934. Ralph Roe was tried and sentenced to a long prison term for one of the bank robberies he had committed with Underhill. Roe was one of the first prisoners shipped out to Alcatraz when the prison opened later in 1934, and he was involved in the first escape attempt off of the "Rock" in 1937. Both Roe and another prisoner named Ted Cole disappeared in the waters of San Francisco Bay and were presumed to have drowned.

January 6, the same day that Underhill died, marked the day that Chicago cops scored a victory in their conflict with the gangs up there by killing "Handsome Jack" Klutas, a professional kidnapper who had many connections in the Chicago area underworld.

Clyde had no connections with either Wilbur Underhill or Jack Klutas and showed no significant emotion concerning the deaths of these two men. Underhill's record of wanton killing repulsed Clyde. It is true Clyde had fired at armed officers coming after him, but Underhill had gunned down nonthreatening shop keepers in temporary fits of rage. Underhill had wanted to kill several of the hostages that were taken during the Lansing, Kansas, prison break but was prevented from doing so by the more stable Harvey Bailey.

Clyde's periodic visits continued into January. My mother's notations concerning the first half of the month include the fact that Clyde visited the home folks twice on the 4th of January, as well as the 7th, 10th, 13th, and the 15th. As far as our family could tell, all continued as quietly as it had for several months with my fugitive brother. In terms of any contributions to the continuing "crime wave," Clyde had become so quiet as to be almost nonexistent.

But there were still enough fugitives from justice around to take up the slack. The excitement concerning the apprehension of both Underhill and Klutas had just begun to die when a new round of criminal activity exploded in the headlines. Bob Brady from Ada, Oklahoma, one of the very few remaining escapees still at large from the Kansas prison break, was shot and killed in Kansas by a posse. Then the "Terror Gang" of Indiana was accused of robbing a bank in East Chicago, a suburb of Chicago just across the state line in their home state. It was during this robbery that John Dillinger was identified as the killer of an East Chicago policeman who had responded to the bank alarm.

Yet, the news of the death of Bob Brady and the East Chicago bank robbery was blasted into oblivion by evening newspaper headlines and radio news bulletins on the night of January 16, 1934. Clyde Barrow had raided the Eastham prison farm and had released Raymond Hamilton. Four other convicts were also freed in the raid. One of the prison guards was mortally wounded by one of the escaping prisoners.

Clyde and Raymond undoubtedly considered the raid on the prison farm as a master stroke against the state penal system. But the attack on the Eastham farm was the beginning of a chain of events that would eventually culminate in the deaths of the infamous Clyde Barrow and Bonnie Parker.

Chapter 18

The news that Clyde Barrow was associated with the Eastham prison break did not come as a complete and total shock to our family. We had an idea what was going on when Floyd Hamilton suddenly popped up in our affairs a few weeks prior. Up until this time, the Barrow family had not had any connection or involvement with Floyd. All of a sudden, Raymond's big brother suddenly expressed an urgency to meet with Clyde.

My brother L.C. had taken Floyd out to meet with Clyde and Bonnie on two or three occasions in December and early January. Raymond's dope-dealing prison buddy had gotten in touch with Floyd, who had contacted L.C., who had in turn set up a couple of meetings just between Clyde, L.C., and Floyd. Floyd and Raymond's friend had been in charge of getting the guns and positioning them just before the escape took place.

Clyde called the afternoon of January 16 and asked for some street clothing to be brought up to a rural location on Highway 114 near the small town of Rhome. L.C. and Floyd Hamilton took the requested items up to the prearanged site. I want to emphasize that the planning and follow-through for the Eastham prison break represented the only face-to-face contact Floyd Hamilton ever had with Clyde and Bonnie. Decades later, Floyd wrote a book in which he said he knew Clyde when my brother was a small schoolboy, and he was the much- trusted middleman Clyde turned towards in order to set up the secret family meetings. These stories are completely and totally untrue; Floyd was never part of any meetings outside of the time period of the Eastham prison farm escape.

All those involved figured police scrutiny would be especially intense in and around Dallas, so Clyde's visit to pick up the street clothes was by necessity a short and fast one. It wasn't until January 18, two days after the prison break, that Clyde, Bonnie, and the majority of the Eastham escapees returned to the Dallas area for another family visit. It was at this time we got a lot of the particulars concerning the so-called "raid."

The series of events which culminated in "Clyde Barrow's Raid" began just after Clyde and Bonnie returned to the Dallas area a week after the failed ambush near Sowers. I have previously mentioned that my brother was very angry over the attempt to shoot him down without warning in our mother's presence. To my brother, the ambush went well beyond the bounds of consideration. Clyde knew what he was involved in concerning his outlaw life was already driving our mother to distraction. He had never wanted any of our family to have any kind of direct involvement in his fugitive activities. The fact that Buck and Blanche had gotten involved with Clyde was only an accident of circumstances. It was strictly because my brother and sister-in-law were in the wrong place at the wrong time when the Joplin incident occurred. The principle behind the Sowers affair, betrayal and ambush, was too much for Clyde to peacefully withstand. To attempt to shoot down, without warning, he and Bonnie before the horrified eyes of their mothers—and possibly shooting their mothers (some of those bullets came pretty close to our car)—was too much for Clyde to accept.

After Sowers, Clyde was looking for a chance to get even. Unfortunately, a chance came his way almost immediately. A convict who had just recently been paroled came into west Dallas, trying to get in contact with my brother. The man had been in contact with Raymond Hamilton, and Raymond had given him directions on where to go and who to talk to in order to make the connection with Clyde. This parolee was already known in west Dallas, and he finally got in touch with Clyde through Floyd Hamilton. Clyde never met Raymond's pal during this time.

Normally, Clyde would not have had anything to do with this particular man because some of this man's previous troubles with the law were due to his involvement in the narcotics trade. Clyde had nothing but scorn and disdain for dope peddlers and drug dealers; my brother neither smoked nor drank liquor. He had very little use for any person who was heavily dependent on booze or dope.

Clyde really shouldn't have had anything more to do with Raymond Hamilton, for that matter, but he was still furious over the audacity of the authorities in Sowers. The concept of engineering Raymond's escape seemed like a good way to even the score, so Clyde fell in with the plot.

The escape plan did not call for Clyde to barrel his way into the prison, firing his machine gun. Rather, his role was a little more indirect. He was to coordinate the placement of a couple of automatic pistols at a strategic place where Raymond and another escapee could get their hands on them. This strategic location would not be in the prison building itself, but would be outside where the prisoners worked every day clearing out underbrush.

This location also had to provide quick access on foot to the one road that ran through the area. Clyde was to be waiting with the getaway car at the point. The expected plan was that Raymond and anyone who was allowed to join him would snatch the automatics from underneath the woodpile near where the convict work crew would be working. The two armed prisoners would then disarm the guards who were on the scene, then flee on foot towards the road where Clyde would be waiting. They would then pile inside the getaway car. Clyde's noted driving skills would insure a safe and successful escape away from the Eastham area, leaving the state prison system officials standing there with the proverbial egg on their faces.

After plans were made, the plan was then put into action. The two automatic pistols were purchased. Both Clyde and Raymond knew the lay of the land where the escape would take place. The parolee who was acting as the go-between had been talking with Floyd Hamilton, with Floyd then using L. C. as a contact. The prison break was set up for the morning of January 16. Clyde and Bonnie made one of their Dallas runs on January 15, but they gave no indication that anything was in the offing. They just came in and we visited with them as everyone had normally done since the previous September.

When they left Dallas on January 15, Clyde and Bonnie got with the contact man and the three of them headed down towards the Huntsville area. Both Clyde and the parolee were familiar with the routine at Eastham, so they knew about when this underbrush-clearing and wood-cutting group would be going out to the fields in the morning. They hid the guns at the prearranged location; Floyd Hamilton had previously informed Raymond where this spot would be. Clyde, Bonnie, and the contact man drove out to the designated spot on the road early on the morning of January 16. Clyde brought along some of his rifles, just in case.

Everyone involved in this plan was hoping that the great Eastham prison break would go smoothly, with no one getting hurt and with no guns going off, just as initially arranged. Unfortunately, this was not to be the case. There were other unforeseen circumstanccs which cropped up, beginning with the heavy fog that rolled in on the morning of January 16. Visibility was reduced to a few yards in either direction, a situation with which Clyde was very uncomfortable. As the three of them waited there on the road, all they could was to hope that things were going smoothly at the place where the prisoners were to be working.

Clyde's misgivings about the raid were not unfounded; things were going awry at the site where the guns were hidden beneath the woodpile. The woodpile was located where Joe Palmer's work detail would be laboring. Raymond was assigned to another detail, but he switched work groups at the last minute and joined Joe Palmer. The trouble started when Raymond's absence from his assigned group was noticed. Someone told the guards that he was over with Joe Palmer. A couple of the guards headed over to Joe's detail to bring Raymond back. This was the worst possible thing that could've happened at that point, as it focused the attention of the guards on both Raymond and Joe. It destroyed any element of surprise that would enable the boys to get the drop on the guards and to disarm them. Both Raymond and Joe saw what was starting to happen and decided it was either now or never.

They dove for the concealed automatic pistols and came up with the guns in their hands. The unanticipated action started immediately. Joe shot one of the mounted guards. This guard's wound was fatal, and he died 11 days later. Joe shot another guard, but this injury was not serious. Some of the other prison guards who were at the scene turned and fled. There was a momentary lull in the action, and the work detail was left alone for a very brief time span.

Raymond and Joe further deviated from the agreed-upon plan by asking the other members of the work detail if any of them wanted to accompany them in their break. Three prisoners stepped forward: Hilton Bybee, Henry Methvin, and a convict named French. The five escapees then fled and disappeared into the fog, heading in the direction where they believed Clyde would be waiting with the getaway car.

Back at the auto, Clyde, Bonnie, and Raymond's contact man heard the shots fired during the melee at the woodpile. They realized immediately something had gone wrong, but they did not flee. Clyde had given his word that he would assist in this raid and he remained at his agreed-upon post. My brother wondered if the thick fog would cause the escapees to lose their way. There was a ditch running from the site of the prison break to the road where Clyde was parked, so all the prisoners had to do was to follow the ditch. But Clyde was concerned about the possibility of the escapees taking a wrong turn in the thick fog, so he picked up one of his rifles and fired several shots in the air. Bonnie began to hit the horn on the car. The sound of both the rifle and the horn gave the prisoners a direction to head towards.

Clyde realized that the sound of the pistol fire from the site of the escape and the sound of his rifle shots would be heard for quite a distance and would be immediately looked into, especially since they were in the vicinity of the prison farm. My brother knew his whole group would have to get out of the vicinity immediately after every one was in the car. The five escapees came into sight through the fog almost immediately after they heard Clyde's gunfire and Bonnie's tooting of the horn. When the convicts came into sight, Raymond's contact man began acting on his own accord. He began to contend with them and told them to go back to the work detail. An argument ensued over the matter, with no one getting into the car to get away.

It was at this point that Clyde took command of the situation. He told Raymond's middleman to shut up and to stay out of the way. My brother then told everyone to get inside the car as best as they could because he was leaving - immediately. Eight people crammed themselves in every available bit of space. Once everyone had squeezed inside, Clyde got behind the wheel and sped off. He knew that the news of the gunfire had probably been relayed back to the authorities, and that action was probably being instigated at that moment by the local police and prison guards.

The group headed back northeast. Of course, their destination was the Dallas area, where both Clyde and Raymond could get assistance from their families. It became necessary to stop on the way back to fill up with gasoline at a service station. Clyde stopped at a station near Hillsboro, Texas to refuel. While they were gassing up, Clyde heard from the attendant that radio news bulletins about the Eastham break were already being broadcast over the airwaves. But the news being broadcast was totally fictional. The radio accounts stated Clyde and Bonnie drove directly up to the prison, snatched Raymond from the guards, and unloaded gunfire on anything that moved. Clyde kept a straight face and agreed with the attendant that it was incredible news. Once they'd filled up, the group began the last leg of their trip back to Dallas.

It was as Clyde's group neared his home area that our family received the phone call concerning the needed changes of clothing for the additional escapees. Clyde and Bonnie had clothing for only two men, with nothing for the unexpected passengers. L.C. and Floyd Hamilton responded to the telephone request for the additional clothing. By the time the group arrived up in Rhome, their party had been reduced by one. Escapee French had separated from Clyde's group shortly after they had gotten out of the vicinity of the prison farm. French's home turf was in the opposite direction from where Clyde was headed, so he decided to make his way back to his safe area as best he could. But he didn't make it very far; he was captured within hours after he left Clyde's company.

After meeting with L.C. near Rhome, Clyde drove his carload of people up into Oklahoma. They made no attempt to contact Pretty Boy Floyd. For whatever reason, Clyde had no further contact with the Floyd family. They did find a place to stay for a couple of days. It was during this excursion that Hilton Bybee split off and went his own way. Clyde had no further contact with Bybee.

Clyde, Bonnie, and their companions returned to Dallas for a family visit on January 18, two days after the Eastham prison raid. During his visit, Clyde told us about his involvement in Raymond's escape plan. We all wished Clyde had told us about what was going on concerning the plot to free Raymond Hamilton. I truly believe that our family would have tried to talk Clyde out of getting involved in such an escapade when we would have found out about the type of people with which he was getting connected. In committing himself to the prison break, my brother was involving himself with a motley collection of dope fiends, snitches, and rats. Raymond's middleman was a dope fiend, Raymond himself turned out to be a snitch, and the "rat" part of the equation can be summed up in two words: Henry Methvin. The character of these men and some others will gradually unfold as their experiences with Clyde developed.

After the family visit on January 18, Clyde and his group headed back up into Oklahoma, but this time the purpose of the trip was strictly business. The boys were making a bank run. The group had been getting by on what funds Clyde and Bonnie had with them, but now it was time to have everyone's treasuries replenished. Robberies of grocery stores and filling stations would not be enough now. Banks would be the desired targets.

Clyde's group drove up through Oklahoma and went further north. It was just a very few days after they left Dallas that they robbed their first bank. I can't recall where the first bank was located, but afterward my brother and his people came back down into Oklahoma. They were planning another bank robbery, but they needed another car with which to do it. Clyde's group robbed a filling station in Oklahoma and stole a 1933 Dodge sedan during the holdup. They used this new acquisition when they robbed the bank in Poteau, Oklahoma which was located just south of Ft. Smith, Arkansas.

These two banks were just a beginning for Raymond Hamilton. He was wanting to rob banks as fast and as frequently as he could for two different reasons. The first reason was that Raymond was obligated to pay $1,000 to the man who acted in his behalf in arranging the logistics of the Eastham prison break. Raymond wanted to get this go-between taken care of as soon as he could do so.

Secondly, Raymond brought his girlfriend, Mary O'Dare, into the group. Mary was the wife of Gene O'Dare, Raymond's former partner who was arrested with him in Michigan back in December, 1932. Gene was still in prison for the bank robberies he committed with Raymond during the autumn of 1932. Raymond saw nothing inappropriate about consorting with his one-time partner's wife, and she saw nothing wrong with it either.

O'Dare's introduction into Clyde's group was a definite step in the wrong direction. What led to immediate trouble between Mary and rest of them (not including Raymond, of course) was the fact that she had definite ideas concerning the lifestyle she should maintain. Clyde and Bonnie had been living on the road for almost two years, and they had that lifestyle down to a fine art. They both knew what to do and what not to do in order to avoid being noticed and identified by the people they met in their everyday travels. They knew how to play it safe in terms of getting food at cafes and eateries, getting their grooming needs like haircuts and permanents, and getting their clothes cleaned. Clyde and Bonnie knew enough to get everything they ate in the form of take-out food. They would put in an order at a cafe and then drive around until their food was ready. Then, they would return to the cafe and pick it up.

Mary O'Dare had other ideas on the matter of how fugitives lived on the road. She expected to be able to go inside nice cafes and restaurants and to sit down to a leisurely, expensive dinner. O'Dare expected to be put up in nice hotels and to go out to nightclubs. Clyde knew better than to make an appearance at a nice restaurant, hotel, or nightclub; people wanted for what Clyde and Raymond were wanted had no business socially mixing. Such caution was a principle with which Mary O'Dare was not familiar, however, and she continued to voice her expectations to everyone. She had Raymond wrapped around her little finger, but the rest of Clyde's group got to the point that they were ready to wrap their little fingers and the rest of their fingers around Mary's neck and squeeze. Tension between Clyde and Bonnie on the one hand and Mary and Raymond on the other steadily increased as the days passed. Joe Palmer and Henry the Rat seemed to back Clyde's perspective concerning Mary. They began to refer to Mary as "The Washerwoman" among themselves.

While internal relations within the so-called "Barrow Gang" were worsening as January came to a close, public conflict between cops and robbers was still a regular feature of the newspaper headlines. It was at this time that officers in two separated states arrested two of the most widely sought gangs in the country. These two groups of fugitives were arrested in winter vacation spots within a very few days of each other.

In Tucson, Arizona, local police apprehended six members of the "Terror Gang" from Indiana. Those arrested included John Dillinger, Harry Pierpont, Charles MacKey, Russell Clark, Evelyn Frechette, and Mary Kinder. They had been vacationing in the sunny Southwest until a fire at their hotel began a series of events which eventually led to their arrest. Some of Dillinger's group had offered firemen an exorbitant amount of money to rescue their luggage (which contained their guns and loot). Their generosity was duly noted and remembered by one fireman in particular who saw the very same men in a photo section of fugitives in a detective magazine the very next day. The local police were notified and a subtle canvas of the rented bungalows and tourist camps in the Tucson area was instigated and the gangsters were arrested, one by one, without a shot being fired by anyone. Clyde pointed out the apprehension of the "Terror Gang" as an example of what could happen when fugitives tried to live like monied people in public places where they could be recognized. However, Raymond and Mary the Washerwoman still didn't get Clyde's point, however.

The second band of fugitives arrested in late January struck closer to home. Clyde, Dock Potter, and Henry Massingale were mistakenly identified as Blackie Thompson, Whitey Walker, and Roy Johnson during their ill-starred trip to Enid, Oklahoma back in September. The three McAlester escapees were arrested in Florida within a very few days of Dillinger's arrest in Arizona. Whitey and Blackie were brought to the Texas penitentiary at Huntsville because they were wanted in connection with capital offenses in Texas. Both of them wound up on "Death Row" at the "Walls" near downtown Huntsville.

Of course, whenever our family read in the newspapers about the arrest of such outfits as the "Terror Gang" and the McAlester escapees, our concerns and fears always focused on Clyde. We knew he would never let himself be taken alive, unlike John Dillinger and Whitey Walker. The calculating mentalities of the professional bank robbers like Dillinger and Blackie Thompson accepted the possibility of arrest as an occupational hazard; if apprehension did occur, their next priority became to escape and to resume robbing banks. For Clyde the situation was much more personal; my brother could not, and would not, accept the concept of surrender. He felt that he had surrendered enough in the past when he was continually being arrested out in west Dallas and when he experienced the horrors of prison life. Clyde didn't classify himself as a "big time" bank robber by choice. Instead, he felt his way of life was a circumstance related to the pressures of the authorities. Our family understood Clyde's perspective and felt that my brother had good reasons for feeling as he did.

Raymond Hamilton, however, aspired to the lifestyle which he felt people such as John Dillinger and the Barker-Karpis gang of kidnappers represented. Raymond wanted to be recognized as a "big time" bank robber, whereas Clyde was just trying to stay alive as long as possible. Their difference in opinion was creating a widening breach between the two boys every day they were traveling together.

January, 1934, with all of its tumult and excitement, finally came to an end and the month of February opened. It had been over two weeks since Clyde had last visited our family. We knew that Clyde's less frequent visits was a bad sign. It was the longest time he had stayed away from his family since he and Bonnie had returned after Buck's death. Another sign indicating things were turning sour was Clyde's increasing dependence on Raymond Hamilton and Henry the Rat. For several months, Clyde's family had been the only 100% dependable party on which he could rely. The further my brother was straying from his only reliable support, the more danger of betrayal he was creating.

Clyde's situation was becoming parallel to that of Jesse James just 55 years earlier. Jesse James rode roughshod over the Federal troops, the carpetbaggers, the rich bankers, the railroad tycoons, and the Pinkerton detectives for over 10 years after the end of the Civil War. Jesse was able to do this because of the quality of his fellow raiders. His brother Frank, the Younger brothers, and others of Quantrill's raiders were all true-blue to Jesse and to each other. But this original group was destroyed in the Northfield, Minnesota bank robbery in 1876. When Jesse began robbing trains again in 1879, he was forced to align himself with a bunch of adolescents who were in grade school when he was initially riding with the Youngers. This new group knew nothing of the old loyalties. As a result, the second James Gang wound up consuming itself. Jesse James himself supposedly killed another gang member named Ed Miller because Jesse suspected Miller of being disloyal. Dick Liddil and Bob Ford shot and killed Wood Hite, Jesse's cousin, in a disagreement over a woman. Liddil surrendered, rather than meet the fate of Ed Miller. Bob Ford went to the governor of Missouri and offered to betray Jesse for the reward and for pardon of past offenses. Ford assassinated Jesse James, and became known as a "dirty little coward" for all time.

CHAPTER 19

LEE SIMMONS WAS THE director of the Texas prison system at the time of Raymond Hamilton's escape from the Eastham prison farm. Simmons was originally from Grayson County, Texas, where he served as sheriff. He was appointed as chief of the state penal system in 1930.

Simmons has been portrayed by his supporters as a shining light in the area of prison reform, leading the penal system in Texas out of the barbarities of the 19th century into the glorious enlightenment of the 20th century. Yet, those of us with family members in the prison system during Simmons's control ever saw any of these reforms. The only change that was made was that 19th century barbarities were replaced by 20th century barbarities.

Whenever any of our family went down to the Huntsville area to visit with either Clyde or Buck at whatever prison farm they were incarcerated, we were always appalled by what we saw in terms of the treatment of the prisoners. Both my mother and Blanche recalled seeing the prisoners being forced to run every morning all of the way out from their dormitories to their work areas in the fields. While the prisoners were running, the guards were riding horses. If any prisoner was unable to keep up with the others, one of the mounted guards would ride down on him, trampling the unfortunate individual. It was the same situation in the evening when the prisoners were being brought back to their dormitory building.

Reference has already been made to Clyde's experiences in this new, enlightened prison system, about how he was made to do the "barrel cavalry" for hours and even days on end. The only enlightenment that my brother received from such revolutionary new concepts in penology was that it was a "burning hell" and that he'd rather die than go back there.

Lee Simmons considered Clyde as the main culprit in terms of placing the blame for the Eastham prison break. He later referred to the episode as "Clyde Barrow's Raid," despite the fact that Clyde really only provided the getaway. The plot itself was originated by Raymond Hamilton and carried out through both Raymond's middleman and Floyd Hamilton. Yet, Simmons, like so many other people over the years involved in something that was only remotely connected with my brother, believed that the Eastham escape would only be significant if Clyde's name was attached to it.

Simmons felt a personal affront because the "Raid" had occurred under his tenure as director of the prison system and because one of his guards had been slain - by Joe Palmer, not by Clyde Barrow. I've read somewhere that Simmons supposedly took an oath on behalf of the fatally wounded guard to avenge his death. The prison director purportedly decided that it was personally up to him to get Clyde and he began to cast about for ways to get this feat accomplished. According to most popular accounts, Simmons decided to find one or two qualified individuals to stay on Clyde and Bonnie until they could be put on the spot

According to the accounts that I've read over the years, Simmons supposedly listed a series of qualifications that his ideal man-hunter should possess. Of course, this person had to be a good and fast shot. Since Clyde was noted for his driving prowess, this person had to be able to drive for long intervals and to live out of a car as my brother and Bonnie were doing. Finally, this individual had to be an already proven tracker of fugitives. It is said that Simmons could only find one man that embodied all of these qualifications: Francis Augustus "Frank" Hamer, a long time Texas Ranger. Simmons approached both Hamer and the state government officials on the matter. According to the popular stories, all agreed that this should be done and "Project Hamer" was off and running.

But the fact is that the version of events which I've heard from various sources throughout the years is somewhat different from the accounts by the Simmons-Hamer partisans. Simmons was indeed embarrassed by the fact that the Hamilton-Palmer escape took place while he was head of the prison system. He did consider it as imperative that the prestige or the prison system be restored by the apprehension of those who had shattered the illusion of his progressive penology.

But where the accounts by the Simmons-Hamer supporters and what I've heard from my sources go their separate ways is the point that Hamer received the designation as the only living person capable of accomplishing the job of catching Clyde. It's been said that Simmons actually talked to several other noted officers about the offer of playing state-sponsored man-hunter. The men the prison director had supposedly approached were tough individuals, men who had dealt with the riotous conditions in the oil "boom towns" of the 1920s like Borger, Ranger, and Mexia. These officers were indeed tough, but they were also fair. They refused to get involved with Simmons' plot to deliberately put somebody on the spot. Therefore, Hamer was merely the first one to purportedly say "yes" to Simmons.

Lest anyone be skeptical about the possibility of what I've just described, let me say that what I've just discussed here has its known parallel in another prominent case during this same time period. I have already called attention to the fact that in later years I came to become acquainted with John Dillinger Sr. I shared the experiences of the Barrow family with him and he spoke of his experience with his fugitive son. One of the things that he related to me concerned the machinations of the two East Chicago police officers who were working with the so-called "Lady in Red" to set up his son's killing. Mr. Dillinger heard these two officers went to the "Dillenger Squad," an organized group solely devoted to capturing John Dillinger, Jr. The East Chicago officers offered to lead the "Dillinger Squad" to the wanted man on the one condition that the Chicago cops would have to agree to kill Dillinger with no allowances for any live surrender. The head of the "Dillinger Squad" refused to take part. The two East Chicago cops then went to the G-Men, who apparently had no reservations about any conditions. The Feds thereby received the opportunity of getting Dillinger.

So it was that Frank Hamer agreed to go out on the road to capture Clyde. Of all of the individuals who have entered the story of Clyde's life, Frank Hamer is one of the best known and is probably the most overrated. Hamer is well-known to a lot of people because of the character bearing his name in the noted 1967 film *Bonnie and Clyde*. Of course, this particular film had a tremendous popular impact and reintroduced Clyde, Buck, Bonnie, Blanche, and the others back into the mainstream of American social culture. Hamer was one of the others whose name reemerged from obscurity. Due to this movie, Hamer has been frequently associated with Clyde in the minds of many people, much as Al Capone and Eliot Ness are mentally associated.

This 1967 film shows the personages of my brothers and Hamer having a personal run-in early in Clyde's career, with Hamer getting the losing end of the deal. The Hamer character swears personal vengeance for the humiliation he receives at the hands of the "Barrow Gang" characters. Like just about everything else in this show, this run-in was a piece of Hollywood-created fiction. Frank Hamer had no personal grudges to settle with Clyde; he went after my brother and Bonnie only at the instigation of Lee Simmons. There were also rumors that Hamer agreed to only take the job with the stipulation that he could keep whatever of Clyde's and Bonnie's personal possessions he wanted when he apprehended them. Subsequent events have caused me to lend credence to this rumor.

While the forces of law and order were gearing up towards a single-minded and dedicated pursuit of Clyde, the object of their interest was still out on the highway. It seemed to be that my brother was having to watch out for some of the people with whom he was traveling as much as he had to keep an eye out for the police. Tempers and tensions within Clyde's group were beginning to reach dangerous levels, and it was all Clyde could do to keep a semblance of peace amongst those supposedly on his side.

It was becoming apparent that the true nature of Raymond Hamilton was not what Clyde had hoped. It turned out Raymond had developed the reputation of a snitch during his time in Eastham prison. Tempers flared between Raymond and Joe Palmer on one occasion and Joe let it be known to the rest of the group that Hamilton was a snitch, which didn't surprise Clyde at all. Raymond seethed over this characterization, but did nothing about it immediately. A very short while afterward, while the group was driving along and Joe was napping, Raymond made like he was going to shoot Joe in his sleep. Clyde had to immediately grab Raymond and slug him to stop him from murdering Joe. This was a very precarious move on Clyde's part because my brother was driving at the time, and their car ran off the road before Bonnie could grab the wheel.

Another example of Raymond's true character came to light during the same time period. Clyde's group was driving through the Ozarks after the Poteau bank robbery. Somehow, their vehicle had been sighted, and the police had set up roadblocks everywhere. Clyde unexpectedly drove up on one of these barricades, and it looked like a close-quarters gunfight was imminent. Raymond hit the panic button and dove down on the back floorboard, where he cowered while the group was in immediate danger. Clyde's driving skills were able to get them out of their predicament without anyone on either side getting wounded or killed, but they all remembered Raymond's display of cowardice. The rift between Hamilton and Mary and the rest of them continued to grow.

It was about this time that Joe Palmer took a sabbatical from traveling with Clyde's group. It was nothing personal against my brother, however; Joe was a 100% stand-up guy. It just so happened that he had one personal complication that adversely affected his ability to travel with Clyde all of the time: Joe suffered from easily induced car sickness. Joe would have gotten ill after riding with anybody over a period of time, but the speeds and recklessness with which Clyde drove would make even a normal person queasy. My brother's style of motoring greatly hastened the development of Joe's carsickness and there were times that Joe couldn't handle any more of it, so he would leave the group for awhile until he recovered.

After Joe Palmer temporarily left Clyde's group to deal with his acute carsickness, Raymond undoubtedly felt as relieved about it as did Joe. Now the chief witness to Raymond's snitchery in prison was gone and Hamilton tried to restore his shattered reputation with the others. He began to emphasize his ambitions towards robbing banks. Raymond also began to belittle Clyde's holdups of grocery stores and gas stations. Raymond conveniently forgot that Clyde was certainly not reluctant to rob banks whenever he had the qualified personnel with which to do it. He had robbed a number of banks with Buck and W.D. and he had no reservations about their first two post-Eastham bank heists. But when it was only he and Bonnie out on the road, however, Clyde usually just robbed the stations and groceries to supply their everyday needs. Due to her injuries, Bonnie was no longer physically able to actively contribute to any major robberies, such as one involving a bank. Clyde was a realist concerning the outlaw life, while Raymond was a romanticist who was coming to believe his own newspaper publicity.

It was after all of this had happened that Clyde made his next visit home on February 13 to west Dallas to see his family. We could tell that things were much different between the members of the group from when they were here last on January 18. There was a discernible tension concerning the subject of Raymond Hamilton and his Washerwoman. No one was directly saying anything about it. Everyone had their best faces on for the sake of the family get-together. However, we could see that the current arrangement between Clyde and Raymond was not going to last. All we could do was to hope that my brother would part company with Hamilton before Raymond and his Washerwoman would lose another confrontation with Clyde, Bonnie, and Henry the Rat. We knew that once this happened, Raymond might very well try to play the snitch on Clyde and the others. Our family also noticed that Clyde seemed to be growing much closer with Henry Methvin as he was gravitating further away from Raymond Hamilton. Methvin was a spur-of-the-moment addition to the Eastham escape group, but my brother was beginning to think very highly of Henry by then and was starting to put a lot of trust in him. Our family felt that if Clyde was happy with Methvin, then we would be happy with him too, especially in light of the way that Raymond was going. Clyde had very few people in his life in whom he trusted that we were willing to embrace anyone who seemingly earned my brother's confidence. Little did we know what lay ahead.

Clyde's visit on February 13 represented the first of his three trips home during the middle of the month. My brother's next visit occurred five days later on February 18, but between these two family get-togethers there occurred an event of interest in eastern Oklahoma. A massive police dragnet of literal military proportions was instigated by the state of Oklahoma. It was intended to eliminate the usage of the mountainous areas along the Oklahoma-Arkansas border as an outlaw sanctuary.

Throughout 1933, many of the most wanted men in the country were seen throughout this region. This group included Clyde and Buck, Pretty Boy Floyd, and the prison escapees from both the Lansing, Kansas and McAlester, Oklahoma crashouts. The state of Oklahoma finally figured that it had seen enough of outlaws and outlawry and so it called out the troops. This military-type expedition utilized the state guard units as well as peace officers at every level of jurisdiction (village constables through federal agents). Actual machine gun nests were set up at intersections, and all cars were stopped and searched. Roving bands of troops went throughout the countryside, searching any and all places where fugitives might be hiding. A lot of people who were suspected of being sympathetic towards the wanted men were roughed up. It was a "scorched earth" policy, designed to eliminate any tolerance towards fugitives. After this happened, the Cookson hills area of eastern Oklahoma was not nearly as attractive as a hideout as it was throughout 1933.

Of course, none of the nationally important fugitives, such as

Clyde or Pretty Boy Floyd, were apprehended in any of the Oklahoma activity. Clyde showed up again in the Dallas area on the day after the big manhunt and was merely one more interested newspaper reader concerning the affair. But we did feel that what happened on the Arkansas- Oklahoma border did represent a change in the intensity of the attitude that the authorities were displaying towards the so-called "crime wave." By mid-February, Clyde was probably the best-known fugitive still out on the highway. Many of those who were notable throughout 1933 were gone by this time. The three McAlester escapees (Blackie Thompson, Whitey Walker, and Roy Johnson) were back in prison. John Dillinger and his pals who had been arrested in Arizona were back in jail in their home states of Indiana and Ohio. The Urschel kidnappers (Machine Gun Kelly and Albert Bates) were in federal prison. Just about all of the Kansas prison escapees were either back in jail (Harvey Bailey, for example) or dead (Wilbur Underhill, for example). Pretty Boy Floyd had not been heard from for quite some time, and it was conjectured that he may have either died or fled the country to Mexico or South America. We were afraid that Clyde and Bonnie would be considered as the next major targets on the law's list.

Clyde's last visit for the month took place on February 22. This get-together went just like all of the other family gatherings with personal news and small talk. My brother did not tell any of us that he, Raymond, and Henry the Rat were going to hold up the R.P. Henry Bank in the small town of Lancaster in a just a few days. This robbery was being planned by the trio at that very time although none of them ever let on that any thing was up.

Lancaster was located just a few miles south of Dallas. Raymond Hamilton had spent many of his childhood years in the area of southern Dallas county around towns like Lancaster and Cedar Hill. The village of Cedar Hill had already suffered for its acquaintanceship with Raymond in the course of the two 1932 bank robberies. Now, it was Lancaster's turn.

The R.P. Henry bank in Lancaster was located just a few yards east of the small town square. This financial institution was located on a small side street that connected the town square with Henry Street. It was a private bank owned by one of Lancaster's leading families. The Henry family had played quite a role in the history of Lancaster. Clyde's visit to the Henry bank would make their family's institution a noted site in local history.

Joe Palmer was still not well enough to actually participate in the hold up, so it would be up to Clyde, Raymond, and the Rat to pull this job off while Bonnie and the Washerwoman waited with the "clean" getaway car several miles away. The three boys would use one car to rob the bank. The make and model of this immediate getaway car would probably be taken down and would be given to the authorities by someone who actually witnessed the robbery. Just outside of town, Clyde and his associates would switch to the long-term getaway car. While the police were looking for the auto seen at the bank, the boys could make a more leisurely getaway in an unidentified car. It was just five days after Clyde's last February visit that the trio hit the Lancaster bank. February 27, 1934 was a bitterly cold day. The three boys had to wear their overcoats. This represented an advantage to Clyde because it meant that he could carry his sawed-off shotgun under his arm beneath the overcoat.

Bonnie and the Washerwoman were left in their long-term getaway car on a country road to the east of Lancaster. The three boys drove their immediate getaway car into Lancaster. The Rat would act as the driver while Clyde and Raymond would enter the bank to make their unauthorized withdrawal. The R.P. Henry bank was located on a corner. Clyde directed Methvin to pull up to the side door of the bank building, so not to be seen by anyone in the town square. Clyde and Raymond entered the bank by this side door, which led to an office area. The two boys ordered those people who were in this area to go up front with them. The small group walked up into the bank lobby. Clyde ordered both the bank employees and the customers to sit down on the bank's black and white patterned tile floor.

Clyde then went over to the front door of the bank and kept a lookout. This vantage point enabled my brother to keep an eye on every aspect of the situation. Clyde could see the town square, the bank lobby, and the Rat in their getaway car at the side of the building. Raymond had already taken what money he could find in the tellers' cages and was inside the vault cleaning out the safe. Once Hamilton had gotten all of the money he could find, he, Clyde, and a couple of the bank employees retraced their steps back towards the office area of the bank from the lobby. None of the people who were sitting on the cold tile floor had moved.

Clyde warned the two bank employees that he and Raymond were leaving now and that there must be no quick response or heroics from anyone inside the bank building until their getaway car was out of sight. Clyde and Raymond then left the building by the side door and jumped into their car. The trio fled out to where Bonnie and the Washerwoman were waiting with their secondary car. The boys transferred the guns, the loot, and themselves to this new vehicle. Clyde got behind the wheel, and they were gone.

At that time, the robbery of the R.P. Henry bank was considered a major calamity for both the business itself and the town of Lancaster. The Henry bank went out of business just two months after the robbery. But then the changes which the passage of time generates began to take place, albeit slowly. Exactly 53 years after the original bank robbery, the "R.P. Henry bank building" was "robbed" again by "bandits" who had drove up to it in a 1933 automobile. But the 1987 "robbery" was presaged by the mayor of Lancaster publicly acknowledging it with a proclamation, and it was advertised in the newspapers beforehand. This 1987 "robbery" was a reenactment performed by living history performers. This reenactment was considered such a success that it was done annually for several years afterwards.

After the Lancaster robbery, Clyde's group left the North-Central Texas area, coming back into west Dallas for a quick family visit on March 3. While Clyde was away from the Dallas county area immediately after the Lancaster job, a tank in the small town of Mesquite, located just East of Dallas, was held up on March 1. The Mesquite robbery took place just two days after the activity in Lancaster.

The names of Clyde Barrow and Raymond Hamilton were not immediately associated with the R.P. Henry job, but the Dallas newspapers ran headlines like "BARROW GANG ROBS MESQUITE BANK." It seems that the Mesquite raiders walked into that bank and immediately introduced themselves to all inside as Clyde and Raymond. The newspapers took these men at their stated word and proclaimed that the"Barrow Gang" was at it again. Our family knew Clyde wasn't even in the area when the Mesquite bank was robbed. The Mesquite bandits were later apprehended and were found to be four men from the Mesquite area who tried to confuse the issue concerning their identities. Yet, it was the initial headlines that have stuck in people's minds and many Mesquite residents have proudly noted over the years that their downtown bank was once held up by Clyde and Raymond.

So it was that two small-town banks in Dallas County had been held up in just three days. The county authorities began to envisage bank heists occurring regularly, and they began to panic. The sheriff's department announced that deputies armed with machine guns were going to be placed in every small Dallas county bank. The usual "shoot to kill" orders would be given to these machine gunners in their quest to end what was expected to be a tidal-wave of bandit raids on these Dallas county banks.

Clyde read all about the Mesquite holdup and the county's bad intentions towards holdup men when he came back to visit with us on March 3. Since the authorities were so agitated about the two bank robberies, Clyde thought that he and his group would get out of the North-Central Texas area for a little while. My brother figured they would go up to Indiana, which was considered as being pretty quiet at that time due to the arrest of John Dillinger and his friends five weeks earlier in Tucson. With Dillinger and associates safely out of the way, Clyde figured that no one would be on the lookout for any fugitives.

Clyde decided that his group would hide out up around Terre Haute. My brother's group traveled towards the northeast, hoping to spend a few days of peace and quiet in that area. Let me say right now that it has been noted that Clyde had a girlfriend on the sly who lived in Terre Haute, and this girlfriend was the reason that Clyde took his group up there. Nothing could be further from the truth; Bonnie was the one true love of my brother's life, and he had no other sweethearts after they fell in love in January, 1930.

Unfortunately, the same day that Clyde's group began their journey towards Terre Haute, John Dillinger electrified the country by pulling off his famed "wooden gun" escape. Instead of being an area where the population would not be on edge concerning fugitives from justice, Indiana was now one of the hottest states in the nation. Clyde was going into an extremely volatile part of the country.

The external volatility of central and northern Indiana during the first week of March, 1934, was reflected by the internal edginess with Clyde's group. Relationships between Clyde, Bonnie, Henry the Rat, and Joe on the one hand and Raymond and Mary the Washerwoman on the other hand were reaching the breaking point. It was during their visit in Terre Haute that the final separation between Clyde and Raymond took place.

Tensions had been building up for some time. Both Mary O'Dare's nonstop whining about life on the road and Raymond's fantasies about being a "big time" bank robber were really starting to get on the nerves of the others in the group. Then, Raymond's attempt to shoot the sleeping Joe Palmer and his cowardice in the face of the police roadblock in the Ozarks totally disgusted Clyde and the others. It was up in Terre Haute that things finally came to a head.

The kids' visit to Indiana started off fairly well. Clyde's group acted like the "ordinary citizens" to whom Bonnie would later refer in her poem. Clyde and the other men acquired new tailored suits and were photographed wearing these new outfits. Both Clyde and Bonnie also acquired other articles of clothing in Terre Haute. Bonnie bought an all-red outfit with color-coordinated silk undergarments, riding pants, beret, and dress. My brother got himself a "Wasson's Towneshirt," manufactured in Indianapolis. This "Towneshirt" was a light blue cotton shirt of the western style. It had one patch pocket and pearl buttons. Clyde also got himself a pair of dark blue woolen pants.

Despite the change in geography, the personalities of Raymond Hamilton and Mary O'Dare remained unchanged. Clyde did not trust Raymond because my brother had seen him hold out on $600 from the money taken in the Lancaster bank robbery. Raymond owed his go-between in the Eastham break preparations a substantial amount of money. Hamilton tried to escalate his freedom from debt by lifting additional money from the Lancaster loot. As Clyde was watching Raymond in the rearview mirror, he witnessed him pocket cash from the R. P. Henry bank proceeds.

There were other ways in which Hamilton and O'Dare were rapidly exhausting the others' goodwill. Raymond and the Washerwoman tried to drive a wedge in the relationship between Clyde and Bonnie while they were up in Terre Haute. Hamilton and O'Dare were witnesses to an argument between them. They attempted to exploit this argument in order to get even with Clyde. Raymond and the Washerwoman conferred between themselves as to how to twist this circumstance to their own benefit. The Washerwoman later approached Bonnie after she had withdrawn herself from Clyde after their argument. Mary appeared to be a sympathetic supporter on behalf of Bonnie and commiserated with her anger and distress. O'Dare said that Bonnie should not tolerate such things from Clyde and that she had a perfect plan to get even with him. The Washerwoman told Bonnie that she should either poison or drug Clyde and then clean him out financially.

O'Dare then suggested that she, Bonnie, and Raymond could then immediately hit the road, leaving Clyde to his just desserts.

Bonnie was indeed temporarily angry, but she wasn't so angry that she had lost all sense of perspective. If she hadn't already been severely injured by the burns from the Wellington accident and the bullet wounds, she would've knocked Mary O'Dare into the middle of next week. The Washerwoman had sadly misread the depth of Bonnie's relationship with Clyde. Theirs was not the shallow relationship of that between Hamilton and O'Dare. Bonnie was so shocked and surprised by Mary's suggestion that she immediately forgot her disagreement with Clyde and told him about what had transpired. The split between Clyde and Raymond was continuing to grow wider.

But the final split between the two factions in Clyde's group came as a result of the division of money. The people in my brother's group had always maintained a general fund out of which expenses that involved everybody were paid. This "kitty" covered things like gasoline for their car. It was kept in a cloth bag and was maintained by equal contributions from everybody. This arrangement was agreed to by all in Clyde's group. But it came to the point that Raymond was even abusing this aspect of their life on the road. Mary O'Dare began to complain again about her lack of money and about Bonnie's share of the proceeds from the Lancaster bank robbery. Raymond decided to shut her up by reaching into the group's kitty and giving Mary a handful of money from the cloth bag, totally disregarding the group's agreement concerning this mutual fund.

This small action was the final breaking point between Clyde and Raymond. My brother had finally come to the end of his patience with Hamilton and his girlfriend. Clyde had gotten tired of Raymond's braggadocio and the Washerwoman's whining. Hamilton's big talk was belied by his cowardly actions and his behind-the-back maneuvering. My brother told them all right then and there that the two couples would have to go their separate ways, which was immediately done. Clyde and Raymond, with their women, each went their own ways. They never saw each other again.

Chapter 20

Both factions in Clyde's group went their separate ways after the final split in Terre Haute. Raymond stole a car with which to provide transportation for he and the Washerwoman. Shortly after Hamilton and O'Dare took off, Clyde, Bonnie, and Henry the Rat left central Indiana. None of them trusted Raymond Hamilton, and they felt that he might contact the officers concerning where Clyde and Bonnie were staying. The three of them headed back to Texas for a family visit.

According to my mother's notations on the wall of our house, Clyde's next visit to his old home occurred on March 12. It was at this time that we got the story behind the split between Clyde and Raymond. None of our family were saddened to hear that Clyde had ordered Raymond out. All of us felt that Raymond was a fit companion for Mary O'Dare, since Joe Palmer had told us that Hamilton had turned into a snitch in prison. We knew that Mary the Washerwoman came from a long line of snitches and rats. There was always a fear in the back of our minds that O'Dare just might betray the whole group to the police, with or without the cooperation of Hamilton. She was fully capable of turning Raymond in with the others, if the price was right.

It was good that Clyde chose March 12, 1934 to make his visit with our family. That same day, there was a double bank robbery in the town of Atchison, Kansas. It was a dual bank robbery because both banks were located in the same building. The gang of bandits got around $25,000 in a violent holdup that involved the wounding of the Atchison police chief and the kidnapping of eight bank employees. The state of Kansas was having a rough time of it. The state prison at Lansing was the site of the famous Memorial Day mass jailbreak in 1933. The task of rounding up the escapees generated headlines throughout the rest of that year. But the year of 1934 did not bring any relief for the state of Kansas. There was a series of twelve bank robberies in the late winter and early spring that kept the Kansas authorities hopping. Clyde and Bonnie had nothing to do with the Atchison robbery, but their names were connected with it anyway because someone saw a woman smoking a cigar in an Atchison hotel within a few hours of the robbery.

Clyde made his next visit with our family just one week later on March 19. Naturally, his visit coincided with another bank robbery. My brother was not involved in this heist either, although there was a tenuous connection: the robbery was committed in Grand Prairie, a town near Dallas, and Raymond Hamilton was the perpetrator. After separating with Clyde, Hamilton also headed back towards Texas and he left Mary O'Dare off at Wichita Falls while he and another man committed the Grand Prairie holdup.

Clyde's visits home were becoming more and more frequent. After the March 19 meeting, Clyde returned again on March 24 and March 27. Of course, we were always glad to see him as often as we could. With everything he was being sought for by the police, we could never tell when our last visit would take place, and we always enjoyed our meetings with Clyde and Bonnie to the fullest. Our family always had a heavy heart when we saw the kids drive off into the darkness and we always silently prayed for the opportunity to see Clyde and Bonnie alive just one more time.

The month of March, 1934 was relatively quiet as far as any major news concerning Clyde's activities. But that did not mean there was no news concerning the continuing "crime wave." During that month, the nation's attention was directed away from the Southwest towards the Midwestern states of Indiana, Minnesota, South Dakota, and Iowa. These states were the playground for the activities of John Dillinger and a group of his associates. After breaking out of the Lake county jail in Crown Point, Indiana, Dillinger drove into Chicago and then up into the "Twin Cities" area of St. Paul and Minneapolis.

While in the Minnesota cities, Dillinger joined forces with a new group of fugitives. One of these men, Lester Joseph Gillis, would later be as famous as Dillinger. He used the alias of George Nelson. Gillis always desired to be known as "Big George" Nelson, but his medium height of five feet, five inches, seemed to preclude this possibility. Another nickname, "Baby Face," seemed to stick better than "Big George," and so Lester Gillis became popularly known as "Baby Face" Nelson in the underworld of the Twin Cities. Nelson's activities with John Dillinger would make his name well-known to the whole country.

Dillinger's Crown Point escape caused both Clyde and Hamilton to depart the area of central Indiana, duc to the police heat being generated in that locale. But Dillinger didn't stick around there any longer than did Clyde. As I have already mentioned, Dillinger went north to Chicago and then on to Minnesota. Mr. Dillinger's boy was in the newspapers for something just about every day. On March 3, he escaped from the Crown Point jail. On March 4, he was with Baby Face Nelson in Minneapolis when Nelson shot and killed another driver after a minor fender-bender. On March 6, Dillinger, Nelson, Homer Van Meter, Tommy Carroll, John "Red" Hamilton (no relation to Raymond and the only one left from the "Terror Gang"), and Eddie Green robbed a bank in Sioux Falls, South Dakota and got over $49,000. Exactly one week later, on March 13, Dillinger's group robbed a bank in Mason City, Iowa of $52,000. Now is as good as time as any to stop and digress on a particular point concerning the bank robberies of that era.

In an earlier part of this story, I made reference to the Barker boys' robbery of a bank in Concordia, Kansas, in 1932, where they got $240,000. I have just referenced two of John Dillinger's robberies which averaged just over $50,000 apiece. When holdups like these are compared against the likes of Clyde's Lancaster robbery, some people may get the impression that Clyde was a highly inefficient bank robber. Raymond Hamilton's bank robberies in Cedar Hill and Grand Prairie never surpassed $2,000 for either of them. Many of Pretty Boy Floyd's robberies with George Birdwell never garnered more than just a very few thousand dollars at the best. It could be inferred from the above facts that Clyde, Floyd, and Hamilton were not successful when contrasted with the Dillinger and Barker gangs.

But the truth is that any time a person read of seemingly successful bank robberies in the newspapers, the chances were extremely good that these "big money" holdups were really inside jobs and that the estimates of the proceeds were highly inflated due to the fact that the missing bank funds were already missing when the bandits walked through the front door of the bank.

There was more money embezzled by crooked bank officers than was ever taken by Clyde, Pretty Boy Floyd, John Dillinger, and the other much publicized fugitives of the early 1930s. Whenever it looked like these embezzled funds might be discovered, the guilty bank officials often made contact with the lawyers who represented the wanted men like the Barkers and Dillinger and who acted as their "mouthpieces." These crooked bankers would explain their situation and would propose that the bank be robbed in order that the embezzled shortages be lumped in with the loot taken by the bandits. A date would be determined for the raid by the bandits, often with the local police chief in on the plot. The police chief would get a cut of the swag by being slow in response and even slower in pursuit, allowing the bandits to make a clean getaway.

Another aspect of these big money holdups were the bonds and securities that were often taken by the bandits. These items were always insured by the bank, which meant that the insurance company had to pay up when these items were stolen. However, accommodations involving the robbers' lawyers came into play here also. These insurance companies would contact the lawyers of the bandits and arrange to buy back these bonds and securities at less than their face value to return to the bank. It was a way to cut the losses by the insurance companies and was the icing on the cake for the robbers, along with the money they actually got, which was never as much as what was announced by the newspapers.

These prearranged bank robberies were typical for the fugitives who headquartered in the big northern cities like Chicago and the "Twin Cities" area. Outfits like those of the Barker boys and John Dillinger had all kinds of contacts through their lawyers. Fugitives like Clyde and Pretty Boy Floyd were never really part of the big city underworld, although Pretty Boy used to headquarter at times in Kansas City and in some of the underworld hideouts in Ohio. Clyde's bank jobs were typical of what Jesse James and Cole Younger would commit: "honest" bank robberies in which as much cash as possible was sought. The smaller banks in the southwest never carried as much cash as did the bigger banks in cities like Mason City, Sioux Falls, and Concordia. There were two totally different world of outlawry in the early 1930s.

Clyde was perfectly willing to let John Dillinger have all of the headlines he wanted during the month of March. My brother was not connected with any new atrocities during that month. I do suppose that he, Henry the Rat, and Joe Palmer (when Joe was well enough to be riding with Clyde) probably did commit robberies during that time, but there were no gunfights or killings charged to my brother.

This period of relative quiet after Raymond left the group seemed too good to last very long. After Clyde's visit on March 27, he said he would try to get back on the following holiday weekend. The next Sunday would combine two different holidays which were at opposite ends of the spectrum: Easter and April Fool's Day.

All of us were looking forward to seeing Clyde and Bonnie again. Bonnie said that she would be bringing in a surprise for her mother on the occasion of Easter. We expected their Easter visit to be typical of their other trips back home, when a group of us would meet them on an isolated stretch of road in a rural area near Dallas around dusk when there would be less people about.

Clyde's scheduled visit came close to coinciding with yet another bank robbery. Raymond Hamilton was at it again, robbing a bank in the small town of West, which was located a few miles north of Waco. Raymond entered the bank by himself, although Mary O'Dare was outside in the car. He got a little more than $1,800 and then the two of them disappeared into the countryside, for only a little while. Hamilton's car ran off the road and could not be extricated from the ditch. He commandeered the car of a woman and her little son. Raymond took the woman along as a hostage, leaving her child in the hands of some farmers who had initially tried to provide assistance at the scene of the wreck. The Hamilton robbery had taken place on Saturday, March 31. Raymond and O'Dare released their hostage the following morning in Houston.

All Saturday evening and Sunday morning, the radio bulletins and newspaper "extras" dealt with the bank robbery in West, the abduction of the woman by the bandits, and the big manhunt for Raymond Hamilton. We were relieved that the hostage had been released down around Houston because it meant that the focus of the police dragnet would be down in that area. Our family was hoping we could have a nice quiet holiday get-together with Clyde and Bonnie while the cops were hunting for Hamilton and O'Dare down towards South Texas.

There have been many accounts published about what happened on Easter Sunday, 1934. All of these stories are riddled with misconceptions and errors. These fabrications usually begin with Joe Palmer coming into Dallas to leave word at our service station for Clyde's family to meet him out past Grapevine on the highway. Joe Palmer wasn't with Clyde that day, first of all. Joe did not travel with my brother as much as everyone seems to think, due to Joe's propensity towards carsickness. His particular illness and Clyde's dependence on his automobile did not mix at all.

It was Clyde himself who came into west Dallas, as he usually did, on that Easter Sunday. It just so happened that, because of the holiday, most of us were not at home. The rest of the family was scattered out over the Dallas area, each one celebrating Easter in their own way. After leaving word at the service station, Clyde, Bonnie, and Henry the Rat headed on out to that particular spot along Highway 114. Let me say right now that my brother did not have any intentions of meeting Raymond Hamilton out there. Clyde was not out there to deal with Raymond in any fashion. I've read stories and articles about my brother choosing that particular spot because it was a favorite vantage point of Raymond's. These accounts state that Clyde was either going to rejoin Raymond or was waiting out there to kill him and Mary O'Dare. Neither one of these surmises are correct. My brother never said anything to any member of our family about getting even with Hamilton or wanting to shoot him down on sight. Raymond was regarded as past history by all of us, which was to our satisfaction. None of us trusted Mary O'Dare at all, and we had our doubts about Raymond Hamilton. We all felt that Clyde and Bonnie were better off without them.

I don't know where my mother was on that particular afternoon, but L.C. and I arrived back at our service station at about mid-afternoon. We got word that Clyde and Bonnie were awaiting us out by Grapevine. L.C. and I jumped into his car to go on out there. We began to drive northwest on Highway 114. Both of us knew where Clyde would be waiting to visit with his family; we were familiar with the spot.

L.C. and I were within just a very few miles of the agreed-upon spot when we both saw a car approaching us from the other direction at a very high rate of speed. We recognized the approaching automobile and slowed down. The other car did the same, having recognized us. It was Clyde's car.

Both automobiles stopped in the middle of Highway 114, and Clyde and L.C. rolled down their windows to speak to each other. We already realized that something was amiss upon seeing our brother speeding back towards Dallas. When we saw the strained looks on all three of their faces, we knew that something was drastically wrong. Clyde's message was terse and to the point: "You'll have to get out of here. Henry's just killed two cops back there."

Clyde didn't elaborate and L.C. and I didn't ask any questions. After giving this brief and to-the-point message, Clyde sped back east on Highway 114. L.C. hurriedly turned his car back around, and we headed back towards Dallas ourselves. Clyde had already disappeared from sight by the time we got turned around, and we were never able to catch up with him. When Clyde meant business, no one could keep up with him.

All L.C. and I could do was wonder what happened up there at the intersection of Dove Road and Highway 114, just a few miles west of the town of Grapevine. We knew we would be hearing plenty from the radio bulletins and reading plenty in the newspaper "extras" which would be appearing later that evening. We also thought that much of what we would be hearing and reading would be nothing more than sensationalized garbage. L.C. and I were right on both counts.

To describe what did appear in the papers and on the radio as "sensationalized garbage" would be charitable. Clyde and Bonnie were demonized in the Dallas-area media of that period to the point that they were not recognized as being anything which remotely resembled a human being. Ironically, neither Clyde nor Bonnie ever killed anybody that day near Grapevine.

Of course, the fact that her son was even remotely associated with an outrage such as that which occurred near Grapevine on Easter Sunday acted as a sword through my mother's soul. The things that Clyde had already been charged with were weighing heavily on our parents, but the Grapevine killings caused their despair to hit a new low. As I have previously mentioned, my mother noted the dates Clyde had come back to visit. But for the first time in four months, she didn't note a visit. April 1, 1934 never appeared on the wall, and none after that day either.

The screaming headlines of the Daily Times Herald did not provide any reassurances for our mother: "$1,500 OFFERED FOR CAPTURE OF BARROW." The newspaper stories contained the usual accounts of "grim faced" federal, state, and local officers, carrying machine guns and bulletproof vests, eager to put an end to "the crimson career" of Clyde and Bonnie. Our family was used to such purple prose in the papers in general, but what was said about Clyde and Bonnie concerning the Grapevine killings went beyond the bounds of logic and common sense.

The newspaper reporters tailored their stories to satisfy the appetites of those who wanted lurid tales. But these accounts belied the truth of what happened in several different areas. The primary area in which the newspaper stories were in error was that these stories only described a couple on Dove Road that day. There were actually three people out there: Clyde, Bonnie, and Henry Methvin. Yet many of the "eyewitness accounts" featured only two people: Clyde and Bonnie. Henry the Rat was too tall for anyone to miss and would have surely been noticed if anyone had actually been watching the people parked there.

The second area in which the newspapers erred concerned how the "couple" occupied their time and amused themselves. The people parked there on Dove Road supposedly spent the whole day smoking (Clyde didn't smoke), drinking moonshine (Clyde didn't drink), hugging, and taking potshots at the birds which flew overhead.

Clyde was not in the habit of making himself conspicuous to passersby by firing off guns within their plain sight. The sound of the gunfire would have drawn attention to where he was parked, which was the last thing that Clyde wanted to do.

One of the most obscene pieces of fiction connected with the terrible killings near Grapevine was the story that had Bonnie Parker walking over to one of the already-prone officers and shooting him with a shotgun point blank. This story then has Bonnie squealing with delight and saying something like this to Clyde: "Looky there! His head just bounced up and down like a rubber ball!"

The primary source for the "rubber ball" comment was a farmer who lived on the same road where the killings took place. Most people believe that the man's farm was where the shootings took place and that he was easily able to hear and see everything that happened. But this was not the case. This man's farm was at the bottom of the hillside, too far away to hear what was being said by the people parked on the crest of the hill. In fact, in the early accounts of the Grapevine murders, the people down at the man's farm were even too far away to determine whether the people by the car were men or women. It was not until the residents of the farm saw one person put his arm around one of the others that they even surmised that there may have been a couple up there. By the time the newspapers got through with it, the arm-around-the-shoulder embrace turned into "love-making," which gave the reader's imagination much with which to play. Both Clyde and Bonnie were pretty conservative in this area of their lives and neither of them were anything remotely resembling exhibitionists.

Nothing in the newspapers sounded anything like my brother and Bonnie, but we knew they were there on the scene due to Clyde's statement that Henry had shot the two men. The actions of the people on Dove Road had nothing in common with the Clyde and Bonnie that I knew. All our family could do was endure the outlandish stories on the radio and in the newspapers until we could get the true story of what happened from Clyde himself.

Needless to say, we did not expect to meet Clyde back at our house on Eagle Ford Road when L.C. and I returned. Clyde had gotten out of the area in a hurry; he knew that there would be a firestorm in the media concerning Henry's killing of the two officers. He also knew that the name of Clyde Barrow would sell many more newspapers than the name of Henry Methvin and that the newspapers would convict him of this double murder with no regard for the truth of the matter. All he could do was to run, and my brother headed north. Oklahoma was the closest state line and Clyde knew that all state and local pursuit would stop when he crossed the state line.

As I said, my mother stopped keeping track of Clyde's visits home after Sunday, April 1, 1934. It was a few days after that tragic Easter Clyde came back into Dallas. It was at that time that we got the true story behind what had happened there on Highway 114 and Dove Road. I can't recall the exact date, but I do recall what Clyde told us. Clyde, Bonnie, and Henry the Rat had come into west Dallas Easter morning and left word where they would be. After they left our service station, they immediately headed up to the meeting place to wait for the rest of the family to arrive. It was a quiet Easter morning with very nice weather. Clyde did not feel that he would attract any attention by parking on the Dove Road and Highway 114 intersection. Nothing was more common back then than for people to picnic and relax by the side of a road, especially on a Sunday holiday. Nobody thought anything of an automobile parked along a roadside.

The news that Raymond Hamilton had apparently headed down towards Houston added to Clyde's feelings of ease. It meant the attention of the police would be directed down there. My brother was feeling so relaxed and comfortable about things that he actually did something we all take for granted, but something which was a luxury for him: Clyde laid down on the back seat to take a nap.

A nap seems like a small thing for any of us, but for Clyde it was a rare occasion when he could get comfortable and relax. My brother had not slept in a bed since the previous July, when he and Buck were renting cabins at tourist courts. Since Buck's death, it had been nothing but running for Clyde, and an entire night of sleep in a comfortable bed became a thing of the past. It is a tribute to Bonnie's affection for my brother that she chose to share this miserable way of life with him. But that Easter morning of 1934, he was feeling good enough about things that he indulged himself with a much-needed nap. Bonnie later followed Clyde's lead and lay down in the front seat to take a catnap herself. Henry the Rat was still awake and remained outside of the car to keep watch.

It was while both Clyde and Bonnie were catching up on their sleep in their car that three members of the Texas Highway Patrol came past on motorcycles. The three motorcyclists were transporting a scale from one place to another. This scale was being carried in the lead motorcycle, equipped with a sidecar, where the scale was laying. The officer driving the lead motorcycle was a veteran Highway Patrolman named Polk Ivy. The two younger men who were following him were named E.B. Wheeler and H.D. Murphy. Wheeler had been on the State Highway Patrol for only a short while. Murphy had just started his career as a motorcycle patrolman. I am sure that all three of the officers noticed Clyde's car sitting up on top of the hill. Ivy continued to drive straight ahead on Highway 114. Wheeler and Murphy, apparently following a sudden impulse, turned their motorcycles right on the Dove Road and began to come towards Clyde's car.

Henry Methvin saw the three officers appear on Highway 114 and began to move back towards Clyde's car. By the time the two young men had turned on Dove Road, Henry was already back by the kids' car. Henry told Clyde "It's the law!" Clyde bolted up in the back seat and looked out the window of their car. My brother sized up the situation in a very few seconds. He saw that neither officer had any weapons in their hands and that the two young men were not anticipating anything extraordinary. Wheeler and Murphy were casually racking their cycles and were beginning to get off of them. Clyde figured he could get the jump on them and disarm them, as he had done so many times before with other policemen. My brother then told Henry, "Let's take them."

Clyde had been in this very same situation with a motorcycle officer in the past. When the Missouri Highway Patrolman Thomas Persell accosted Clyde, Bonnie, and W.D. back in January, 1933, Clyde had told W.D., "Let's take him." W.D. promptly got the drop on Persell and disarmed him. The Missouri officer was released a short time later with no harm done. Clyde had ordered W.D. to capture the two Wellington officers with the same command, "Let's take them." The two officers were later released in Oklahoma after Clyde had rejoined Buck. Even Raymond Hamilton had understood what Clyde meant when he said "Let's take him" when they abducted the deputy at Bonnie's aunt's house in New Mexico.

Unfortunately, Henry Methvin was not W.D. Jones or even Raymond Hamilton. At the command to "take them," Henry grabbed up a rifle and started firing at the two young officers. Neither of the patrolmen had a chance to pull their own guns; they just barely had time to look up at Henry's motion before he began to shoot. It was the last thing they ever saw in life. As the shots rang out, both officers crumpled to the ground, fatally wounded.

The newspaper reports the following day included the account of passersby who had stopped at the sound of gunfire and drove into Dove Road to see what had happened. They saw a tall man standing over the bodies of the two highway patrolmen. Henry had heard one of the officers groaning and decided to "put him out of his misery." The Rat grabbed another gun and walked over to the two prone men. It was Henry Methvin who fired into the motorcycle officers, not Bonnie Parker, after the two young men were gunned down.

Bonnie was so weak with shock after seeing the wanton murder that she was unable to get out of the car. Clyde had gotten out of the car after Henry the Rat had already done his initial shooting. My brother followed him down to where Henry finished his act of mayhem by firing down into the officers. All they could do after that was flee the area. Clyde got Henry back into the car and took off back towards Dallas, which is where L.C. and I met him on the highway.

Many try to portray Henry Methvin as a "scared kid" who didn't have the capacity to be a cold-blooded killer. Those who believe Methvin was merely a country boy gone wrong should consider the crime that put him in prison in the first place. Methvin had hitchhiked out to west Texas in order to try to find work. On the way back to his home in Louisiana, Henry thumbed a ride with a driver. Methvin repaid this driver's kindness by cutting his throat. He was indeed capable of gunning down a couple of motorcycle officers on a sudden impulse.

CHAPTER 21

THE SERIES OF MEETINGS between Clyde and his family that culminated in the killings of the two highway patrolmen were not the only meetings Clyde was the subject of interest during this time period. On March 24, the same day Clyde, Bonnie, and Henry the Rat met with the Barrow and Parker families near Dallas, another meeting was occurring in northwest Louisiana, the home area of Henry Methvin. It was Henry the Rat who was the causative factor.

This Louisiana meeting occurred in the office of Bienville Parish Sheriff Henderson Jordan. Those present included Jordan; the deputy sheriff of Bossier Parish, Steve Norrid; and a federal agent, Lester A. Kendell. I would like to point out that neither Frank Hamer or Ted Hinton were at this meeting, despite their claims that they were the instigators of the Louisiana activity concerning Clyde and Bonnie.

Division of Investigation operative Lester A. Kendell was one of the relatively unknown individuals who played a big part in the final few weeks of my brother's life. Yet he was probably more instrumental in putting together the series of events which led up to what happened eight miles south of Gibsland, Louisiana, on the morning of May 23, 1934. Certainly G-man Kendell actually played more of a direct role than either Hamer or Hinton.

It was in this short meeting on the afternoon of March 24, 1934 that the seeds were planted for the awful harvest of May 23. The federal agent and the Bossier Parish deputy had called on Jordan in order to discuss the whereabouts of "Old Henry" Methvin, the father of the Rat. It seems Old Methvin had been residing in Bossier Parish until he suddenly disappeared a short time before the officers' meeting. Old Methvin had been traced by G-man Kendell down to southwestern Bienville Parish, which was under Jordan's jurisdiction.

Agent Kendell told Sheriff Jordan he knew that Henry Methvin was running with Clyde and Bonnie. As the G-men typically kept surveillance on the families of fugitives, they knew when Old Methvin disappeared. Agent Kendell operated out of the New Orleans office of the Division of Investigation, and therefore, any activity of Clyde's in Louisiana would come under his jurisdiction. I'm sure the Dallas G-men had our family under surveillance as well. The Dallas office of the Division of Investigation was headed by a man named Frank Blake, who would have been involved in any action involving Clyde in Dallas. However, the Dallas-area G-man office kept itself occupied with things like the Charles Urschel kidnapping and not Clyde Barrow. J. Edgar Hoover kept his agents busy with his "war" on kidnappers like Machine Gun Kelly and Verne Sankey.

The federal agent asked the Bienville parish sheriff to initiate an investigation to find out exactly where Old Methvin was currently living and report back on his findings. Jordan began to circulate in that part of Bienville parish, trying to gain a lead on the Methvins. Jordan was still searching on the day Henry Methvin killed the two officers near Grapevine. With the dreadful and untrue stories that appeared in the newspapers about the double murder on that Easter Sunday, I have no doubt that Jordan was wondering what G-man Kendell had gotten him into.

I would imagine that Jordan was thankful Clyde, Bonnie, and Henry the Rat didn't immediately head over to his part of Louisiana after the slaughter of the two highway patrolmen. Clyde headed immediately for the closest state line, Oklahoma.

The next appearance the newspapers reported occurred on April 4 at DeKalb, Texas, a town close to where Oklahoma, Arkansas, and Texas joined together. My brother supposedly abducted and robbed a service station attendant. The attendant purportedly began to pay too close attention to two men and a woman who had pulled in to buy gasoline. The trio told him to get into the car with them. The attendant was robbed of $40 and was released unharmed several miles out of town afterward.

Our family was too upset and overwhelmed by the firestorm that occurred in the aftermath of the Grapevine killings to wonder about a service station holdup many miles away. All of us were still dazed by the level of vituperation unleashed at Clyde Barrow. By now, the totally false version of the double killing was becoming established in the public mind, the story where Clyde and Bonnie got publicly drunk, took potshots at birds, and made love there by their car. The third man on the scene totally disappeared in these news accounts; it was now just Clyde and Bonnie who wantonly murdered the two men. All of us were just sick about it. It was hard to imagine how things could have gotten any worse in that first week in April, 1934, but it did. Just five days after the murders on Dove Road, Clyde's name was connected with another killing of a peace officer.

Like the Grapevine outrage, this killing was the result of an almost accidental meeting between Clyde and the officers. The incident took place in the northeastern corner of Oklahoma near the towns of Commerce and Miami. Clyde's car got stuck in the mud on a mining road. My brother initially tried to get the auto out of this predicament by adroitly steering and maneuvering the vehicle. All Clyde succeeded in doing was to churn up bunches of mud and attract the attention of a few passersby who volunteered to help in pushing the car out of the mudhole. Clyde had reservations about letting too many people get too close to where he, Bonnie, and Henry the Rat were stuck, due to the possibility of being recognized from all of the publicity generated by the Grapevine killings. But Clyde also knew that they had to get back on the road as soon as possible. My brother accepted the proffered help of the passersby.

Clyde was behind the wheel of the car, steering as the men tried to push them out of the mudhole. Bonnie was sitting with Clyde, while Methvin was in the back seat. Apparently Henry thought some of the people who were pushing on their car were getting a little too inquisitive. The Rat began to curse and swear at them. At this exercise of ingratitude and castigation by Henry, some of the people who were close to him began to back away, and then someone made a movement that set Methvin off.

Henry grabbed one of the Browning Automatic Rifles and pointed it at the retreating people. He told all of them to stay right where they were. Methvin then heard the sound of a large truck corning down the mining road and went out in the middle of the road to intercept it. The truck driver saw Methvin pointing the business end of the BAR directly at him and stopped.

Methvin ordered the truck driver to get a rope and to tie Clyde's car on to his much larger truck. Henry told the truck driver to pull them out when the rope was secured. Together they were able to easily pull Clyde's car from the mud.

Clyde was telling Henry to get back into the car when the unexpected happened. Two local officers from the Commerce-Miami area were approaching the scene. They had received a report rcgarding some kind of commotion on the road and were coming out to investigate. The two officers were walking over to the site from their own parked car when they saw Methvin waving his machine gun around. Then, they pulled their guns from their holsters and began to fire.

When Clyde saw the two local officers come toward the car with guns drawn, he grabbed a rifle himself and threw open the door of their car. By this time, both the officers and Methvin were blasting away at each other.

Each officer was able to get off several rounds before hitting the dirt to avoid the machine gunfire come from Clyde and Henry. The first officer fell voluntarily, while the other fell as a result of a fatal wound. When the two officers dropped, Clyde and Methvin ran over to where they were lying and covered them with their BARs.

Clyde could see that one of the officers, an older man named Cal Campbell, was severely wounded and could not be moved. This time my brother was able to stop Methvin from "finishing him off." The other policeman, a younger man named Percy Boyd, was not severely wounded, and Clyde ordered him to get into their car with them. Once Boyd was put into his car, Clyde took off.

The after effects of this gunfight were the same as all of the others: motorized posses swarming about, roadblocks set up on all of the major roads, nonstop radio bulletins about the manhunt, and newspaper "extras" hitting the streets. The officers like Frank Hamer who were supposedly right on Clyde's tail had to drive in from other states where they were looking for him while he was in the Commerce-Miami area.

Since the area the killing took place was at the convergence of four different states (Arkansas, Kansas, Missouri, and Oklahoma), policemen from each of these states swung into action in case Clyde chose to come their way. Even Texas lawmen set up roadblocks at every bridge spanning the Red River between Texas and Oklahoma in case Clyde and Bonnie tried to return to Dallas.

Clyde actually drove north from the site of the shooting. The quartet entered the state of Kansas. Clyde, Bonnie, and Methvin kept Percy Boyd with them for several hours while they laid low in the southeastern Kansas countryside. They attempted to treat Boyd's scalp wound with some antiseptic. When they felt the coast was clear, Clyde and Bonnie released Boyd just after midnight on the morning of April 7, less than 12 hours after he was abducted near Commerce.

After letting Boyd go, Clyde did something totally unexpected.

Instead of trying to get away from the area of northeastern Oklahoma, my brother drove into the largest city in the area, Tulsa. Clyde looked up one of the Newton boys of Uvalde, Texas, who happened to be living and operating a business in Tulsa at that time.

The Newton brothers were already legendary characters in the southwest by 1934 due to their involvement in what was considered the nation's largest train robbery near Rondout, Illinois ten years earlier. There were four of these brothers who involved in this train robbery in which the loot amounted to more than two million dollars. All four brothers were arrested shortly after this holdup. This particular Newton boy had already served his time and was operating some kind of a drive-in. There was a little house located in back of this business. Clyde, Bonnie, and Henry the Rat stayed in the little house for two days after they turned Percy Boyd loose. This Newton brother advised Clyde and Bonnie to surrender, otherwise they were certainly going to get killed. Both Clyde and Bonnie fervently wished they could somehow surrender, but they knew their surrender would inevitably result in the electric chair. All they could do was to thank Mr. Newton and give him what money they could spare for his consideration before they went back out on the road.

There was a guessing game going on among the newspapers and the lawmen as to the identity of the man who was traveling with Clyde and Bonnie. Many people thought Raymond Hamilton was again riding with my brother, but neither Clyde nor Raymond ever had any inclination to associate with each other again. Some people thought that the unidentified man might have been Jim Clark, who was about the last remaining escapee from the 1933 Memorial Day jailbreak from the Kansas State Prison. In early 1934, Clark was as badly wanted by peace officers as Clyde himself. But my brother never had any connection with Jim Clark at any time.

Of course, federal agent Lester Kendell had learned the identity of Clyde's associate. Because of Kenell's identification of Methvin, Sheriff Henderson Jordan became involved in the search for Clyde. Jordan's investigation uncovered a Methvin relative, a Judas Iscariot-type, who was willing to talk. Henderson Jordan never identified his source publicly, but I know now that the first people to talk to Jordan were in-laws of the Methvin family with the name of Joyner. The Joyner family member told the sheriff that Clyde, Bonnie, and Henry the Rat were visiting with the Methvin family about every other week.

Jordan contacted Kendell with this bit of news and the two men began plotting how to get Clyde through his friendship with Henry Methvin, using the information supplied by the Joyners. It is interesting to note that Jordan was not calling in officers such as Frank Hamer who were purportedly hunting Clyde full time. I have no doubt Hamer was poking around northwest Louisiana, trying to pick up some piece of information, but at this point in time Jordan had been working with the G-men as exclusively as possible.

It was not surprising that Henderson Jordan chose to deal with the federal agents when one considers what was going on in the headlines in March and April of 1934. Even the Attorney General of the United States, a man named Homer S. Cummings, was jumping on the "Get Dillinger" bandwagon. Cummings was quoted in the newspapers as saying he hoped the federal agents would get John Dillinger in a way that would make a trial unnecessary. Of course, the policemen in Texas, Oklahoma, Missouri, and Arkansas had already been saying such things about Clyde for a year.

Anything John Dillinger did in this time period attracted national attention. I have already referred to Dillinger's bank robberies in Sioux Falls, South Dakota and Mason City, Iowa. On the same weekend Raymond Hamilton robbed the bank in the town of West, Texas and Henry Methvin killed the two motorcycle patrolmen, Dillinger was involved in a shooting affair at the apartment house where he and Evelyn Frechette, his girlfriend, were temporarily residing. Two federal agents and a local officer were checking out a tip on suspicious tenants. The three lawmen were not expecting any trouble and did not bring any bulletproof vest, machine guns, or riot guns as they would have on a serious raid. They expected another false alarm, but they hit the motherlode: the current hideout of Dillinger and his moll. Not only that, but Homer Van Meter, a long-time associate of Dillinger's, chose to make a friendly visit at the very same time the three officers came to call. This accidental three-way convergence erupted into a firearms free-for-all between Dillinger, Van Meter, and the small posse of lawmen. No one was killed in the affray; in fact, Dillinger was the only one affected when a bullet struck him in the leg. Both Mr. Dillinger's boy and Van Meter got away.

There was a follow-up investigation for days afterward. But even this follow-up investigation got bigger newsprint in the New York Times than did Henry Methvin's murdering the two motorcycle officers.

Any incident in the "war" between the so-called Dillinger Gang and the G-men always got big play in the press during that spring. By the way, the gunfight at Dillinger's apartment paid unexpected dividends for the federal agents. When they went through everything that Dillinger and Frechette had to leave behind due to their unexpected checkout, the G-men found a street address that they decided to follow up. It turned out to be the residence of Eddie Green, an associate of Dillinger's. The federal agents set an ambush for Green and shot him down, fatally wounding him. It took a while for Eddie Green to die from his wounds, and, in his delirium, he gave the G-men a lot of information concerning the activities of the Barker boys and Alvin Karpis. Before this, the only thing Fred Barker and Alvin Karpis were publicly wanted for was the murder of a sheriff in West Plains, Missouri in late 1932.

Of course the Barkers had been involved in much more than the killing of a sheriff. They had been involved in many bank robberies, including some of the prearranged ones that I spoke of earlier. Fred and Arthur Barker were also involved in two kidnappings which had been publicly blamed on other gangs: the William Hamm, Jr., snatch in June, 1933, and the Edward Bremer abduction in January, 1934. The federal government had prosecuted Roger Touhy for the Hamm kidnapping, but Touhy was found not guilty in a jury trial. The Bremer kidnapping was believed to have been done by members of John Dillinger's gang. Arthur Barker's finger-print was found on a piece of evidence, but all that had previously meant was Barker was considered an associate of Dillinger. Then Eddie Green's disoriented talk before he died informed the G-men that both Arthur and Fred Barker were involved with Alvin Karpis and others on several pretty big capers.

Clyde had begun the year as the only major fugitive still uncaptured by the authorities. Then, he was joined in the public's perception by John Dillinger and Baby Face Nelson. Now Clyde and Dillinger were going to be joined in the public eye by Ma Barker's two boys and their friend Alvin Karpis.

But while the Dillinger-Nelson and Barker-Karpis gangs were creating waves up in Chicago and St. Paul, the Southwest was still primarily concerned with Clyde and Bonnie. That first week of April was especially devastating for our family and Bonnie's relatives. Clyde and Bonnie were connected with the deaths of three peace officers within less than a week. Although they had been at the scene on both occasions, the Grapevine killings had been directly committed by

Henry Methvin, and the shooting of the Oklahoma constable had been initiated by him. Clyde was still convicted in the Texas newspapers of all three murders. That tumultuous first week in April had created a change in the mindset of our whole family.

Our mother had stopped keeping track of Clyde's visits as of that fatal Easter Sunday. We were hoping against hope that something would happen that could cause Clyde to evade his inevitable end. But the grim events of the first full week of April destroyed these hopes. All we could do was to live from visit to visit with Clyde and Bonnie.

It was about two weeks after the tragedy near Grapevine when Clyde returned to pay another family visit. My brother could never stay away from his home area for longer than two weeks. It was the public outcry concerning the murders of the two highway patrolmen that caused him to avoid the Dallas area for so long.

Clyde's visits in mid-April were like his previous visits. Clyde would drive by our service station and drop off a note as to where they wanted us to meet him and Bonnie. L.C., our mother, Billie Jean, and myself would get into one of our cars to meet them at the appointed place. We would look at our latest photographs and even take some pictures. My mother would always take food for Clyde out to these meetings; Clyde could never get enough of his mother's cooking.

The Barrow and Parker families were not the only parties who were wanting to meet with Clyde and Bonnie. Federal agent Lester Kendell was still working behind the scenes in attempting to set up an ambush for my brother. About the same time Clyde made his first April appearance in the Dallas area since Easter Sunday, Lester Kendell and Sheriff Henderson Jordan were organizing a raiding party for an anticipated visit by Clyde, Bonnie, and Henry the Rat. The trio was expected to make one of their periodic visits with Methvin's family in Bienville Parish. Jordan was still getting information from the Joyner family as to Clyde's movements in Louisiana. Clyde's visit with the Methvin family was expected to take place on April 13.

Not surprisingly, Jordan contacted other county officers in northwestern Louisiana and Kendell brought in a party of federal agents. Neither one of the two officers ever gave Frank Hamer any consideration concerning Hamer's participation in this particular raid. The federal agents and Louisiana policemen gathered together on the afternoon of April 13. Jordan decided to make one last check with the Joyner family. They told him that Clyde's visit would be delayed until a later date. The raiding party disbanded.

At this time, Frank Hamer was showing no particular interest in pursuing the Methvin angle in Louisiana. The one-time Texas Ranger was primarily dealing with the Dallas County officers in order to set up a plan to try to catch Clyde. Hamer supposedly did quite a bit of investigation out in west Dallas, visiting places where Clyde was seen and talking to people who knew my brother. Hamer certainly never came to our service station to get information about Clyde. I don't know of anybody that knew Clyde who gave Hamer any information. People along Eagle Ford Road who were friendly with my brother certainly didn't make him a casual topic of conversation, especially with snoopy strangers.

Hamer's sleuthing ability is best summarized by his interpretation of one of Clyde's idiosyncrasies with Bonnie. After the Sowers ambush in which Bonnie's burned leg was reinjured by the officers' bullets, Bonnie could not walk and had to be frequently helped about. She was able to hop somewhat on her good leg, but getting about was still extremely difficult. Clyde always helped her, lifting her out of the car during our family visits. Clyde carried Bonnie around in his arms on many occasions. Frank Hamer discovered the fact that Clyde was always seen helping Bonnie and carrying her. Hamer came to the rather stupid conclusion that Bonnie was always in a drunken stupor and was unable to walk due to being in a constant state of inebriation. This conclusion was totally contrary to the facts: Clyde absolutely did not drink, and Bonnie did not drink because she knew what Clyde thought of it. With faulty reasoning like that on the part of all of Clyde's pursuers, my brother would have died of old age in bed. Unfortunately for Clyde, Lester Kendell did not think like Frank Hamer thought. The federal agent was working on the one weak area in Clyde's defenses: my brother's complete trust in Henry Methvin and Methvin's family. This one weakness would make all of the difference.

Chapter 22

By mid-April, Clyde knew that there were a couple of Texas Ranger-types assigned the task of bringing him in, dead or alive. My brother did not know much beyond that particular fact, however. I don't know how he learned this bit of information, since the fact of Hamer's assignment was supposed to have been a secret, known only to a very few individuals in the state government in Austin.

Frank Hamer's involvement was also known by the Dallas County Sheriff's Office. Smoot Schmid's department was one of the first places that Hamer contacted when he began his so-called manhunt in early February. But I don't believe that there were any leaks in the sheriff's office from which Clyde could have directly received this information. Deputy Sheriffs Bob Alcorn and Ted Hinton had been appointed by Smoot Schmid to work full-time on Clyde's case. Alcorn and Hamer were traveling together on a regular basis by mid-April. Again, I want to point out that Ted Hinton was not known by the Barrow family until he received this full-time assignment. The ambush at Sowers was the closest contact that Hinton had previously had with the Barrow family. Our family did know Bob Alcorn. But I don't believe that either Alcorn or Hinton ever tipped anyone concerning Hamer's interest in the pursuit of the so-called "Barrow Gang."

The tip concerning Hamer's assigned task most likely came from Hamer's own "investigative efforts" in west Dallas. According to what I have read over the years, Hamer supposedly spent a lot of time along Eagle Ford Road talking to the business owners who knew our family. People along west Dallas' main street did not easily volunteer information concerning Clyde's activities and whereabouts in casual conversation amongst themselves and they sure were not going to speak of those things in the presence of inquisitive strangers. In my opinion, Frank Hamer probably gave up as much information about himself as he learned about my brother. Hamer's ramblings up and down Eagle Ford Road stuck out like a sore thumb in west Dallas, and his interests were undoubtedly related to Clyde by one of my brother's old friends.

From what I have learned in the years since, it was Hamer's intent to learn everything he could about Clyde, including his mannerisms and habits. The ex-Ranger believed that, by learning all he could about his quarry, he could come to anticipate Clyde's next movement and then be there to arrest him when he showed up.

Frank Hamer honestly came to believe that he would eventually be waiting for Clyde and Bonnie at one of the campsites he believed they frequented. The lawman thought he could remain hidden in a nearby blind while Clyde and Bonnie settled in for the night. Then, when the two kids finally drifted off to sleep, Hamer thought he could storm into their camp, snatch their guns from beyond their reach, and then arrest the two of them before they would be able to realize what was going on.

I have no doubt that Frank Hamer may have apprehended some individuals in this fashion before he got on Clyde's trail. But Clyde would prove to be the exception to the rule; in fact, when it came to my brother, the rule book would have to go flying out the window. The reason why Clyde's behavior could not be reliably predicted by Frank Hamer or any other lawman was that my brother firmly believed in playing his hunches - and Clyde's hunches almost always proved to be correct. In fact, there was only one hunch on Clyde's part that proved to be wrong - trusting Henry Methvin and Methvin's family - and it proved to be fatal for him and Bonnie.

Clyde's correct hunches were the reason the law was never able to catch up with him. Trying to anticipate Clyde's next move was futile to anyone attempting to catch my brother. Although Frank Hamer claimed several near misses in his search for Clyde, the hard fact of the matter is that the only time Hamer ever got anywhere close to my brother was on the morning of May 23, 1934. Before that day, the only places Hamer ever narrowly missed my brother were in the lawman's dreams.

Clyde knew there were two Ranger-types after him because Hamer had acquired an associate to go on the road with him in pursuit of my brother. By mid-April, an officer named Manny Gault was traveling with Hamer, Alcorn, and Hinton on their excursions. Now, it seemed that there were five men pursuing Clyde full time: Hamer, Gault, Alcorn, Hinton, and Lester Kendell. Ironically, while the Texas Rangers and Dallas County Deputies have received the most publicity in the years since, the federal agent probably did the most deliberate and deadly work in terms of what did finally happen. While the four Texas officers were running all over the southwest to places where Clyde was allegedly seen, G-man Kendell continued to operate with Henderson Jordan, the Joyner family, and the Methvin relatives in northwest Louisiana.

By mid-April, it didn't really matter to Clyde who was chasing him. My brother knew better than anyone that he would eventually and inevitably be put on the spot. Clyde figured that he would probably be betrayed by someone who was close to him. But he knew our family would never turn him in to the law. It was doubtful that the Parkers would now ever try to betray Clyde and Bonnie, due to Bonnie's continued insistence that she would never leave Clyde's side and that she would rather die with him than live without him.

But Clyde continued to believe that someone outside the Barrow and Parker families would sooner or later put him on the spot. The public outrage and the ever increasing reward amounts described in the newspapers acted as guarantees that someone who had some familiarity with Clyde and Bonnie would inevitably go to the authorities. By then, more rational individuals were questioning the sincerity of some of those who were offering hundreds and even thousands of dollars for Clyde's apprehension. It was apparent that some people were acting out of emotion and a desire for newspaper publicity in offering money for Clyde's arrest. It was believed that when my brother and Bonnie were finally run to earth, most of these reward offers would not be worth the price of the paper in which they were advertised.

The only people in the world that Clyde seemed to trust, outside of his own family, were Henry Methvin and Methvin's family. Clyde was helping Henry the Rat's family in terms of finances. My brother gave Old Henry Methvin the money to purchase a pickup truck and was helping the family out in other ways. The Methvin family was gratefully accepting Clyde's assistance with one hand while using the other hand to let the Joyners know about Clyde's appearances.

My brother figured that Henry the Rat would be last person in the world who would be instrumental in betraying him. Clyde figured since Henry actually killed the two motorcycle officers and had most likely been the one to slay the Oklahoma constable, Methvin was in too deep to ever be able to get out of any of the murder charges. These were the crimes that had the press screaming for Clyde's blood, and my brother figured that anyone else who had been involved was in too deep to be able to make a deal or a bargain with the law. The last thing in the world Clyde expected was the Methvins and their relatives working with the law.

Since my mother stopped keeping records on the wall of our house as of that "Black Easter," I cannot recall the actual dates of Clyde's visits during April, outside of the first. I do know that he was gone for about two weeks after the Grapevine killings, which would have made his next visit occur about April 15. During mid April he made a series of quick visits over the period of about a week. These April visits took the same form as did all of the previous visits: Clyde would leave a message for our mother as to where he and Bonnie would be waiting, our mother would get L.C. or Joe Bill Francis to drive a group of us (including Emma and Billie Parker) out to where they were told us they would meet us, and we would follow through. We always took food and our cameras, as I mentioned previously.

It was always Clyde, Bonnie, and Henry who were there at the appointed meeting place. We saw very little of Joe Palmer; his particular illness consistently prevented him from traveling with Clyde on a regular basis. One of the topics of conversation at these meetings was the letter which was written by Raymond Hamilton to his lawyer in Dallas. Hamilton's lawyer had released this letter to the newspapers.

In this particular piece of communication, Raymond stated that he and Clyde had been separated for several weeks. Of course, Raymond did not go into the truth of why they parted company. Raymond said nothing about the fact that Joe Palmer had pegged him as a snitch in prison to the others in Clyde's group. Raymond said nothing about how Clyde saw him swiping additional amounts of money beyond his recognized share out of the Lancaster robbery loot. Raymond said nothing about the fact that none of the others liked or trusted Mary the Washerwoman. Raymond said nothing about his plundering of the group's kitty in order to placate Mary O'Dare, which proved to be the last straw. All Hamilton said was that he didn't "go Clyde's speed." Coming so soon after the three killings during the first week of April, Raymond's statements sounded like the self-proclaimed aristocrat of highwaymen cavalierly brushing off a barbarian (which is undoubtedly what Hamilton was hoping the public would perceive).

Raymond's letter was given much publicity in the newspaper. The public was being treated to daily accounts of the depredations of the so-called "Barrow Gang," so Raymond thought he would take advantage of this circumstance to distance himself from Clyde. Raymond stated that he was staying in a hotel in New Orleans while Henry Methvin was committing mayhem at Grapevine and Miami-Commerce. Hamilton said he could provide documentation to substantiate his claim. There was an implied request to the public by Raymond that they should please differentiate between Raymond Hamilton, the spiritual descendant of Claude Duval and Dick Turpin, and Clyde Barrow, the spiritual descendant of Attila the Hun and Genghis Khan.

Clyde could certainly understand about Raymond wanting to supply an alibi for himself on that Easter Sunday. My brother would have loved to have been elsewhere himself. It was Hamilton's cavalier insinuations that were under question by those of us who knew the truth of the matter.

Responses to Hamilton's letter which were signed with some variation of Clyde's name began to be mailed in to newspapers and police agencies. One such letter was mailed to a Houston paper in mid-April. It was a short, one paragraph message which confirmed that Clyde and Raymond were no longer running together. It also said that if one of the two were arrested, the other might assist in breaking him out. This short message also referred to a warning to tourists to be careful and stop when the police told them to stop. The writer said that the police should be careful in determining who they would be asking to stop. This letter was signed "Clyde and Bonnie."

This letter was not written by my brother because he had no plans of ever assisting Raymond Hamilton again in any more prison breaks. There was no agreement for Clyde and Raymond to provide assistance for the other in case either of them was apprehended by the police. Clyde was through with Hamilton for good. The other reason why this letter could not have been written by my brother was because Clyde had no intentions of being arrested and imprisoned. Clyde was very clear on this issue: he would not be taken alive. One time, Clyde told our mother that if he was ever surrounded with no way out, he would shoot himself before he would let himself be arrested. Our mother begged him not to commit suicide. My brother finally agreed not to shoot himself, but he again reemphasized that he would never be taken alive.

There were a couple of other letters written in early April which were credited to my brother and Bonnie. One letter is not too well known, but the other is very famous. I'll deal with the little known letter first. It was mailed from Decatur, Texas a couple of days after the killings at Grapevine and was addressed to Mr. Amon Carter, the publisher of the Ft. Worth newspaper. The writer of the letter threatened Mr. Carter for publishing the falsehood that Bonnie smoked cigars. The writer also threatened Miriam "Ma" Ferguson, the governor of Texas at that time, for authorizing a reward for the parties who killed the two highway patrolmen. The letter was composed of threats against many prominent people and of vulgar descriptions of sexual activity.

This letter to Amon Carter was certainly not written by Clyde because my brother did not stay around the area long enough to mail off any letters from Decatur, which is not too far away from Grapevine. The vulgar content of the message concerning sexual activity (the letter said that the two motorcycle officers were killed because they stumbled across Clyde and Bonnie making full-fledged love there by the side of Highway 114) was strictly out of character for Clyde. My brother was very straight-laced in many of his personal activities, despite his career as a fugitive. Clyde didn't smoke or drink, and he was very circumspect in terms of any romantic behavior with Bonnie.

The second letter in early April was also written to a prominent man. It was mailed from Tulsa, Oklahoma on April 10 and was received in Detroit, Michigan a few days later. It was written to Henry Ford. This letter was a glowing testimonial to the good qualities of the Ford automobiles. Clyde did prefer the Ford V-8 for several reasons, but the hard truth of the matter is that Clyde never wrote this letter or any other letter to Henry Ford. The Ford company has gotten a lot of mileage out of this particular letter in terms of public response. Copies of this little message currently hang all over north-central Texas. A copy of the Henry Ford letter was hung in the Tarrant County Sheriff's office. Photocopies made by the Ford Motor Company are proudly displayed in antique stores, shoe repair shops, and offices. But my brother did not mail this letter to Detroit and really had nothing to do with it.

There were other letters purportedly sent by Clyde and Bonnie during the month of April, but before addressing these other communications, another occurrence must be described. Raymond Hamilton, who perceived himself as the modern Claude Duval, was arrested after he and another man robbed the bank in Lewisville, Texas. Hamilton and his associate were chased by a posse which immediately appeared on the scene. The pursuit began on Lewisville's main street and ended near the small town of Howe in Grayson County, two county lines away. Hamilton and the other man were brought back to the town of Denton. I stated that there was a posse on the scene immediately. The posse's presence was not an accident. Mary O'Dare had informed the authorities that the robbery was going to take place. Clyde had been right about Mary the Washerwoman all along.

It was Hamilton's arrest that occasioned the next wave of letters that were purportedly sent in by Clyde. The newspapers reported that Raymond Hamilton was transferred from the Denton county jail to the Dallas county jail. It was at the Dallas County "bar hotel" that a letter was received at the very end of April. It had been sent from Memphis, Tennessee on April 27, when the news of Hamilton's arrest had appeared in the national newspapers.

There have been different versions of this letter that have been published in written accounts of Clyde's life. Some versions of this letter are full of bluster, swagger, and threats. But the version of the Memphis letter that I accept is the one that begins with an expression of the lack of sympathy concerning Raymond's arrest. It mentions several things that Raymond neglected to address in the letter to his lawyer: Hamilton's wanting to shoot Joe Palmer while Joe was napping, Hamilton's cowardice at the roadblock in the Ozarks, the theft of the money from the Lancaster bank robbery, and the conflicts due to Mary O'Dare. Of all of the letters that were written during the month of April that purportedly were composed by my brother, this particular version of the Memphis letter is the only one that actually may have been written by him. Clyde finished this particular message by telling Hamilton that Raymond could not expect any further assistance or regard from my brother. This sign-off highlighted the fact that Clyde wanted nothing more to do with Hamilton.

Raymond was tried and found guilty on the Lewisville bank robbery, but he did not receive the death penalty on this charge on the basis of the habitual criminal statute or the robbery-with-firearms laws. Raymond avoided a death sentence during the many trials with which he was involved throughout 1933. But the authorities announced that they were planning to try Hamilton for his participation in the escape at the Eastham prison farm. The law held that everyone who was involved in this jail break were equally liable concerning the killing of the prison guard. The fact Hamilton would be going on trial for his life had no impact whatsoever on Clyde. Since Raymond had surrendered, my brother figured that Hamilton had asked for it by giving up so easily. Clyde also took no interest in Raymond's predicament because his mind was on other things. After his quick series of visits back home, Clyde went back out on the road to generate some more funds. Somewhere along the line, Joe Palmer rejoined Clyde and Henry the Rat and the three men began to investigate potential robbery sites up in the Midwest.

The group of law officers who were pursuing Clyde and Bonnie were also doing some traveling. Hamer, Gault, Alcorn, and Hinton were still driving over five different states, checking out every report of Clyde's presence. It was about the same time that Clyde, Bonnie, and Methvin went north that the four Texas law officers made one of their periodic stops at Shreveport. They contacted the sheriff as they usually did to see if any new leads had popped up. Since the sheriff had been involved in the April 13 preparations with Henderson Jordan and Lester Kendell, the sheriff advised the four men to get in contact with Jordan.

Apparently, Hamer and Alcorn decided to check out this possibility, and they met with Henderson Jordan at Arcadia, the county seat of Bienville Parish. Jordan told them of his connection with the Methvin and Joyner families and of his previous activities over the past four weeks. The three officers exchanged all of the information that they had accumulated. The two Texas officers agreed that this Louisiana set-up represented the best opportunity they would have to catch up with Clyde. Of course, his plan was completely contingent on someone Clyde trusted ratting him out to them. The officers' attempts to catch Clyde by anticipating his next move had failed miserably and they were as far from apprehending Clyde in late April as they had been on the day they all accepted the task of trailing him. Alcorn and Hamer asked to be included in Jordan's next move. It is interesting to note that Henderson Jordan did not seem overly enthusiastic about working with Alcorn and Hamer. The Louisiana sheriff told them that Hamer should go back to Austin, Alcorn should go back to Dallas, and that whenever something new came up, Jordan would contact them. In short, Jordan told them, "don't call me; I'll call you."

In late April, Hamer and Alcorn made a follow-up visit to Bienville Parish. Jordan took them around the southern part of the parish, giving them the general lay of the land. Interestingly enough, Jordan did not let the Texas officials talk to either the Methvin or Joyner families. The Louisiana sheriff was keeping himself as the central figure in this particular aspect of the manhunt for my brother. Jordan also did not offer to set up a meeting with Lester Kendell and the Texas officers. After seeing the terrain in Bienville Parish, Alcorn and Hinton began to talk about setting up a raiding party. Jordan immediately vetoed the idea, saying it would endanger women and children, even though Jordan and Lester Kendell had set up a raid on April 13 with the large posse of federal agents and Louisiana officers. Jordan was intent on associating himself with the G-men on the case. Alcorn and Hamer returned to their respective cities in Texas after their tour of Bienville Parish.

Henderson Jordan's desire to exclusively operate with the nationally-recognized federal agents was tested in late April. The federal agents were undergoing some ridicule and criticism during that period of time. The G-men had attempted a raid on a hunting lodge in northern Wisconsin which had ended in disaster. This particular affair had nothing to do with Clyde, however. A group of fugitives, including John Dillinger and Baby Face Nelson, were reported to be frequenting a certain hunting lodge and a horde of federal agents from Chicago and St. Paul-Minneapolis had responded to the report. The federal agents did not bother to contact the local police when they organized their raid, and their neglect showed up in the results. The G-men shot down three men who had emerged from the lodge when dogs began barking at the agents' approach. The agents believed these men could have been some of the fugitives who were alerted by the barking. The trio proved to be innocent bystanders; two of them were wounded, and one was killed. Dillinger, Nelson, and the other wanted men were alerted by the officers' gunfire and fled out the back.

The lodge owner called the local police, and a couple of these officers met one of the G-men at a neighboring lodge where another report of trouble was relayed. The nature of the trouble turned out to be Baby Face Nelson, who shot down the three officers, killing the federal agent. Baby Face, as well as the others, made a successful escape.

There was an immediate uproar over this affair; some newspapers demanded the resignation of J. Edgar Hoover and Melvin Purvis, who headed the party of G-men on this raid. Will Rogers, a popular newspaper columnist, said that the G-men were waiting to shoot Dillinger, but when the innocent bystanders came out instead, the agents shot them. Rogers continued his account by stating that Dillinger would get shot only when he mixed in with innocent bystanders, as they were the ones receiving the biggest part of police gunfire. Despite the ridicule and criticism the federal agents were receiving in the national media, Henderson Jordan continued to focus on Lester Kendell and not the Texas lawmen in his plans to catch Clyde.

My brother became a regular feature in the editorial cartoons in the newspaper in Dallas. Back in the early 1930s, the *Dallas Morning News* had a companion newspaper published as an evening edition, called the *Dallas News Evening Journal*. The front page of the *Dallas*

Journal always featured a prominent editorial-type cartoon. During 1934, the cartoon regularly dealt with the “crime wave” in general and Clyde in particular. One such cartoon during this time period show a nonchalant Clyde Barrow walking away from the state penitentiary with release papers prominently poking out of his coat pocket and then firing a machine gun out of the window of a speeding auto.

Another cartoon concerning Clyde appeared in the *Dallas Journal* during this same period. This caricature showed an old-time sheriff-type sitting up in his bed, trying to remember exactly what it was that he was intending to do that day. Hidden beneath the lawman’s bed were gangster-types and machine guns. Caricatures of Clyde, Bonnie, and Raymond Hamilton were poking out from beneath the end of the bed, grinning at the newspaper reader.

Yet another cartoon of this type from the *Dallas Journal* showed Pretty Boy Floyd. Pretty Boy was hopping up-and-down in one of his hideouts, waving his fists in the air. Floyd was surrounded by newspapers with headlines dealing with Clyde, Bonnie, Raymond Hamilton, and John Dillinger. Pretty Boy was caricatured as screaming and shouting about his lack of newspaper publicity during the past few months.

There was yet another cartoon showing an angry citizen shouting about why the authorities had not done anything about the depredations of Clyde, Bonnie, and Hamilton. Then the cartoon showed the citizen more concerned about the horse races in the racetrack in Arlington, Texas than he was about Clyde, Bonnie, and Raymond. I suppose it was meant to illustrate that the public’s concern with Clyde was vacillating and half-hearted.

But our family knew that the officers’ attitudes towards Clyde and Bonnie were anything but half-hearted. We knew my brother was being purposefully sought by lawmen at the federal, state, county, and local level - and that these officers’ jobs would not be concluded until Clyde was brought in, dead or alive. And we knew which part of the “dead or alive” equation Clyde would accept.

What our family did not know was that Clyde’s quick series of mid-April visits was the last group of get-togethers that my brother would ever have with his family. Our mother, who so adored her fugitive son and was adored in return, would never see him again. The series of events which would result in an ambush on a country road eight miles south of Gibsland, Louisiana, was accelerating towards that inevitable conclusion.

Chapter 23

By the beginning of May, Clyde had been on the run for just over two full years. Those two years culminated in more heartbreak for our family than most people have seen in a lifetime. We continued to bear up every time when the latest tragedy with which Clyde was connected exploded into the headlines. But it wasn't just my brother's involvement which caused the Barrow family to grieve. We felt sorrow for every family involved in these tragedies.

But there were many people whose emotional involvement in Clyde's activities were of a different sort than that of the Barrow family. People across the country followed the careers of fugitives like Clyde, John Dillinger, and Pretty Boy Floyd in the same fashion as they followed the weekly movie serials or the continuing episodes of radio shows like "Jack Armstrong, the All American Boy." It all seemed like just one big, exciting, adventurous, grown-up game of "cops and robbers" to some segments of the American public. But to the families of these wanted men, who knew and loved the flesh and blood personages behind the sensational headlines, the movie house newsreels, and the hysterical radio bulletins, it was one big, long-running tragedy with no glamour attached to it, whatsoever.

Early May also brought the news that a series of new crime fighting laws would soon be passed by Congress. There had been some initial resistance to this new legislation, due to concerns regarding the broadening of the federal government's police powers. Some people felt that these new crime laws might infringe on the rights of the states. Hatton Sumners, a congressman from the Dallas area, was one of those legislators who felt that these new laws might conflict with states' rights and his congressional committee managed to delay the passage of these laws during the spring of 1934.

There was agitation across the country for the passage of these crime laws from newspaper editors, bankers' organizations, and politicians. For example, the Texas Bankers' Association ran an editorial in the April, 1934 issue of *The Texas Bankers Record*, the official publication of the state's bank officials, titled "Let U.S. Catch Bandits," in which it welcomed these new crime laws. The article also asked those politicians who were delaying the passage of this legislation to stand aside and to quit interfering.

This edition of *The Texas Bankers Record* did not stop there. The April issue also published pictures of Clyde, Bonnie, and Raymond in a "wanted poster" fashion. It characterized the three of them as "Public Enemies 1 - 2 - 3," saying they had "robbed four banks and killed at least three good men" since February. Ironically, the true murderer of the "three good men" was not mentioned at all in this magazine. Henry Methvin was still getting away with his bloodletting at Clyde's expense.

Clyde was also becoming a regular feature in the "true crime/detective" type of magazines. For example, the June issue of *Startling Detective Adventures,* which actually hit the newsstands in early May, contained the second installation of an article supposedly co-written by W.D. Jones and a professional writer. The two-part series was titled "I Saw Clyde Barrow, Terror of the Southwest, Kill Five Men!" Of course, W.D. was just faithfully repeating the alibis that Clyde had instructed him to tell. It was hard for those of us who knew the truth about W.D.'s involvement to keep a straight face while reading his alibis, but we were all hoping he would be able to avoid the electric chair.

Obviously, Congress was paying more attention to the items in *The Texas Bankers Record* than *Startling Detective Adventures* articles. It was the activities of John Dillinger in the Midwest and Clyde Barrow in the Southwest that acted as an impetus in getting action going again on the logjammed crime laws. There were several of these bills that seemed aimed directly at the interstate automobile bandits. Under these new laws, it would become a federal crime to rob a bank that was insured by the federal government. It would also become a federal crime to cross a state line in order to escape prosecution.

Since both Clyde and John Dillinger continuously traveled in and out of several states, it meant that the G-men could use this law to go after them. Up to this time, the only crime the Division of Investigation had on either of them was driving a stolen car across a state line. It also became a federal offense to assault or murder a federal agent. The killings of the G-men in the Kansas City Massacre of June, 1933, and the Dillinger-related Wisconsin lodge raid in April, 1934, were felonies only on the state level; it was not a federal crime to shoot a federal agent on a federal case.

Before Lester Kendell got involved in pursuing Clyde, there was no continuous, coordinated federal pursuit of my brother for any of the federal crimes he had committed. That was somewhat surprising because Clyde had been involved in some things that should have brought federal scrutiny. His raids on National Guard armories to get automatic pistols and Browning Automatic Rifles were technically federal offenses. Clyde continuously drove stolen cars over state lines, which were violations of the Dyer Act. On the few occasions when Clyde had to temporarily abduct both officers and citizens, state lines were frequently crossed. The deputy at Carlsbad was taken from New Mexico to Texas. The two people in Louisiana were taken into Arkansas and released. The two officers from Wellington were taken from Texas into Oklahoma. The officer from Miami-Commerce was driven into Kansas and released. These interstate abductions were technically violations of the Lindbergh law, which made taking a kidnapping victim across a state line a federal offense.

The Division of Investigation issued a wanted poster for Clyde on October 24, 1933. The G-men issued it on the basis of a warrant for the "National Motor Vehicle Theft Act," which was the formal title of the Dyer Act. But there was never any follow-up by the federal government until Lester Kendell was assigned to the case.

Clyde did not care if Lester Kendell, Frank Hamer, J. Edgar Hoover, or Wyatt Earp was after him; it was all the same to my brother. At this point in time, Clyde was involved in other things, which became somewhat apparent when my brother made his final visit home on May 7, 1934.

Henry Barrow, our father, was the last member of our family to see Clyde alive. The visits Clyde and Bonnie made with our mother and Mrs. Parker are well known to all who have any familiarity with my brother's story; but what is not so well known is that Clyde also visited a number of times with our father. The meetings between Clyde and Henry Barrow were carried out in a different fashion than were the get-togethers between Clyde and Bonnie and their mothers.

When Clyde wanted to have a visit one-on-one with his father, my brother would drive by our father's filling station and toot his car horn in a certain fashion. When we heard this particular sequence of horn-tooting, all of us knew it was Clyde. My brother did it in this manner to avoid having to stop in front of the service station. If Clyde would have stopped in front of the station, which was in full view of passersby on Eagle Ford Road, it would have been the equivalent of advertising his presence to everyone in west Dallas. We would then meet with him wherever he parked, providing Clyde was at ease with the situation. However, if my brother had one of his hunches, he would drive on down Eagle Ford Road and come back later or would make several trips past the service station to make sure the coast was clear.

When our father was aware that Clyde wanted to talk to him, Henry knew just where to meet with his fugitive son. They always met at the intersection where the road to the west of the service station (known today as Borger Road) crossed the Texas and Pacific rail-road tracks in west Dallas. Our father would always start walking south on Borger Road to where Clyde was waiting for him, and they would talk there. On the evening of May 7, Clyde drove up in front of the service station and "tooted" the horn until my father responded and went to the front where my brother was waiting. Father and son talked with each other for a short period out in front of the station and then agreed to meet down by the railroad tracks. Our father walked off across the road towards the Texas and Pacific tracks. Clyde drove around until Henry had enough time to travel down there. My brother then drove down to where his father was waiting.

By May 7, Clyde was traveling in what was a fairly recent acquisition for him: a 1934 Ford V-8 Four door Deluxe. The color of the car was really rather hard to define. The color has been characterized as some variation of tan, grey, or brown. However, the color which best describes this auto is "Desert Sand." Clyde had gotten this off-color Ford V-8 about nine days earlier on a Sunday afternoon in Topeka, Kansas.

My brother felt the need to make a switch from the car in which they were traveling. Clyde changed cars often because it was one way of keeping a step ahead of the officers. While the police were broadcasting bulletins concerning one make and model of automobile, Clyde would have already gotten another car of a different type.

On this Sunday afternoon, Clyde and Bonnie were driving around Topeka, looking around for a desirable automobile. My brother found what he wanted in the driveway of a residential neighborhood, which belonged to a couple named Warren who had recently purchased it. Clyde and Bonnie circled the block. When they felt the coast was clear, Clyde jumped out of their car and ran over to the Warrens' vehicle. He got it started and drove off, following Bonnie, who was driving their old car, out into the countryside. There they transferred all of their clothes and belongings from the old car into the new one. Neither Joe Palmer nor Henry Methvin were with them when they took the Warrens' auto in Topeka.

The new car wasn't the only thing our father noticed when he and Clyde met by the Texas and Pacific tracks on the night of May 7. My brother had a suitcase full of money in the back seat of the auto. Apparently, his trip up into the Midwest to generate funds with Henry the Rat and Joe Palmer had been successful. Ironically, one of the banks the boys had robbed was in the town of Stuart, Iowa, which was just a very few miles west of Dexfield Park. This park, located between the towns of Dexter and Redfield, was where Buck had been fatally wounded almost 10 months earlier.

Clyde's visit was not completely social in nature; he had some legal papers that he wanted to sign and to send to our mother. My brother grasped a suitcase that was on the back seat of his car and got it out. Clyde opened the suitcase and piled the stuff that was in it on the running board of the car. While Clyde was doing this, our father was holding a flashlight to assist his son in what he was doing. Clyde finally found the paperwork he was hunting for, but then the unanticipated happened: my brother found that he had run out of ink and couldn't sign any of the documents. Clyde wasn't too upset by this setback and felt that it was only a minor inconvenience He said that he would be back in two weeks and would get the matter fixed up then. Clyde told our father that he wanted to put his fingerprints on the documentation to prove his identity. Since my brother could hardly seek the services of a notary public due to his status as a wanted fugitive, he had to devise some other fashion of establishing his identity. Leaving his fingerprints on the documents was the one definitive way Clyde had in verifying the authenticity of his signature. Our father saw that only two pieces of documentation were involved in this matter and he never really got a chance to take a good look at them to see exactly what was involved. None of our family ever really learned what this matter was about, but we somehow gained the impression that it involved some land or money.

There was one possible explanation for the paperwork. Our family did find out later that Clyde was financially assisting the Methvin family. I have already mentioned that he had purchased a Model A pickup truck for Old Henry Methvin. It is also believed that my brother was involved in the purchase of property from which the Methvin family benefited. Clyde was always open-handed and generous with both his own family and the families of those few people whom he felt he could trust. It is possible the paperwork they discussed on May 7 might have involved the purchase, in his mother's name, of some land over in Louisiana.

There has been one persistent rumor connected with Clyde's possible buying of Louisiana property which should be put to rest. This rumor deals with the scenario of Bonnie being pregnant, of Clyde buying property where Bonnie could be situated during her pregnancy, and of Clyde and Henry going on a bank-robbing binge to accumulate funds so that the three of them could go to Mexico where Bonnie could have her baby and where the three of them could live happily ever after. This scenario is pure poppycock. It's already been established that Bonnie was incapable of having children. But, what many do not know is, due to a childhood illness, Clyde also could not reproduce.

Nevertheless, this scenario has been relayed as the truth by many people in northwest Louisiana for well over 60 years. Even in the 1990s, there were people who will adamantly argue that Bonnie was indeed pregnant during the spring of 1934. It is one more unfounded rumor that will probably never go away, despite the hard facts of the matter.

Whatever the unsigned documentation dealt with, Clyde put it back in his suitcase and returned the suitcase to the back seat of the car. He then visited with our father until about one o'clock in the morning. Clyde told his father that he ought to be getting back to the service station, since the police were watching the movements of both of our parents and his absence may have been noticed. Clyde hugged his father before they separated, never realizing it would be for the last time. Then Clyde drove the four-door Deluxe off into the night. Our father watched his fugitive son disappear into the darkness and then walked back to the service station.

Clyde's hunch that the authorities were watching our parents was confirmed just a very few days later when a carload of officers drove up to the service station and asked to speak with our mother. When Cumie came to the officers' car in response to their request, they hustled her into the car and hurriedly drove off. No one had the slightest idea where the cops were taking our mother. Of course, our family was very concerned about what happened. Word of the abduction was somehow relayed to Texas Governor "Ma" Ferguson, who immediately ordered the law enforcement officials involved to return our mother to her home, which was done. Cumie was not harmed during her ordeal. All of our family felt this was an ill-advised attempt to draw Clyde out of hiding. After the failed ambush near Sowers in the previous November, someone had told the Dallas county officers that Clyde had threatened to get anyone who attempted to harm as much as one hair on our mother's head. The officers figured Clyde would angrily storm back into the Dallas area when he had heard that his mother had been arrested. The officers figured that Clyde would be coming to them at that point, a situation in which they felt they would have the upper hand. But Clyde knew that this was an attempt to draw him out of hiding and he didn't respond to their attempt.

It was during this same time frame that yet another letter purportedly written by Clyde was received by the authorities. This piece of correspondence was poorly typed on the back of a Western Union telegram form. This message was addressed to Winter King, an assistant district attorney in Dallas. The letter was mailed from McKinney, Texas on May 11, 1934, and was received by King the following day. The letter accused Raymond Hamilton and Mary O'Dare of shooting the two motorcycle officers near Grapevine, Texas, on Easter Sunday. The tone of the letter was extremely bitter and vindictive towards Hamilton.

While we knew that Clyde had no use for Raymond anymore, we did not believe he and Bonnie wrote this letter. Clyde never returned to the Dallas area after May 7, and McKinney is only about 30 miles north of Dallas. If my brother would have been that close to home, he would have contacted his family concerning the signatures he needed on his paperwork. Clyde had told our father he would not be back in the area for at least two more weeks. All I can say is that whoever wrote this letter had no use for either Raymond Hamilton or Mary the Washerwoman, which meant that anyone of quite a number of people could have written it. One of the reasons why Hamilton was publicizing his role as lone gentleman highwayman was that very few people who knew him wanted anything to do with him.

The group of officers working full-time pursuing Clyde continued to focus their attention on the one weak spot in my brother's defenses: his fondness for Henry Methvin. The four Texas officers made their third excursion to Bienville Parish to see Sheriff Henderson Jordan at about the same time Clyde made his last visit home. Jordan was as vague about what was going on as he had been previously, telling the four Texans that something might break during the next three weeks and that they should wait until he called them.

The four Texas peace officers then went back out on the road, trying to anticipate my brother's next move, and, as usual, getting nowhere. It turned out that it wasn't one of Clyde's moves that caused the next development in the case. Old Henry Methvin was the person who made a move that got the attention of Henderson Jordan. Old Methvin moved from his place in the extreme southwestern end of Bienville Parish to an old cabin located more towards the center of the parish. The old man's relocation took place around Wednesday, May 16. Located deep in the woods, Methvin took up residence in an old cabin, "Cole Place," there was only one rather primitive road connected it to the highway.

Many people have considered the "Cole Place" as my brother's Louisiana hideout but nothing could be further from the truth. From Clyde's point of view, it was a death trap: anyone could be bottled up in there if the one road out was blocked. My brother depended too much on his driving ability to allow himself to be sequestered in a situation where his automotive getaway options were as limited as they were at the "Cole Place."

Some have said that Clyde had planned on using the Cole cabin as a place where either he and Bonnie or he and our parents could have spent the entire summer of 1934 together. My brother had no such illusions about being able to settle down for such a long period time at a single location. Clyde knew his best chances of surviving depended on being fast and flexible, which meant living out of his car as much as possible. Truthfully, there was no benefit for Clyde if he established a semi-permanent hideout. The sole beneficiaries of this latest move were likely the senior Methvins, who had probably never before lived as well as they were living courtesy of Clyde's assistance.

Three days after the move into the Cole cabin, two opposing forces converged in this northwestern corner of Louisiana. On the evening of Saturday, May 19, the first contending force, consisting of the four Texas officers, had pulled into a Shreveport hotel to rest from 10 days of unsuccessfully attempting to catch up with Clyde and Bonnie. Their previous visit to Henderson Jordan had taken place on May 9, resulting in absolutely no definitive results from Jordan's surveillance of the Joyners. The four officers wanted to follow up with Jordan.

The second contending force, consisting of Clyde, Bonnie, and Henry the Rat, had also driven into Shreveport that same evening. Ironically, the trio had pulled into a restaurant which was only a few doors away from the hotel occupied by Alcorn, Gault, Hamer, and Hinton. Clyde stopped in order to purchase some take-out sandwiches. Henry was sent inside to pick up the sandwiches while Clyde and Bonnie waited outside in the car at the curb.

Then the unexpected happened: a Shreveport police car came cruising down the street where the officers' hotel and the restaurant were located. Clyde saw the police car approaching their location. My brother did not know if any of the people who were coming and going at the restaurant had recognized either he or Henry the Rat, but he did not wait around to find out; Clyde whipped his car out into the street and sped off. The Shreveport officers saw Clyde's car suddenly pull out into traffic. The police car attempted to catch up with my brother's vehicle, but Clyde easily lost them. The officers were not aware of who it was that they had surprised at the restaurant, as they were out on a routine patrol and were not looking for anything in particular. If Clyde and Bonnie had just remained inconspicuous in their car, the Shreveport officers probably would have just passed them by. Clyde's reaction to the Shreveport officers would set off a chain of events which would have fatal consequences for my brother and Bonnie.

Henry Methvin, who was inside the store purchasing the intended meal for the trio, made the second mistake. He saw what had happened outside the restaurant between Clyde and the Shreveport police and hit the panic button. Henry dashed outside the restaurant and disappeared, leaving his order untouched just as he was just preparing to pay for it. If Henry had just remained composed and watched to see if the police car was just cruising by, events might have turned out drastically different. The cashier at the restaurant thought Henry's reaction was very unusual. The incident at the eatery was reported by both the restaurant people and the officers in the prowl car to those in charge at the Shreveport police headquarters. But none of those involved still had any idea of the identities of the people who fled at the approach of the officers. It was just regarded as a rather suspicious occurrence, something to be written up in a report and forgotten shortly thereafter.

On Sunday, May 20, one of the Texas officers contacted the

Shreveport police. There was no particular reason for making this contact, outside of professional courtesy in letting the local cops know that Alcorn, Gault, Hamer, and Hinton were in town. It was during this informal meeting that the Shreveport officers told the Texas lawman about the incident at the restaurant on Saturday night. The description of the man who rushed out of the eatery without picking up his order rung a bell with the Texans - it sounded a little too much like Henry Methvin. The Shreveport police were asked to go back to the restaurant and show a picture of Methvin to the people who had waited on him. Of course the restaurant employees positively identified the photo of Henry the Rat. The photo was not labeled with Methvin's name, and the restaurant people were not told the identity of the man in the photo.

The lawmen from Texas began to get excited about this accidental discovery. They had finally hit the northwestern Louisiana area at the same time Clyde, Bonnie, and Henry Methvin were in the same region. They made immediate preparations to get in contact with Sheriff Henderson Jordan on Monday, May 21.

According to what Ted Hinton later related, the quartet of officers drove from Shreveport over to Bienville Parish to see Jordan on Monday. The two Dallas County deputies were in one car, while the two state officers were following them in another automobile. On the way, a detour had to be made around some type of road construction, with the traffic being routed by state highway employees. There was a continuous line of autos traveling in both directions on this detour. It made for tedious traveling for Alcorn and Hinton until they recognized Clyde driving toward them in the line of traffic going west. But there was nothing they could do about it with so many other cars so close to them inching their way along until the traffic snarl gave out on the highway. It was only Clyde and Bonnie in their car - Henry the Rat was not riding with them on this trip.

By the time the four Texas officers reached Arcadia, they were undoubtedly high with excitement. They had finally caught up with Clyde. But Henderson Jordan might have had mixed feelings about the matter with the four Texans accidentally getting their own lead on Clyde's whereabouts in the Caddo/Bossier/Bienville parish area. Up until this weekend in May, Jordan had been the pivotal individual in the northwestern Louisiana manhunt for my brother. He had carefully protected his connection with the Methvins and the Joyners from both the federal agents and the officers from Texas. Now, the Lone Star lawmen were calling on him with their own suggestions on setting up an ambush for Clyde and Bonnie along one of the country roads in the vicinity of Old Henry Methvin's current residence at the Cole cabin. They had learned enough on their guided tour three weeks previously that they had already put together their own plans to ambush Clyde in Henderson Jordan's territory. Things were not working out as Jordan had initially envisioned.

Henderson Jordan handled the situation by saying he would check with his contact to see when Clyde and Bonnie would be making their next trip to the old Cole place. Once Jordan ascertained this precise time, it meant that the officers could set their trap with the full expectations of quick and definite results. Jordan also told the Texans that he had definite information that Clyde and Henry the Rat were planning to hold up the bank in Arcadia sometime during the next few days. Jordan felt it important that he take measures to protect the property of his constituency. The sheriff advised the Texans to go back to their hotel in Shreveport and wait until he gave them the word on Clyde's next visit to Old Henry Methvin's place - and then to be ready to leave on a moment's notice. The quartet returned to Shreveport.

On the morning of May 22, Henderson Jordan contacted the banker in Arcadia about the rumored robbery. Armed men were set up in the immediate vicinity of the bank, with an armed guard placed inside the bank. Guns were given to the bank officials. Whether this was a real rumor or just a dodge by which Jordan could again delay the quartet of Texas lawmen is not known. I do not believe that Clyde ever had any intentions of robbing that bank in Arcadia; it would be foolish to commit a major crime like bank robbery within a very few miles of where he was allegedly setting up a long-term hideaway.

The banker was not the only person Jordan attempted to deal with on that Tuesday. The sheriff also tried to contact Lester Kendell at his New Orleans office of the U. S. Division of Investigation. But the unexpected again happened: Kendell was not in his office. The federal agent was out of town in connection with another case. I am sure Jordan spent the better part of the whole day desperately trying to make contact with Kendell to give the famous G-men the first opportunity to be involved in the apprehension of Clyde Barrow. Jordan also made contact with the Joyner family to get information concerning the next expected visit by Clyde and Bonnie to the Cole place. The Joyners said my brother and Bonnie would definitely be in that area of the morning of May 23.

By the evening of May 22, it was apparent that Jordan was not going to make contact with Lester Kendell in enough time to allow a heavily armed squad of G-men to quickly travel to Bienville Parish from New Orleans. If Henderson Jordan wanted to ambush Clyde Barrow at this time, he would have to use the only armed officers available: the quartet of Texas officers sequestered at the Shreveport hotel. Jordan called them and the four officers responded.

Jordan and one of his deputies named Oakley sat down with Alcorn, Gault, Hamer, and Hinton. The six men made their plans concerning the deaths of Clyde and Bonnie. The Louisiana officers knew of movements which would be made by Old Henry Methvin early the next morning and plotted accordingly.

While the lawmen were planning and plotting on that Tuesday evening, Clyde and Bonnie were meeting with Henry Methvin and a few of his relatives in a rural area of northwestern Louisiana. It seems that after Clyde and Bonnie drove off from the Shreveport eatery, Henry the Rat stole a car in Shreveport and drove over to relatives of his in a nearby town. I can't definitely say where Clyde and Bonnie went immediately after leaving Shreveport, but they probably went to one of their regional hideaways. Stories that Henry Methvin intentionally separated from Clyde and Bonnie at the restaurant and disappeared on his own volition are belied by his meeting with Clyde and Bonnie on the evening of May 22.

Of course, that does not mean Henry the Rat wasn't connected with the plot in which his parents and the Joyners were so deeply involved. Sometimes it seems that Clyde and Bonnie were the only ones who weren't aware that the elder Methvins and Joyners were working with the officers. Methvin and some of his cousins met with my brother and Bonnie. Henry apparently was not intent on immediately rejoining Clyde and Bonnie in their auto. Methvin arrived with the relatives with whom he was staying, and he drove off with those same relatives after that evening's get together. Clyde and Bonnie were probably the only ones present who didn't know that they only had about 12 hours to live.

Chapter 24

Before going into what I believe occurred at about 9:15 a.m. on the morning of May 23, 1934 at a site on Louisiana State Highway 154 (around eight miles south of the small town of Gibsland), let me quickly summarize the three widely different versions of what happened as related by those individuals who were directly involved.

The first version, which has appeared in many books and articles dealing with that particular individual, is Frank Hamer's. Hamer's story states that his shrewd detective work, deductive reasoning, and dependence on snitches uncovered the location of Clyde's "mailbox" on that particular Louisiana road. It was simply a matter of being there with a posse at the same time that Clyde pulled up to see if any messages were left for him. In Hamer's version of events, when the ex-Ranger sees Clyde and Bonnie pulling up to his roadside "mailbox," he swiftly strides out into the road with his trusty rifle pointed directly at Clyde's car. Hamer yells for my brother to surrender, but Clyde chooses to go for his gun. Hamer therefore has no choice except to shoot down both Clyde and Bonnie, with the rest of the posse, who remain hidden in the roadside shrubbery, joining in after Hamer begins to fire. Neither Old Henry Methvin nor Young Henry are part of Hamer's scenario.

The second version is that of the Methvin family, which was featured in the 1967 movie *Bonnie and Clyde.* Old Man Methvin, wanting to get his son off the hook, approaches the officers with a plan to set up Clyde and Bonnie. Henry the Rat is fully cooperative in this plan, hoping to be free of "the nightmare life" in which his association with Clyde has placed him. Henry separates from Clyde and Bonnie at the first opportunity, with my brother trying to find him again. Clyde gets in contact with Old Henry Methvin to see if Henry the Rat had returned home. The old man agrees to meet Clyde on May 23 to give him an update on Young Henry's whereabouts. Old Henry Methvin puts himself out on Highway 154 with the Model A truck which my brother purchased for him jacked up, waiting for Clyde to show up. The posse of six officers are also nearby with their guns at the ready. Clyde and Bonnie drive up to see what is wrong with Methvin's truck.

The officers see their moment and yell for my brother to surrender. Clyde doesn't, and they fire on him.

The third version belongs to Ted Hinton. In this version, the officers learn of Clyde's presence in the area through the affair at the restaurant in Shreveport. The four lawmen from Texas go out to Bienville Parish on Monday evening to set up the ambush on the highway. The six officers spend the entire night out there. They spend all day Tuesday at the same spot. The sextet continue their vigil all that night into the morning of May 23. Early that morning, the officers catch Old Henry Methvin driving along Highway 154 and shanghai him, tying him up in the woods while using his allegedly disabled truck for bait. The peace officers figure Clyde would recognize the vehicle and would naturally stop to see what was wrong, giving them the opportunity to order him to halt before they shoot him. Clyde shows up, does exactly what they anticipate, and is shot dead. Jordan, Hamer, and Old Man Methvin concoct the betrayal story right then and there to cover up what really happened.

These three stories cannot all simultaneously be true. Hamer's account may be rejected immediately, due to its sense of exaggerated self-importance and the fact that the Methvins were definitely involved. There is some degree of truth contained in both the Methvin and Hinton versions. I have already given what I believe to be the truth concerning the events which built towards the assassination of my brother and will now relate what I believe happened at 9:15 a.m. on the morning of May 23, 1934 on that stretch of Louisiana highway.

I do not know where Clyde and Bonnie spent the night of May 22 after they met with Henry and his cousins. It had to be north of the area where the Cole cabin was located due to the fact that he drove into the meeting with Old Henry Methvin from the north. That morning of May 23, Clyde and Bonnie were purportedly seen in the small town of Gibsland at a cafe where they frequently stopped. This cafe was located on Gibsland's main street next to the local movie theater. Over 60 years afterward, Gibsland residents who were children in 1934 could still remember seeing Clyde and Bonnie on Saturday nights. These kids were standing in line at the movie house when they watched Clyde carry Bonnie into the cafe to grab a Saturday night dinner while he waited in the car. Then he would carry her back out to their auto to keep watch while he grabbed a bite inside the cafe.

Clyde and Bonnie got some food at this cafe and then started driving on what would unknowingly be their "last mile." Both of them were wearing clothing which they had purchased in Terre Haute, Indiana, in early March. Bonnie was wearing a matching red outfit and Clyde was wearing a blue western-style shirt and dark blue pants. Clyde's tan hat was sitting the car, with his jacket laying over the driver's seat and his necktie draped around the rear-view mirror. One of Bonnie's tams lay in the seat with Clyde's hat. Their other possessions, from their guns to Clyde's fishing tackle box and Bonnie's makeup case, were also in the car. The suitcase containing the substantial amount of cash that Henry Barrow saw on May 7 was also in their auto.

Clyde and Bonnie drove south on Highway 154. But my brother was not driving along at 80 miles an hour, as Frank Hamer allegedly said later. It would not be possible to navigate that narrow, winding road at such an excessive speed. Clyde's speed was likely in the 30 to 40 miles-per-hour range. They were feeling perfectly secure in northwestern Louisiana but were undoubtedly wanting to get back to visit their parents in the Dallas area. I am sure they were talking about the need to get back to see the home folks. It had been a little more than two weeks since Clyde and Bonnie had seen their families They had spent at least the last four days in Henry Methvin's home area, but it was time to attend to their own parents.

About eight miles south of Gibsland, Highway 154 straightens out for a few miles, beginning at a bend in the road which turns into a long incline up a hill. When Clyde came to this point in the road, he saw something that caught his attention, Old Henry Methvin's jacked up truck over on the side of the road. The truck was parked on the west side of the north-south Highway 154, pointing north. The officers were crouched in the brush behind an embankment on the east side of the road. Our family always believed that Old Henry Methvin was out there with his seemingly disabled vehicle.

Upon seeing the Model A pickup, and Old Henry, Clyde of course slowed down to see if he could be of any help. Old Methvin admitted that he was having trouble with his vehicle. Clyde, Bonnie, and Old Henry talked for a few seconds until a large truck hauling logs (logging was a big industry in this part of Louisiana) came into sight. It was traveling north on the highway.

Clyde told the old man to wait for a moment as he began to pull his car past the Model A truck. Clyde was attempting to give the log truck enough room to pass both vehicles. It was just after Clyde got beyond the Methvin truck that the hidden officers opened fire from the foliage on their side of the road.

Despite what has been printed in many of the accounts of my brother's assassination, there was no command to "halt" or "stick 'em up" or anything of the type from any of the lawmen. Some stories say that Hamer stepped into the road or that Jordan yelled something or that Alcorn yelled an order to stop. No warning of any kind was given by the police. Oakley, Jordan's deputy, hit the panic button and popped up out of the weeds and got off two shots, hitting Clyde in the back of the head. All Bonnie had time to do was to scream as Clyde slumped to his left side and the other officers joined in firing. Their car rolled forward towards the east side of the highway as Clyde lost consciousness after the impact of Oakley's first two shots. Their car rolled several yards before it hit the embankment and stopped. As the car slowly rolled, the officers continued to fire a steady stream of bullets from their rifles, shotguns, and pistols. After they'd emptied their guns into Clyde's car, the officers cautiously approached the auto.

Bob Alcorn later told us that he believed that he had been the first one to hit Clyde and Bonnie with his gunfire. He also said that he'd ran after the car as it rolled slowly forward and that he told the others to stop firing at this point, as they'd already killed Clyde. Ted Hinton later said that it was he who ran after the car. Frank Hamer later said that he was already out in the road when the firing began. I don't believe any of them tried to chase after Clyde's car on foot. But whether or not any of the officers were actually out in the road, the others continued to fire their weapons until they ran out of ammo.

When the gunfire was over and the car had stopped rolling, the officers cautiously gathered around the riddled Ford. Clyde still rested against the car door; Bonnie was slumped forward with her head between her knees. Ted Hinton later said that he lifted her up and placed her against Clyde. The officers also later claimed that Clyde's door was open and that he had a shotgun on his lap, but my brother never had any time either to grab for a shotgun or to open the car door after the Louisiana deputy's first two shots struck him in the back. Clyde probably never knew what hit him.

Shortly after the gunfire stopped, half of the officers left the killing site. One of the Dallas county deputies had to find a telephone to call Smoot Schmid. One of the Texas Rangers had to call Texas prison Chief Lee Simmons. Sheriff Henderson Jordan had to go arrange for the parish coroner and a coroner's jury to verify and make official the assassination of Clyde and Bonnie. The other officers remained at the site of the ambush in order to "inventory" the possessions Clyde and Bonnie had in the car, and maintain order of the ever-growing crowd that appeared due to both the sound of the gunfire and the rapidly growing word-of-mouth communication.

Let me say a word about those who were attracted to the scene by the sound of the gunfire. Every person within earshot of the noise, later said that they clearly heard the sound of two shots at the beginning of the fusillade. This fact squares with the knowledge that the Louisiana deputy panicked and shot Clyde in the back without any warning.

Before the crowd managed to get too great, Ted Hinton took out a 16mm movie camera and began to record the scene for posterity. The car doors on Bonnie's side of the vehicle were opened so Hinton could film the bodies in the front seat and their possessions in the back seat. Bonnie's body can be seen on the seat, propped up against Clyde. Mercifully, the film was shot from a few yards away and there is no up-close gruesome detail. Even more mercifully, it is hard to even distinguish Clyde in the front seat. But the film unintentionally gave away some of the other officers' intentions. One of the other members of the firing squad can be seen rummaging through Bonnie's purse. This recorded action would be a portent of what would happen with their personal items a little later.

The Hinton film was later seen as newsreel footage in movie theatres. Apparently other lawmen saw this footage and got ideas from Hinton's camera work at the site of Clyde's death. When federal agents shot it out with Ma and Fred Barker in Oklawaha, Florida, several months later, one of the G-men remembered to bring along a photo camera. He took pictures of the bodies of Ma and Fred in the room where the two fugitives made their last stand. The bodies were sprawled on the floor, machine guns by their sides.

When the Dallas County sheriff's office was informed of the news, pandemonium resulted. The work for that day was immediately stopped. Smoot Schmid and Chief Deputy Bill Decker made immediate arrangements to travel over to Bienville Parish to take advantage of the national publicity which they knew would result from Clyde's death. It was the same with Lee Simmons; when he received the call from one of the Texas Rangers, he immediately hit the road to drive over to Bienville Parish.

I remember that morning very well, as it was during a very significant week in my life. I had just gotten married to Joe Bill Francis, the young man who had driven us over to meet with Clyde and Bonnie the night of the Sowers ambush. The wedding had taken place on that previous Sunday. On that morning of Wednesday, May 23, I was driving in the area of Cement City. I had just stopped in at a service station when I heard the news blaring over a radio at that establishment. I immediately got back into my car and drove back over to the service station on Eagle Ford Road to be with my family.

My parents had already been informed of Clyde's assassination by a reporter who had gotten the news at the Dallas County sheriff's office. It is ironic to note that neither the deputies over in Louisiana nor anyone we knew at the sheriff's office had the courage to inform my parents of their son's death. It was up to a newspaper reporter to report the sad news, and it was indeed tragic news for our family. No matter what Clyde had already been convicted of in the newspapers, we knew the real flesh-and-blood boy behind the sensational headlines and grieved for his passing. My oldest brother Jack had been informed of what had occurred with his younger brother, and he and our father were making plans with the undertaker at the Sparkman funeral home in Dallas to travel over to Bienville Parish to bring Clyde home for the final time. I stayed with my mother, who was understandably devastated by the news.

The Parker family had been informed of Bonnie's death by another newspaper reporter. They were already in the midst of another tragedy when news came of the ambush in Bienville Parish. Billie Jean Parker had been arrested just a few days earlier in connection with the murder of the two motorcycle officers near Grapevine on Easter Sunday.

The police had also arrested Floyd Hamilton on this same charge. Buster Parker had returned to Dallas when he heard of Billie Jean's trouble. Buster was home with his mother when the news came, and he began to make plans to travel to Louisiana to pick up Bonnie's body. The Parker family contacted the McKamy-Campbell funeral home on Forest Avenue in south Dallas for this sad duty.

Things in Dallas came to a momentary standstill when the news of Clyde's and Bonnie's deaths were broadcast over the radio. The newspapers began to chum out "extra" after "extra" as more and more details of the ambush came in from Louisiana. The newsboys who hawked these papers on the street were very busy for the rest of the day. It is believed that the daily circulation of the Dallas newspapers almost doubled on May 23. People stopped in the streets when the news was overheard and inquired for further details of Clyde's slaying.

Back in Bienville Parish, the coroner and his jury demonstrated a thorough grasp of the obvious when they concluded that Clyde and Bonnie met death due to the gunfire of the six-man posse. With that bit of business finished, preparations were made to transport the bodies to Arcadia in order to be made ready by the local undertaker for transportation back to Texas. But Clyde and Bonnie were not removed from their car for this purpose. Their Ford Four Door Deluxe was hooked up to a wrecker with their bodies still in the front seat.

The wrecker towing the car and bodies was accompanied by the six officers who made up the firing squad and a couple of hundred other automobiles containing sightseers and inquisitive residents who wanted to be a part of this bit of history. The wrecker drove about eight miles on Highway 154 until it came to the town of Gibsland, where it stopped in front of the school. Some accounts say that the wrecker broke down momentarily, but this is not the case. The stop was intentional and was made on behalf of the graduating seniors at the Gibsland High School. The class of '34 would be given something to really remember about their graduation. The seniors were allowed to come down to the road and view the remains of Clyde and Bonnie. When the students in the lower grades saw what was going on out in front of the school, the whole student body came pouring out of the building to see the bullet-riddled, bloody bodies. Many of the school kids found the scene shocking and had nightmares for years afterwards as a result of their close-up glimpses of the shattered bodies in the front seat of that automobile.

The wrecker, "death car," officers, and ever-growing line of sightseers made the turn onto Highway 80 from Highway 154 in Gibsland and began the ten-mile trip towards Arcadia. Arcadia was also the destination for law enforcement officers from all over the southwest, reporters from all over the country, and thousands of people from the tri-state region of Texas, Arkansas, and Louisiana. The relatively small town was already dealing with an influx of visitors, something it had never seen before and which it would never see again.

Then, the wrecker and the "death car," with its attendant entourage of hundreds, pulled into downtown Arcadia, with its thousands of waiting people. The influx of people had already brought traffic to a standstill. The wrecker and the "death car" slowly made its way to the street in front of the combination furniture store and funeral parlor. At that point, the vehicles stopped and Clyde and Bonnie were removed from their Ford, about three hours after they had been killed around 9:15 that morning. Their bodies were lifted out of the front seat and placed on gurneys, then wheeled into the back of Conger's Furniture Store, where the embalming apparatus was located. The Conger's funeral home itself was next door to the furniture store and both were located directly across from the Arcadia train depot.

The local undertaker began to do what he could on the bodies to make them fit for transportation back to Dallas. The crowds which were filling the embalming area, the furniture store out front, and the sidewalk outside made it extremely hard for the embalmer to do what he wanted to do. It got to the point that he had to squirt formaldehyde on the bystanders when they crowded in too close. The bullet-shattered "death car" was surprisingly able to run on its own after it was lowered from the wrecker and the bodies were removed. It was driven over to the courthouse where it was placed behind a chain-link fence. The six officers now began to do some serious "inventory work" on Clyde's possessions. The firing squad had its own plans for most of the things that Clyde and Bonnie had with them.

Somewhere along the line, Frank Hamer had made a request of Lee Simmons, asking if Simmons would back him up if Hamer took and kept anything of Clyde's after my brother was apprehended. Simmons told Hamer that he could take and keep anything he wanted of Clyde's when he caught up with my brother. Some say that this request was granted when the car was finally secured at the Bienville Parish courthouse. But there are others who say this request was actually a condition that Hamer demanded of Simmons before he would agree to go on Clyde's trail. Either way, it was undoubtedly perceived at the time that Frank Hamer just wanted to keep one or two of Clyde's weapons in his own gun collection as souvenirs of the chase. Frank Hamer and the others did keep some of Clyde's weapons for themselves - but they didn't stop there. The six officers appropriated everything they could get their hands on.

There has been much condemnation of the people who descended on the ambush site on Highway 154 while their car with their bodies was still there. These people got little pieces of both Clyde's and Bonnie's clothing, strands of their hair, small patches of the upholstery of their car, and many other small items. The officers kept the sightseers under enough control that the people were unable to take the guns or anything else of substance from the "death car." The officers maintained this crowd control out of more than just propriety - they had their eyes on Clyde's and Bonnie's possessions themselves, knowing that these items would be of great monetary worth due to their historical value. At the Bienville Parish courthouse, the six officers divvied up what possessions Clyde and Bonnie had at the time of their deaths.

It seems that those officers affiliated with the Texas Rangers (Hamer and Gault) wound up getting the lion's share of Clyde's things. Over the decades since the Bienville Parish ambush, the Texas Ranger Museum in Waco has auctioned off many items taken by those two individuals, from the guns taken from National Guard Armories (the Browning Automatic Rifles and automatics) and the guns legally purchased by Clyde (the shotguns) to Clyde's fishing tackle box and Bonnie's overnight case. One of the two Texas Ranger-related officers even got my brother's socks that he was wearing when he was killed. These socks are purportedly still kept by the Ranger Museum.

Bob Alcorn decided he wanted to keep Clyde's saxophone and the saxophone case. To Alcorn's credit, however, he later returned the instrument and its case to our family. But none of the other members of that six-man firing squad ever returned any of Clyde's personal belongings taken from the "death car."

Among the many things which disappeared was the suitcase full of money that my father saw on Clyde's last visit home on May 7. Officially, it was claimed that about $500 was found on my brother's body. Only a very few dollars were found on Bonnie. No one in Louisiana ever admitted the existence of that suitcase containing thousands of dollars. But I know it existed because my father saw it on the back seat of Clyde's car on May 7.

Henry and Jack Barrow arrived with the hearse from the Sparkman funeral home in the afternoon. They were appalled at the three-ring circus my brother's assassination had become. But our father and Jack were not there to stir up any trouble because of what had happened. It really hit our father pretty hard when he finally saw the shot-up body of his son. Henry went out into the furniture store section of the Conger establishment, sat down in a rocking chair, put his head in his hands, and just cried. The man from Sparkman's helped get Clyde's body ready for transportation. Jack did what he could to support his father's grief and to get things ready for Clyde's last trip home.

Henry and Jack were also given a few of Clyde's personal effects. They received the blue western-style shirt, the dark blue pair of pants, and the underwear that my brother was wearing when he was assassinated. My father was also given Clyde's tan hat (which was hit by one of the officers' bullets) and my brother's wristwatch (also creased by a bullet) which he was wearing when he was killed.

It was later in the evening, after dark, when the Arcadia undertaker finally got Clyde's body in good enough shape to allow the man from Sparkman's to make the return drive back to Dallas. About the same time as the Barrow family was preparing to leave, Buster Parker and the representative from the McKamy-Campbell establishment arrived. Some observers have noted this after-dark activity from both families and concluded that the Barrow and Parker families were so ashamed of their slain loved ones that they only came into town under the cover of darkness. This assumption is totally scurrilous and untrue. The representatives from both families left Dallas for Louisiana as soon as they were able to do so, and Jack and Henry Barrow made it to Arcadia while it was still daytime. It just so happened that Buster and the McKamy-Campbell people erroneously traveled over towards Acadia, Louisiana instead of Arcadia. Acadia is a parish in the southwestern part of the state. By the time Buster's party discovered their error, they had to backtrack for several hours and didn't arrive at Arcadia until around 10 p.m. that evening.

Buster Parker reacted differently to the sight of Bonnie's bullet-shattered body than Henry Barrow. While my father gave way to sorrow and grief, Buster was angry and outraged over what the six officers had done to his sister. He stalked up and down in the furniture store, shaking his fists. Buster verbally castigated the members of the firing squad in front of anyone who would listen to him. At that time of night, I don't believe any of the six officers was still around. It is probably for the best that they were not on the scene; Buster was so livid with rage that he was ready to physically confront any of those officers. Eventually, the body of Bonnie Parker was made ready to be transported back home.

Bonnie had previously expressed two requests to her mother concerning her funeral and burial. Bonnie had not wanted to have her final services conducted in a funeral home, but she wanted her visitation and memorial rites to take place at her mother's house. After this first request was agreed upon, Bonnie asked to be buried next to Clyde. However, Mrs. Parker was unable to bring Bonnie's body to their home due to the crowds hovering around Lamar Street (where Mrs. Parker was living at the time) and was unwilling to have her interred next to Clyde.

I believe Mrs. Parker held my brother responsible for Bonnie's slaying. Mrs. Parker believed her relationship with Clyde was the direct cause of her death. The Barrow family agreed with both Clyde and Bonnie in their wishes to be buried side-by-side, but we knew that it didn't matter that much to Clyde. However, we respected Mrs. Parker's wishes in her grief and did not try to talk her into allowing the double burial. It was probably better in the long run that both Clyde and Bonnie were laid to rest in their own respective family plots. Mrs. Parker did not try to bring Bonnie to their family home on Lamar Street and left her body at the McKamy-Campbell chapel after Buster returned from Bienville Parish.

On Thursday, May 24, both bodies were open to public visitation, but no one really expected the massive crowds of people that continuously filed through both funeral homes to see Clyde and Bonnie. It would be too much to hope that these visitors came out of profound respect for the deceased. To most of these people, Clyde and Bonnie were figures they only knew through the newspaper reports, radio bulletins, and newsreels. The Barrow family and their memories of Clyde were subjected to a lot of crude behavior and coarse comments. The situation got so bad that my father requested the Sparkman establishment terminate public visitation for a little while.

The funeral home sightseers weren't the only people by whom the Barrow family was subjected to harassment concerning Clyde's death. That Thursday, a man telephoned and asked to talk to Henry Barrow. My father took the call. The man was some type of showman, and he had a "business" proposition. He wanted to buy Clyde's body from the Barrow family for $10,000, and exhibit my brother's body to the public for an admission charge. Henry angrily refused this offer, telling him that it was the family's intention to give Clyde the best Christian services and burial they could afford. This man grew angry in return and told my father that if the family wouldn't sell Clyde's body, then this man would take it anyway.

This outrageous demand upset our family. We had no idea whether this offer was serious or was some kind of a cruel joke, but we could not afford to take any chances. My father went to the Dallas police with the news of this man's telephone call and asked for their assistance. A police guard was assigned to the Sparkman funeral home for the duration of Clyde's visitation time on Thursday and Friday.

This unfortunate circumstance concerning the police guard almost had tragic results late Thursday. The son of one of the employees of the Sparkman funeral home went out drinking with a couple of friends earlier in the evening. Later that night, the three young men came back to the undertaking parlor inebriated. The drunken trio was not too subtle in their efforts to gain entrance to the funeral home. The Dallas police officers standing vigil over Clyde's body were not aware that these boys belonged to someone at Sparkman's, and the policemen came close to firing on the trio before their identities were established by other Sparkman personnel. Fortunately, the rest of that Thursday night came and went with no further crises at the funeral home.

Clyde's services were scheduled for late Friday afternoon, May 25, 1934. Some visitation was again allowed during that day. Newsreel cameramen were there filming the seemingly endless lines of people on the sidewalks in front of the Sparkman funeral home. This visitation continued throughout Friday morning and into Friday afternoon. Our family alternated between our individual homes and the undertaking parlor, but as the time for my brother's final service drew closer, the Barrow family gathered at the Sparkman chapel. There were a number of family friends there, and attendance at the actual funeral was restricted to just the family and close friends. When it came time for Clyde's funeral, the sightseers were cleared out, and the musicians and minister were ushered in. The family and friends were settled in their seats, but we could still hear the shouts and taunts of the disgruntled people who were removed from the chapel. There was nothing we could do except grit our teeth and focus on the comforting words of the minister and the songs of hope performed by the singers. Despite what has been claimed in later years, Frank Hamer was not at the services in the Sparkman chapel. We certainly did not regard Hamer as a friend of the family, and still do not.

Clyde's eulogy was given by the minister, and the singers sang their hymns of future hope. During the minister's talk, he commented on something concerning my brother which would surprise many people. He spoke of the fact that Clyde prayed frequently, even during the months when he was out on the road. This was something that was also noted by both W.D. Jones and Raymond Hamilton. W.D. was impressed by the fact that oftentimes he would see my brother off by himself at night praying while everyone else was asleep. Hamilton said he too frequently saw Clyde and Bonnie praying together. Clyde's early years at the Baptist church near Eureka still exerted an influence.

Then, it was time to take my brother's body to the family plot in the Western Heights Cemetery on Ft. Worth Avenue in west Dallas. The pallbearers carried Clyde's coffin out to the waiting hearse. The family members and friends left the Sparkman building out of the side entrance which led directly to the driveway where the cars in the procession were waiting to pick up their passengers. Many of the spectators and sightseers who were waiting outside the funeral home also got into their cars and fell in line behind the official procession.

There was a much bigger crowd already at the Western Heights cemetery. The pallbearers were just barely able to make their way through the tightly packed mob to Clyde's grave. The heat of the day, the closeness of the crowd, and the emotional intensity of the situation caused some of our family members to feel faint, and some did pass out momentarily. But they were quickly resuscitated and the graveside services were concluded. Clyde's casket was then lowered into the ground next to our brother Buck. During the scene at the graveside, an airplane flew close overhead and released a wreath of flowers. Our family left Western Heights cemetery while the grave diggers began their dolorous duty of filling in the grave. The newsreel cameras were at Western Heights cemetery documenting the burial for local news service companies. People took flowers from the wreaths and soil from the grave as souvenirs. If Frank Hamer was anywhere at Clyde's services, he was with the crowd at the cemetery. Ironically, Joe Palmer, one of the men for whom Hamer and the others were searching, was also out there at the graveside services, unnoticed and unrecognized by the many officers present.

The funeral activities for Bonnie Parker were held the following day. Although Mrs. Parker did not come to Clyde's memorial services, my parents and members of our family did attend the rites held for Bonnie at the McKamy-Campbell undertaking parlor in south Dallas. The minister who gave the eulogy for Bonnie was the same man who had officiated at Clyde's funeral. The pastor spoke words of comfort on behalf of the Parker family, and then, it was time to take Bonnie to her final resting place. She was to be buried next to Billie Jean Parker's two children at the La Reunion cemetery in west Dallas, a few miles north of the Western Heights cemetery.

Mercifully, the crowd control was better at Bonnie's burial. There were large crowds of people outside of the McKamy-Campbell establishment on Saturday, but this mob was a little more orderly than those who were outside of the Sparkman funeral home on Friday. This order was due to the fact that there was much more of a police presence at McKamy-Campbell. This policy was also maintained at the Fish Trap cemetery. The Parkers, Barrows, and other close friends were able to sit on folding chairs under a funeral tent as Bonnie's casket was lowered into the ground.

Mrs. Parker was able to get her remaining daughter temporarily released from the Tarrant county jail in time to attend the services, although Bonnie's sister was accompanied by officers who stayed with her during the funeral. Billie Jean was taken back to the county jail in Ft. Worth after her sister's burial. After Bonnie's services, Mrs. Parker continued her frantic work to get her younger daughter out of the ludicrous charge of assisting in the killing of the motorcycle officers near Grapevine on Easter Sunday. Just a few days later, Billie Jean was cleared.

Perhaps the best way to end this account of Clyde's life story is to quote from my mother in her unpublished manuscript about her son: "And so they brought them down. The officers who performed this grim task did their duty as they saw it, and I hold no grudge—only the regret that my boy had to go that way. We, of course, had long known it would be something like that, but it was harder than anyone who has never experienced such a thing can ever realize ... Out of all of this I try as best I can to gain some consolation through knowing that the end came swiftly and mercifully. After all, the lives of all of us just hang by a mere thread and we should all try to so live that when we come to die we are ready to meet our 'Maker.'"

Chapter 25

So Clyde had finally come to the same end as our brother Buck. Our family had hoped that my brothers' story would end with the burials in Dallas and that everyone would let them rest in peace. But when the flesh-and-blood people were finally laid to rest, their legends were just getting started.

Bonnie had correctly predicted in her poem titled "The Story of Bonnie and Clyde" that their deaths would bring sorrow to a few people and relief to many others. Our family was among the few who were sorrowful. The many who were relieved by what happened on that country highway in Bienville Parish, Louisiana on May 23, 1934 made their relief known shortly after the sound of the gunfire died away.

One of the first and most notable individuals to make his relief known to the public was O.K. Allen, the governor of Louisiana. Allen sent a congratulatory telegram to Sheriff Henderson Jordan as soon as the governor heard the news about Clyde's assassination. The telegram was received in Arcadia just a couple of hours after the ambush. But that was just the beginning of the commentary of the high-and-mighty concerning my brother's slaying.

A congressman from Texas stood up on the floor in the U.S. Capitol building in Washington, D.C., and addressed his colleagues concerning the deaths of Clyde and Bonnie. The congressman announced to the others that the rest of the country ought to express gratitude to Texas for ending Clyde's life. This sentiment is interesting in light of the fact that the ambush actually occurred in the state of Louisiana and was initially conceived by a Louisiana sheriff and a federal agent out of New Orleans.

A major newspaper in New York City at least got the correct state identified. An editorial in this particular newspaper warned of the follies of gangland activity and concluded with the dignified resolution that the nation ought to be gratified because Louisiana "rubbed them both out." Newspapers all over the country ran the same type of crime-does-not-pay editorials. But neither Clyde nor Bonnie had ever said anything otherwise about their lives as fugitives and wanted people; they knew better than anyone else that a life of crime did not pay off in anything except sorrow.

The media of the era continued to publicize any and all aspects of Clyde's slaying. Our family had the latest in a long line of bad moments when a newsreel company got hold of Ted Hinton's 16mm film, which has become the "Zapruder film" of the 1930s. I don't know whether Hinton sold the film to the newsreel producers or they acquired a pirated version. Either way, these films of both Clyde and Bonnie slumped in the front seat of the "death car" were shown all over the country on the big screens of the movie theaters as part of the movie fare.

Then someone made the mistake of booking these "death car" newsreels at the Majestic Theater in downtown Dallas. Our family was outraged that the sensational films were going to be shown in Clyde's home area and be seen by his family and his friends. The publicity outside the Majestic Theater featured gruesome oversized photos of the bloody bodies of Clyde and Bonnie. There was also advertising promising even more sensational sights to be seen on the screen. It was the last straw for the Barrow family, and some of us resolved to do something about it. My mother and I made our way to downtown Dallas in order to personally deal with the insult to our family. She and I marched up to where the sensationalized ads were displayed and ripped all of them down. Cumie Barrow was really a meek person by nature, but when the defense of one of her children was involved, she became as bold as a lioness.

The affair at the Majestic Theatre was not the only conflict in which Cumie Barrow was engaged. Our mother wrote a letter to Frank Hamer asking him to return the guns and other personal possessions he and his crony Gault had taken from the "death car." Deputy Bob Alcorn had apparently felt bad about the way that he and the other officers had plundered my brother's items and returned Clyde's saxophone and its case. We figured the Browning Automatic Rifles and automatic pistols would be returned to the National Guard Armories (they weren't), but we had a right to claim the items that Clyde had legally purchased. It was reported many times in the regional newspapers that Clyde was seen purchasing shotguns in hardware stores and sporting goods establishments. But Hamer and Gault were not made of the same moral fiber as was Bob Alcorn, and the two Austin-based lawmen ignored our mother's requests. Hamer also ignored Mrs. Parker's letter requesting the return of some of Bonnie's things. However, Hamer's refusal was not the end of this particular story; the ex-Ranger's attitude on this matter would have repercussions of a surprising sort with Bob Alcorn and Ted Hinton five years later.

Frank Hamer himself was lionized by the press. The idea of an "old-timey" Texas Ranger being involved in a 1930s manhunt struck a nerve with many people. Hamer said he was capable of bringing in both John Dillinger and Pretty Boy Floyd if he could get the authorization from the federal government. "Fearless Frank" also supposedly told the G-men that he knew Dillinger had recently underwent plastic surgery to change his facial features somewhere close to New Orleans, Louisiana. The federal agents knew that Dillinger did indeed have some plastic surgery done at this time, but they also knew it was accomplished in the Chicago area and not near New Orleans. Tips like those of Hamer's would not help them and J. Edgar Hoover said "thanks, but no thanks" to Hamer's offer of his services in the Floyd and Dillinger manhunts. Hamer's services would not have made much of a difference anyway as the G-men shot and killed both Dillinger (in late July) and Floyd (in late October) during that same year of 1934.

Hamer and Gault were not the only people who had their own angles in their connection with Clyde's story. A few weeks after Clyde's burial, my sister Nell was approached by a writer named Jan Fortune. Ms. Fortune wanted to work with both the Barrow and Parker families in order to write the "true story" of my brother's life. This particular writer also contacted Mrs. Parker in order to get her cooperation. I was not involved, but I approved of the notion of someone making a serious attempt to tell the truth concerning my brother Clyde. I looked forward to the finished product.

Apparently, Jan Fortune did talk to both Nell and Mrs. Parker. Then she took the information and notes she generated in her conversations with our families and went off and wrote the book *Fugitives* on her own. It is this particular work of fiction which has generated much of the misinformation which is taken as ironclad fact by those who have an interest in Clyde and Buck. When I confronted Nell with some of the examples of the romanticized, sentimentalized claptrap of which Fortune's piece of fiction was composed, she told me that she had never told the writer any of that stuff. Jan Fortune was a screenwriter for the movies in the 1930s, and she approached the life story of Clyde and Bonnie in the same fashion as she would a movie script. Ms. Fortune may have thought that if the story of Clyde and Bonnie was romantically approached, it might be an easier "sell" to the movie studios.

If Jan Fortune had any plans to sell *Fugitives* to some movie studio, she was to be in for disappointment. Will Hays, who was the czar of the movie industry, stated in the late spring of 1934 that any movies based on the life of John Dillinger or any other wanted person of his type would be banned. The head of the movie studios took the not-so-subtle hint and scuttled any plans they had of making films based on the noted fugitives of 1934.

The book *Fugitives* was published in the early fall of 1934. Although our family was dissatisfied with the content, a much worse crisis suddenly loomed on the horizon. The federal government had announced that it intended to prosecute any and all individuals who had given aid and comfort to Clyde Barrow and Bonnie Parker. Several of the Barrow and Parker family members and friends were then arrested and incarcerated in the Dallas County jail to await prosecution.

It is still a mystery to me why the federal government made a move to prosecute our families for any contact with our family members. Clyde and Bonnie had been in their graves for almost four months, and our families were just getting settled down to living normal, quiet lives again. The federal government had no reason whatsoever to fear anything from our family. The Barrows just wanted to be left alone and no further contact with anything that involved "cops and robbers."

I also have to note that the federal government showed some discriminating tendencies when it came to whom they chose to prosecute on the charge of harboring fugitives. The G-men had only one man (Lester Kendell) assigned to the so-called "Barrow Gang," but they had a whole special squad organized to go after John Dillinger. The federal agents kept the Dillinger family farm under surveillance during the spring of 1934 and they would watch while family reunions were carried on at which Mr. Dillinger's fugitive son was the special guest. The G-men knew that Dillinger was visiting his kinfolk and that he would spend weekends at the farm. Yet there was never any talk of prosecuting old Mr. Dillinger on harboring charges. The state of Indiana said that Mr. Dillinger was exercising his rights in putting his fugitive son up on the family farm and that the state would not go after the Dillinger family. It is true that Mr. Dillinger was a decent, law abiding, god-fearing person, but so was Cumie Barrow. But my mother's good character didn't matter to the federal prosecutors, so she went to jail for being a loving mother to her fugitive son.

Cumie Barrow wasn't the only member of our family who went

to the Dallas county "bar hotel." My brother L.C. and I were also arrested for visiting with our brother, as was my husband Joe Bill Francis. Ironically, my sister Nell was not picked up for harboring her brother at our family get-togethers, despite what was written in the book *Fugitives*. According to Jan Fortune's account, Nell was meeting with Clyde and Bonnie every time they came in to town. Yet, I don't recall Nell ever going with our group out to see Clyde, although I am sure that she did see him on occasion. Clyde frequently met with his father down by the railroad tracks in west Dallas. Yet, the federal government seemed intent in going after only the members of the group which was associated with Clyde's and Bonnie's mothers.

Initially, my mother and I were separated in the county jail. Since I was only 16 years old at this time, I was assigned to the juvenile section while my mother went over to the adult area. But I knew that she still had not really recovered from Clyde's death and feared for her health and safety. I asked the jailers if I could be transferred over to my mother's section to provide support and assistance for her. This was done, and I spent the last few months of 1934 with my mother in the Dallas county jail awaiting our trial.

All of the family members who were arrested in connection with the "Barrow-Parker harboring case" went on trial during February, 1935. Many other people who played a part in Clyde's life were also included in these charges. W.D. Jones was brought in from the Texas prison system. Blanche Barrow was brought down from the Missouri women's prison. Even Henry "The Rat" Methvin was brought in. L.C. was forced to sit next to Henry the Rat at times during the court proceedings and to endure Methvin's self-serving version of events. Methvin protested to L. C. that he was not involved in any of the machinations going on concerning the ambush in Bienville Parish and could not control anything his parents and the Joyners were doing without his knowledge. (At the same time, Henry the Rat was writing letters to Lee Simmons demanding Simmons' help in exchange for what Henry had said he had done in setting up the killing of Clyde and Bonnie.) L.C. disregarded Henry's "crocodile tears" over Clyde's death, but nevertheless had to tolerate Methvin's presence in the courtroom.

All of the men were chained together by the neck when they were brought into court every day, with handcuffs on their wrists and shackles on their feet. Both the men and women were transported to the court building every morning in paddy wagons and were transported away in the afternoons by these same vehicles. Newsreel cameramen were cranking away while we were led in and out of the building. There was always a large contingent of heavily armed officers standing around, probably as a show for the benefit of the newsreel people. Our entry and exit from the court building always attracted a big crowd of spectators. This was obviously a "show trial" for the benefit of the federal prosecutors.

It was a foregone conclusion that the Barrow family was going to be found guilty of giving what little food and comfort we could afford to our fugitive kinfolk. This conclusion proved to be correct when the verdicts were read. My mother received 30 days in jail, as did Mrs. Parker, for the crime of visiting with their children. L.C. was hit with a severe two year sentence, to be served in Leavenworth prison, for meeting with his older brother. Billie Jean Parker received a year in jail for assisting her older sister. I received a sentence of one hour in the company of a federal marshal, which sounds ludicrous when compared against the other sentences, but I was still considered a "minor" due to my being 16 years of age. But none of these sentences could be considered as being fair; the "Barrow-Parker harboring case" was something that never should have happened. This prosecution accomplished nothing except to bring the Barrow and Parker families more unnecessary grief and to give the federal prosecutors some headlines to keep up with the considerable publicity which was generated by the G-men during those months.

My mother, Joe Bill, and I served our sentences in fairly short order and were released. The "harboring case" proved to be our last dealing with the forces of the law concerning any direct connection with Clyde and Bonnie. But this trial was not our last involvement with the public's interest in my brother. Some time after the harboring trial was over, our family was contacted by an individual popularly known during the middle and late 1930s as the "Crime Doctor."

The "Crime Doctor," whose name was Charles Wiley Stanley, represented an organization called the "National Anti-Crime Association" out of Topeka, Kansas. He contacted my parents regarding a traveling "crime does not pay" show which he was operating. The "death car" that Clyde and Bonnie had stolen from the Warren family and in which they had died was the primary attraction of this anti-crime exhibition. That 1934 Ford Four Door was already a story in and of itself. During the many months which had passed since Clyde's assassination, that 1934 Ford continued to generate trouble and controversy for everyone who had come into contact with it.

This trouble had started immediately after the car was driven behind the wire fence at the Bienville Parish, Louisiana courthouse just after noon on May 23, 1934. The members of the firing squad divided up the personal items which had belonged to Clyde and Bonnie. Of course, the car itself could be considered as the one most valuable artifact, but the fact that it was already registered to a legal owner in Topeka, Kansas precluded any of the lawmen making off with it. But the car disappeared from the courthouse yard anyway.

Mrs. Warren traveled down to Bienville Parish from Topeka to claim her legal property. She initially approached Sheriff Henderson Jordan in order to get her automobile. But Jordan told her that he and five other brave officers had risked their lives to get that car back and that it would not be immediately returned. Mrs. Warren had to get a Shreveport lawyer to file a lawsuit against Jordan before he would turn the car loose. A federal judge ordered Jordan to return the bullet-riddled Ford to its rightful owner. It seems that the "death car" had been hidden in a barn in rural Bienville Parish for several weeks before Jordan was forced to hand it back over. When Mrs. Warren finally got her car in late July, over two months since the ambush had taken place.

Promoters lost no time in beating a path to Mrs. Warren's door, offering various schemes concerning the public exhibition of the auto in which Clyde and Bonnie were slain. Mrs. Warren came to an agreement with one of these promoters, but the arrangement came to a quick end. Then, Charles Stanley, of the "National Anti-Crime Association" out of the Warrens' hometown of Topeka, contacted Mrs. Warren and a fair agreement was reached, giving Mr. Stanley the right to exhibit the auto.

Along with the "death car," Mr. Stanley also had a slide display which he would show in connection with his lectures. These glass slides were projected on a screen and included pictures of Clyde, Bonnie, John Dillinger, Bruno Richard Hauptmann (the purported kidnapper of the Lindbergh baby; my mother closely followed the Lindbergh case in the newspapers), and other noted fugitives of the early and mid 1930s. This was a traveling road show which moved from town to town and state to state. The "National Anti-Crime Association" of Topeka, Kansas was a real organization endorsed by J. Edgar Hoover and other nationally known law officers in the mid-1930s.

Mr. Stanley had taken his anti-crime show around the country without incident until he came to Austin, Texas. Mr. Stanley flatly stated during his lectures that the Methvin family was involved in the plot to set up Clyde and Bonnie. Unfortunately, the city of Austin was the home of both Frank Hamer and Manny Gault at that time, and these two officers went to one of Mr. Stanley's exhibitions. Needless to say, Mr. Stanley's version of events (the Methvins set Clyde up) conflicted with Hamer's reported statements (Hamer tracked my brother down to his "mailbox"). After the presentation, Hamer and Gault confronted Mr. Stanley. According to the pro-Hamer stories, the two men from Austin were supposedly outraged by the "lurid" presentation of Clyde's death. Hamer reportedly pushed Mr. Stanley around and knocked him down.

The slides were "confiscated" by the two Austin-based lawmen. Hamer physically threatened the showman concerning the exhibition and said something along the line that he would be coming after the "Crime Doctor" no matter where he was at if Hamer heard of him talking about Hamer's role in Methvin-Joyner version of the Louisiana ambush. Mr. Stanley immediately left town, knowing that Austin was Hamer's hometown and that the ex-Texas Ranger could do pretty much anything he wanted to there. According to the pro-Hamer accounts, Mr. Stanley immediately closed down his show, dropped from public sight, and refused to comment until Hamer's death 20 years later. I suppose this last fact was to indicate that Hamer's righteous wrath had cowed Charles Stanley into craven submission. However, Mr. Stanley's version of events was different than the pro-Hamer version, and I accept Mr. Stanley's account that Hamer was really more upset about the ambush being described as the result of a betrayal more than his man-hunting capabilities.

The only part of the Hamer story that I can accept as being true is the part about Hamer smacking Mr. Stanley. The part about the show being lurid and sensational was totally untrue and the part about Mr. Stanley going into 20 years of humiliated silence is a flagrant falsehood. "Fearless Frank" may have been trying to protect both his reputation and Henry the Rat. After leaving Austin, the "National Anti-Crime Association" exhibition continued to travel around the country. Fortunately, the showman had a second copy of the set of slides to use and his show continued as before.

Some time after the incident in Austin, Mr. Stanley came up with the idea of using the parents of some of the noted fugitives to give the American public a first-hand message that "crime does not pay." The showman approached John Dillinger Sr., Emma Parker, and my parents on this matter. All of them agreed to work with Mr. Stanley. Joe Bill and I were also hired by the traveling show. Joe Bill did various jobs while I collected admission tickets from the patrons of the exhibit. Mr. Stanley's show was traveling with a carnival at the time. I enjoyed the work; collecting tickets was not a hard task, and I was able to go on many of the rides traveling with the carnival.

While I enjoyed the experience, my parents and the others were somewhat less enthused. Their age played a role. My parents were both in their mid-sixties at this time; Mr. Dillinger was up in his mid-seventies, and Mrs. Parker was somewhat younger than the others, but she was still no "spring chicken" herself. Consistently traveling with a carnival was much harder on them than it was on Joe Bill and me.

It was also hard on them due to the nature of the show. My parents, Mrs. Parker, and Mr. Dillinger had to continually rehash the fugitive careers and violent ends of their children day after day for those who attended the show. They had to regularly see Mr. Stanley's glass slides of their prodigal sons and daughter in both life and death. My parents and Mrs. Parker had to view the bullet-riddled automobile every day in which their children had died. Both the physical strain due to the travel and the psychological strain concerning having to graphically deal with the deaths of their children on a daily basis caused them to eventually sever their arrangement with Mr. Stanley. Joe Bill and I too terminated our jobs with the traveling show when my parents left.

Other changes in our lives continued to take place throughout the rest of the 1930s. A couple of years after Clyde was slain, there was a fire at the family's service station on Eagle Ford Road. Both the "oil room" and the living quarters were completely burnt to the ground. My father rebuilt both the service station and the family residence, although it was just he and Cumie who were living there. Henry continued to operate the service station for a few more years after the fire and rebuilding.

There was one more occurrence which should be related before the story of the Barrow family during the years of the 1930s is brought to an end. A circumstance came about in 1939 which wound up involving many of the people who played a role in the killing of Bonnie and Clyde five years earlier. I believe that this happened at the time of the Texas State Fair at Dallas' Fair Park during October.

As I previously mentioned, Charles Stanley continued to operate his "National Anti-Crime Association" exhibition all over the country after the trouble with Frank Hamer and invited any and all of us to come out to see the exhibition again.

The showman did have one reservation about doing the show at the Texas State Fair. He had remembered Frank Hamer's threat a few years earlier to come after him if the lawman ever heard of Mr. Stanley talking about the betrayal and ambushing of Clyde again. This time the showman was going to hire two security guards to be ready for Hamer if he showed up. Dallas was close enough to Austin that it was deemed very possible that Hamer would pay an unfriendly visit. It was not likely that Hamer would not know of the appearance of the "death car" and the slide show at the state fair. But there was a bigger surprise in store.

Not only would there be security personnel, but the two men who readily agreed to provide protection for the "National Anti-Crime Association" exhibition were none other than Dallas County Deputies Bob Alcorn and Ted Hinton. The scene was now set for a most interesting confrontation and showdown between four members of the six-man firing squad who had shot Clyde and Bonnie over five years previously. If Hamer did show up to make good on his previous threat, he would be standing face-to-face with Alcorn and Hinton - and this time the men would not be acting together on the same side. The Dallas County deputies had no quarrel with Mr. Stanley's presentation and fully intended to protect him and his property. There would be no repeat of the contention which occurred at Austin.

All of us were expecting trouble to occur at Mr. Stanley's exhibition between Hamer and the Dallas County deputies. Our family made it a point to have someone there to provide support for the "National Anti-Crime Exhibit" and Mr. Stanley's truthful and temperate rendition of what happened on May 23, 1934. Either my father or another family member was always at Mr. Stanley's show, waiting to see if either or both of the Austin officers would make an appearance - and hoping they would not.

Our fears of a violent incident were never realized. Frank Hamer never showed up, despite his previous promise. The determination of Mr. Stanley and the Dallas County deputies had ensured that the display of the "death car" would not be marked by any trouble. It is fitting that this final act in the drama involving Clyde's life came at the end of 1939. It meant that with the end of the decade came the end of our fears of continued strife and trouble over the life, crimes, and death of my brother Clyde. The stormy years of the 1930s had finally passed.

Chapter 26

The anticipated confrontation that never occurred at the 1939 Texas State Fair is probably the best place at which to end the story of Clyde, Buck, Blanche, and Bonnie. Although their public "lives of crime" all ended during the 1930s, their legend continues to attract a great number of people. I was continuously asked in the 1990s if there were still any Barrow family members alive or if Bonnie Parker had any family left. To answer questions of this type, I will give an abbreviated account of what happened to the Barrow and Parker families, as well as some of the other people who played a major part in the story of Clyde's life, in the decades since the 1930s.

In 1940, my father finally retired and sold his service station. Henry and Cumie moved from the old family home on Eagle Ford Road. My parents acquired a house on Lawrence Street in the city of Dallas. This Lawrence Street residence represented the first time that my mother would enjoy the relative luxuries of indoor plumbing and running water.

My parents lived together on Lawrence Street for about two years until my mother died of natural causes on August 14, 1942 at the age of 67. Cumie Barrow was buried next to Clyde in the Western Heights cemetery on Ft. Worth Avenue.

I believe the year 1942 also saw the death of the Joyners who were involved in the Bienville Parish plot to set up Clyde and Bonnie. It is said that the Joyner couple died in a murder-suicide killing in Louisiana. Four years later in 1946, Old Henry Methvin also died a violent death in northwest Louisiana as the result of an automobile accident.

It was also in 1946 that Emma Parker, the mother of Bonnie and Billie Jean, died. The previous year Mrs. Parker and Billie Jean had the bodies of Bonnie and Billie's two children removed from the Fish Trap cemetery and reburied in the Crown Hill Memorial Park near Love Field in Dallas. There have been all kinds of dark and sinister reasons conjectured as to why Bonnie's body was relocated. The pure and simple reason is that the Parker family was dissatisfied with the Fish Trap facility, due to the rough nature of the neighborhood and the vandalism which occurred at that graveyard.

The following year of 1947 saw the passing of my brother Elvin. W. "Jack" Barrow at the age of 53. Jack was buried in the Barrow family plot along with Buck, Clyde, and Cumie Barrow. Manny Gault, Frank Hamer's associate in the manhunt for Clyde and Bonnie, also died in 1947.

Henry Methvin died violently in 1948 when he was run over by a train near Sulphur, Louisiana. Methvin had laid low in Louisiana until he was arrested in connection with the murder of the Oklahoma constable. Henry the Rat was never prosecuted in the state of Texas for either the murder of the Eastham prison guard or the two motorcycle patrolmen near Grapevine. It is believed that Hamer was instrumental in getting Methvin a pardon in the state of Texas. But a Texas pardon was of no value to the state of Oklahoma, and Methvin was found guilty of the murder of the constable and was sentenced to death. This death sentence was later changed to a life sentence purportedly through the efforts of Frank Hamer. Henry the Rat received a pardon from the state of Oklahoma (also allegedly courtesy of Frank Hamer) in the early 1940s and returned to Louisiana. Methvin experienced a series of failures concerning businesses; he tried jobs which Frank Hamer had arranged for him. Eventually he began running with untrustworthy ex-convicts, which proved true the old adage that "birds of a feather flock together." Methvin's death was officially ruled an accident, although there have been persistent rumors that Methvin had been murdered by his "friends" and his body thrown on the railroad tracks to cover up his killing. Henry the Rat was buried next to Old Henry Methvin in a country graveyard near Ringgold, Louisiana.

Frank Hamer, Methvin's number one supporter, followed his friend Henry the Rat into the next world seven years later. Hamer died in Austin, Texas during the summer of 1955. It may seem to many that I have been hard on Frank Hamer in this account of Clyde's life. But Hamer's probable "confiscation" of so many of Clyde's things, including my brother's fishing tackle box and Bonnie's overnight case, rubbed us the wrong way. It was also Hamer's self-centered perspective on his role in the manhunt for Clyde which irritated us. The fact that Bob Alcorn and Ted Hinton were willing to provide protection for the "Crime Doctor" against a potential confrontation with Hamer indicates that others were not endeared to him either. It is true that Hamer was portrayed poorly in the 1967 movie *Bonnie & Clyde*, but so was everybody else in that show. After that film, many articles and books were written to correct the erroneous portrayal, but these accounts lionized Frank Hamer at my brother's expense to a level that was beyond both reality and credibility. In later years, Hamer reportedly said that he'd personally killed 52 men (including Clyde) and one woman (Bonnie Parker) and wasn't bothered by any of the killings. Clyde was actually killed by the Louisiana deputy, and there were four other men in that firing squad with Hamer who were firing at Clyde and Bonnie at the same time. When it came right down to the hard facts concerning the ambush, Hamer was nothing but one gun among six.

Henry Barrow, my father, passed away on June 19, 1957 at the age of 83. He had outlived three of his four sons. His memorial service was held at the same Sparkman funeral home where the last rites for Clyde and Buck were held over two decades earlier. Henry was to be the final one who would be buried in the family plot in the Western Heights burial grounds. In fact, he was the last person to be buried in the cemetery altogether.

Louisiana deputy Oakley, the man who had actually assassinated Clyde with the first two shots of the ambush, died in 1957. Oakley later served as sheriff in Bienville Parish after his boss's re-elections had run their course.

Former Bienville Parish Sheriff Henderson Jordan outlived his one-time deputy by only a few months, dying in mid-1958 Jordan was re-elected to his office after Clyde was shot. Both Oakley and Jordan are buried in the Arcadia, Louisiana cemetery.

Former Dallas County Sheriff Smoot Schmid died in mid 1963. Deputy Bob Alcorn died in 1964. After he had returned Clyde's saxophone to the Barrow family, Alcorn continued to assist us whenever he could. He was perfectly willing to help protect Charles Stanley when the "Crime Doctor" brought his traveling show to the state fair in 1939. Alcorn continued to be counted as a friend by the Barrow family until his death.

My sister Nell passed away at the age of 63 in 1968. She had been afflicted with Lou Gehrig's disease.

W. D. Jones died in 1974 when he was gunned down in Houston. W. D. had served eight years in prison before he was released in 1942. He got married and settled down to a law-abiding life for a number of years. But things changed for the worse after his wife died, and W.D.

began to associate with a bad crowd, one of which shot-gunned him to death in the summer of 1974.

Former Dallas County Deputy Ted Hinton died in 1977. After Clyde and Bonnie were killed, Ted Hinton became a friend to the Barrow family, a friendship which lasted for over 40 years. Ted worked with Bob Alcorn when Charles Stanley needed protection from Frank Hamer in 1939. In later years, Ted helped L.C. get his long-time truck driving job at the Overhead Door Company. Hinton had just finished writing his version of the story of Clyde and Bonnie when he passed away as a result of an illness.

My brother L.C. Barrow died of natural causes in 1979 at the age of 66. L.C. had managed to survive whatever the cops and prosecutors threw at him during the rest of the 1930s. He did the two year sentence from the "Barrow-Parker harboring trial" at Leavenworth prison. L.C. was also charged with a drug store robbery in the Dallas area, a robbery with which he had nothing to do. My brother eventually weathered all of the storms of those years and went on to a long career as a truck driver with the Overhead Door Company. My sister Artie tried to get L.C. involved in the barbering trade. (Artie was the first female barber in the city of Dallas.) L.C. went to school to learn the tonsorial trade and made a creditable barber, but L.C. preferred more physical-type work and really seemed to enjoy truck driving.

My last remaining sibling Artie Barrow passed away in 1981. Artie was in her early 80s when she died.

Blanche Caldwell Barrow died in late 1988. Blanche served several years in the Missouri women's penitentiary for her alleged role in the gun battle at the Red Crown Cabin Camp near Platte City, Missouri. She regularly communicated with our family during that period, sending us photographs with notes written on the back and we visited her at the Missouri prison when we could afford to do so. Blanche was paroled in 1939. She later remarried, but Blanche did remain in contact with the Barrow family until she passed away. Blanche always remained a favorite with our family.

Billie Jean Parker passed away in 1993. Her brother Buster and his wife (Clarence Clay's sister) had died decades earlier. There are no remaining members of Bonnie's family who personally knew her. Ralph Fults, one of Clyde's earliest associates, died that same year.

Interviews: the main source for this book was the personal experiences of Marie Barrow. Notes were taken of our conversations during 1996 and 1997. Also extremely valuable were conversations with Joseph Pinkston during 1994 and 1995. Joe was the owner/operator of the John Dillinger Historical Wax Museum in Nashville, Indiana, from 1976 until his untimely death in 1996. He was a friend of both Marie and Charles Wiley Stanley, better known as the Crime Doctor of the 1930s. Joe gave me quite a bit of information regarding Mr. Stanley's activities with the Barrow and Parker families in the years after the deaths of Bonnie and Clyde.

Newspapers: the microfilmed newspaper records in the Dallas Public Library were very valuable. Copies of the following newspapers were heavily utilized: the *Dallas Morning News*, the *Dallas Times Herald*, the *Dallas Dispatch*, and the *Dallas Journal.* Additional information concerning the early years of the Barrow family in Ellis county, Texas, was uncovered in the genealogical section of the Dallas Public Library.

Books and magazines: in order to stimulate Marie's recollection of the early 1930s, I consulted everything I could find which was available at that time. I would outline the different accounts of Clyde's activities (such as the Joplin gunfight, the Dexfield Park shootout, and the Eastham prison break) and present these versions to Marie. I told her: "Here is what the historians and researchers say – review these accounts and tell me what really happened." Here are the writings which Marie and I reviewed:

Barnes, Bruce. *Machine Gun Kelly: To Right a Wrong.* Tipper Publications, 1991.

Barrow, Cumie. Unpublished manuscript (courtesy of Marie Barrow).

Barrow, Nell, Emma Parker, and Jan Fortune. *Fugitives: The Story of Bonnie and Clyde.* Signet Books, 1968.

DeFord, Miriam Allen. *The Real Bonnie and Clyde.* Ace Books, 1968.

Hamilton, Floyd. *Public Enemy Number One.* Acclaimed Books, 1978.

Hinton, Ted, and Larry Grove. *Ambush: The Real Story of Bonnie and Clyde.* Shoal Creek Publications, 1979.

Jenkins, John H., and Gordon H. Frost. *I'm Frank Hamer: The Life of a Texas Peace Officer.* Pemberton Books, 1968.

Johns, Joe. "Kidnapped by Bandits," *True West* magazine, September, 1981.

Karpis, Alvin, with Bill Trent. *The Alvin Karpis Story.* Coward, McCann, and Geoghegan, 1971.

Louderback, Lew. *The Bad Ones.* Fawcett-Crest Books, 1968.

McCormick, Harry. *Bank Robbers Wrote My Diary.* Eakin Press, 1985.

Milner, E. R. *The Lives and Times of Bonnie and Clyde.* Southern Illinois University Press, 1996.

Phillips, John Neal. *Running with Bonnie and Clyde: The Ten Fast Years of Ralph Fults.* University of Oklahoma Press, 1996.

Portley, Ed, Henderson Jordan, and C. F. Waers. "Killer Gang," *Master Detective* magazine, February, 1945.

Quimby, Myron. *The Devil's Emissaries.* A. S. Barnes, 1969.

Simmons, Lee. *Assignment Huntsville.* University of Texas Press, 1957.

Toland, John. *The Dillinger Days.* Random House, 1963.

Treherne, John. *The Strange History of Bonnie and Clyde.* Stein and Day, 1984.

Underwood, Sid. *Depression Desperado: The Chronicle of Raymond Hamilton.* Eakin Press, 1995.

Watson, William P. *Union, Justice, and Bonnie and Clyde.* Everett Publishing, 1989.

Photography Credits

From the collections of the Texas/Dallas
History and Archives Division,
Dallas Public Library

Jonathan Davis Photo - Jim Miller

About the Author

Jonathan Davis was born in Evansville, Indiana. In the early autumn of 1993, he made the acquaintance of Marie Barrow when they both worked on a documentary concerning the Barrow Gang. From that time until her passing in early 1999, Marie and Jonathan worked on several Barrow-related projects, such as the manuscript and the nationally-publicized auction of Clyde's death shirt and other family items. Jonathan has also appeared on several national programs concerning Bonnie and Clyde. He currently resides in Dallas, TX.